Game
and the Gunner

Game and the Gunner

*Observations on Game Management
and Sport Hunting*

by
PIERRE PULLING

(ALBERT VAN SICLEN PULLING)

Drawings by Richard Amundsen

Winchester Press

Library of Congress Card Number: 73–78830
ISBN: 0–87691–121–1

First printing December 1973
Second printing March 1974

Published by WINCHESTER PRESS
460 Park Avenue, New York 10022

Printed in the United States of America

Dedicated to
Samuel T. Dana

Contents

Preface

ANYONE WHO WRITES anything of book size should have a reason or (possibly) an excuse. I disapprove of explanations, but to omit them here would perhaps disclose too much egotism. Even though it is hard to say whether explanations make the situation less or more murky.

The following chapters may be different from most books in print for a couple of reasons:

1. "Game Harvest" means primarily field shooting. I am not familiar with any widely experienced and skilled gun writer who is or was a professionally trained game manager. There may be such, but I have not heard of them.
2. Professional game-management specialists have written well and extensively, but I do not know of any who have made equally careful studies of arms, shooting, and the pursuit of game.

My master's degree was earned in game management, and my practice in this specialty has been extensive indeed. I have hunted since I was big enough to shoulder a gun, and I have studied guns and shooting with great care ever since. My opportunity for this study has happily improved since official retirement in 1961. I currently own over a hundred shooting guns, varying from the most primitive to the most effective (as I view them) for taking game.

This combination of experiences may be a new approach. Everything in "Game Harvest" is viewed as the final objective of "Game Management." With a few purely scientific exceptions, my suggestions in game management lead to harvest.

Naturally, this book could scarcely have been written without gleaning some information from other sources. Where this help has been really important, it is mentioned in the text. I am, however, something of a lone-wolf writer, and take full responsibility for everything I have written, good or bad.

Most conspicuously, I am indebted to Secretary Cherie Kremer for copying my crudely written notes. Secondly, Idaho State University has furnished an office, a library, and certain consultation opportunities with biologist colleagues.

Perhaps this is also the place to list something about technical training and inspiration from the former faculty of the School of Natural Resources at the University of Michigan. I largely worked with Dean Samuel T. Dana and Professors S. A. Graham, H. M. Wight, and Ned Dearborn. All but Dr. Dana have now gone to the Happy Hunting Ground, but their achievements in American wildlife management are immortal. Though long officially retired, Dr. Dana is still working, and I consider him to be the "dean" of the whole field of natural-resources conservation.

I must hark back still further to my senior undergraduate year at the New York State College of Forestry at Syracuse. In the fall of 1914 I was appointed student assistant to a new professor: Dr. Charles C. Adams. Dr. Adams was the first ecologist I had met who had specialized on vertebrate animals. He started the wildlife-management division at Syracuse, and it was my good fortune to become an instructor under his supervision nine years after graduation. Dr. Adams was one of the two or three game-management pioneers in North America. Possibly he was senior to all the others. He sharply influenced all who came within his orbit, and I was fortunate indeed to be among them. Honesty demands that I admit certain disagreement with some of Dr. Adams' views. By 1924, I felt that his politics discorded to some extent with his science, but there was no doubt as to his gigantic stature.

Employment by the U.S. Fish and Wildlife Service, the U.S. Forest Service, and the National Park Service all contributed to my knowledge of how the great federal bureaus handled wildlife. I have not always agreed with them either, but when it seems essential to point out specific zones for disagreement, they are mentioned in the text.

Individually, Dr. Clarence Cottam may have helped me more than anyone else, because his assistance has been recent. I might not have written the book at all if he had not encouraged me to do so. Just as Dr. Dana is the dean of general conservation, Dr. Cottam occupies an equivalent ivory chair in wildlife management. If anyone disagrees with these views, I will cheerfully debate, in lieu of more violent methods for upholding opinions.

Though this book may have some value as an informal text for collegiate training in both game management and outdoors recreation, I have omitted certain common textbook features; most notably, there are no bibliographical references. Possibly the reasons for this should be explained.

I have not read *anything* for specific help in preparing the manuscript. Textbooks are frequently compilations gleaned from other books. This may not be a defect, but even if so, it is not committed here. Errors in scientific texts are not uncommon, but any found in the following pages are *mine*.

Further, I have not followed a typical textbook style. This is largely unavoidable, as anything except direct first-person expression seems stilted and awkward when I try to assume it. Besides, it may be outdated, like the quasi-legal verbiage once so popular in government reports. I deal only with information that I feel is basically sound and hopefully interesting, and generally have strived for brevity (hoping this effort is not conspicuous!) as well as accuracy. If the reader is seeking inspiration for scholarly help in writing a formal term paper, for example, he has already read too far.

While I hope my writing will not be despised by learned scientists, my primary concern is that it may prove useful to guides, farmers, ranchers, woodsmen, and the millions of grass-roots sportsmen.

ALBERT VAN S. PULLING
Professor Emeritus of Biology

Idaho State University
September 1973

Part I
HARVEST

Introduction

SOME PEOPLE, THESE days, have taken to thinking of hunting and game conservation as fundamentally contradictory activities. I happen to have had extensive experience with both sides of this particular coin, and I do not concur, for reasons which the following pages will make clear. Moreover, it is suggestive that many of the greatest naturalists and formulators of conservation policy have also been hunters—Audubon, George Bird Grinnell, Charles Sheldon, and Aldo Leopold are illustrious names that spring readily to mind. Hence I am persuaded that they, too, regarded the management of game and its harvesting as means and ends that were inextricably connected.

Of these two related aspects of my subject, I have chosen to deal with the harvesting of game first, for no other reason than that it probably possesses more immediate interest for more readers. While admitting the basic effrontery of any writer, I must also acknowledge a certain diffidence in writing on this aspect. Sports periodicals have been full of hunting tales ever since their first issues. I have read them by hundreds if not thousands, beginning at the turn of the century, and have read the relevant books by libraries. This has been very entertaining, but whether or not it has made me a better hunter may be open to question. I am skeptical, because the very best hunters I have known never read *anything* about guns or stalking. Of this I am certain, for they could not read!

Still, *you* can read, and I am writing largely for a general public. You may know more about certain details than I have had a chance to learn, and you may disagree, for men disagree about many things, especially guns, horses, and women. I will write little about horses, and less of women, but I am sure many of you will have contrary opinions about guns. Be that as it may, I hope you will enjoy what I have written; and just possibly, you may find some information that will help you find game a bit more easily, or kill it a bit more cleanly.

—1—

Shotguns

As every farmboy knows (and I was one), the harvesting of any crop is made vastly easier by the use of appropriate tools, and game harvesting is no different. Man has devised many different tools for the harvesting of game, of varying degrees of refinement, efficiency, and legality. The earlier ones—club, spear, snare, and bow and arrow—will largely be ignored on the pages that follow, as will such tactics as netting and running off a cliff, for they have no (proper) place in a book entitled *Game and the Gunner*. However, the bow-and-arrow enthusiast will find much of interest even so, and the trapper may find some information of interest in the management section dealing with fur-bearing animals.

Since our primary interest is here and now, I have also chosen to eliminate most references to primitive forms of firearms, though as a sometime muzzleloader enthusiast, I have exempted such forms of them as are in current (and increasing) use. Generally, however, the most important game-harvesting tools within our frame of reference are shotguns and rifles, and since shotguns are and long have been the most important single type, it seems only fair to afford them first priority.

Modern Shotgun Actions

There are only a few types of shotguns, and everyone knows about them:

1. The single-shot
2. The double barrel (side-by-side or over-and-under)
3. The pump, slide-action, or "trombone" repeater
4. The semi-automatic, autoloading repeater, commonly called "automatic"

I am ignoring the cheap bolt-action repeating shotgun, though some exist and apparently fill a certain need. A possible fifth type is the three-barrel gun (drilling) that combines two shotgun tubes with a rifle barrel. These will get some attention later, but from the shotgun angle, they function as doubles.

About the only reasons anyone ever used a *single-shot* shotgun—aside from some high-grade, specialized trap guns—is that he does not have or cannot get anything else, which are tough reasons to argue about. Still, guns were predominantly single-shot for centuries. I go for single-shot kills. A single will take three-fourths of the shots anyone usually gets, especially with game limits low. I acquired a single 12-gauge Stevens about 1903, and sold it in 1919 for more than its original cost. I took everything in the shape of small game with it. Full-choked, it was poor for close-jumping grouse and woodcock, and I did little wing shooting with it anyway—ammunition was too scarce and expensive. Still, one is not in too bad shape with a good single. It shoots as well as anything, but just not as much. On one occasion for a couple of weeks, two of us got half of our food supply and all of our fresh meat with a single smoothbore, and a .410 at that. The birds were largely dumb, young, high-country grouse, and I lined up two when I could, plinking them through their heads.

So, if you cannot manage anything but a single, do not weep. You can get just about anything with it. I did, and still could.

However, *double guns* are my favorites, and double rifles ditto. There is basically only one thing wrong with them: good ones run into money.

In my earliest youth, there were no shotguns worth mentioning except doubles and singles. Repeating smoothbores were largely experimental and not very satisfactory until the '97 Winchester was developed.

Including the relics, the rifles, and the drillings, my collection of shooting irons includes twenty-five double breechloaders and four front-feeder doubles. There are no pumps and no "automatics" in long guns, though I have four "automatic" pistols.

Yes, the expense is the only objection to doubles that I can see. But since many readers may never have used a double, my discussion of them may seem somewhat academic. If so, please skip ahead if you cannot stand it!

When multiple-shooting guns were first developed, they were popular with waterfowl market hunters. You were allowed twenty-five ducks a day, eight geese, and eight brant. The market hunter wanted to get his limit (there had not been *any* limit very long) and get it sold as fast as he could. The guns held six shells.

A double gives a choice of two chokes, and it is often not too difficult to get two sets of barrels.

Doubles are the sportiest guns and the prettiest, as I view them. In a discussion at an annual meeting of the Idaho Wildlife Federation, a questioner once asked famous gun editor Jack O'Connor if the double was a "gentleman's gun." Jack allowed it was (doubles are his favorites) but added that one ought to be something besides a double owner to qualify! This remark got the correct chuckle, and no one disagreed.

Most fine old American doubles (and at their best they were good enough for anyone) went entirely off the market at about the World War II period or earlier. They included the Parker, Smith, Lefever, Remington, Colt, Baker, Ithaca, and Fox. Charles Daly sold some beautiful doubles, but I think they were all jobbed in Prussia. Some fine over-and-under Brownings may have stayed in production, but they also were imports.

Charles Daly has resurged with an import as I write. Browning hung on with the fine over-and-unders, and has now added a side-by-side. Smith (owned by Marlin) has brought back a double, and Ithaca has an imported over-and-under. The Fox name never died, but Philadelphia's A. H. Fox sold out to Stevens and Stevens combined with Savage. Savage-Stevens-Fox continued to put out good, cheap doubles. They still do, but they bear little resemblance to the original Ansley H. Fox jobs. Actually, Fox was a latecomer to the fine U.S. double-gun field, but he had few (if any) superiors.

Scads of relatively cheap American-sold doubles were jobbed from abroad, largely Belgium. There were all sorts of brands and some crude workmanship, but most of them were good enough shooters. The best of the fine U.S. doubles were works of art as well as potent killers.

Peculiarly, as the fine old U.S. doubles like Parker and Lefever were expiring, Winchester came out with one. Really two, though the cheap one, the Model 24, had little significance. But Winchester's Model 21 is a very fine gun, maybe as good as any of the old-timers. Perhaps it is not quite up to the best European double jobs, but it is good enough. Expensive and solely custom at present, you own a real gun when you have a Model 21. The one I have is the best killer I have ever fired at Western open-ground upland birds, such as doves, chukars, Huns, pheasants, and sage grouse.

Returning to the expense of doubles, you can generally manage if you try hard enough. It is comparable to the dedicated alcoholic. This type of drunk manages to stay drunk. Similar singleness of purpose will result in a doubleness of guns. I know, as I have been either a poor college professor or a poor federal biologist through most of my working life. Now a poor retiree, I still manage these double guns, and fodder for them.

Most of my smoothbore shooting is with the Winchester 21 just mentioned, and a 1940 Smith. Both are 12-gauge.

The Winchester, picked up secondhand, has 28-inch barrels. The right barrel is improved cylinder, and the left modified choke. It has taken both pheasants and sage grouse at 50 yards, but is not consistent much over 40 yards. The right barrel is at its best when game is 25 to 35 yards away. That is about where doves and pheasants should be if you plan to always bag them. I have never used anything except No. 7½ and No. 6 shot in this gun. Like all but the earliest 21s, it has a selective single trigger.

The older Smith has two sets of barrels. One set is 30 inches long, both full choke (and how!), and the others are 26 inches long and both improved cylinder. The trigger is single, but nonselective. This trigger got out of whack a few years ago. I managed to find a gunsmith who could repair it, and without being asked, he juggled it so the left barrel now shoots first. Not a bad idea, since that right barrel took a real rim-racking for nearly a quarter-century. Incidentally, that same right barrel has averaged some 86 percent patterns with 1⅝ ounces of No. 6 shot. A waterfowl killer-diller, you have to be very careful if shooting over blocks at under 35 yards. You'd better also fire No. 7½ or 8 shot.

The short barrels are woodcock, jacksnipe, and ruffed-grouse medicine, and not bad for skeet. I use No. 9 pellets for the woodcock and snipe, 7½ for grouse. (No. 6 are also fine for the second barrel on grouse —if there is any second barrel, as generally there is not.) Those short barrels would be equally good for bobwhites, but sadly enough I have not hunted them. My father shot many when I was a small boy, but they went on the songbird list. I have shot Gambel's, valley, and mountain quail, but prefer modified choke in the second barrel when hunting these birds. My 21 is also right for them with 7½ shot.

Pump guns are no doubt the general favorites among American hunters, though I have not studied the statistics. One reason is that you can get an excellent pump gun considerably cheaper than a really good double. Many know little and care little about anything except the pumps. There is the advantage of more shots. Since migratory game shooting has been reduced to three shots this is not so important, but the third shot can still prove valuable in finishing waterfowl, especially geese.

There are some marked *dis*advantages to both pump or "automatic" smoothbores, if one would analyze them carefully. They are longer, because of the breechblock. You are restricted to one choke, unless you install a variable-choke device. And a pump or "automatic" gun is not as safe as a double.

Automatic guns have the same disadvantages as the pumps, but enjoy the advantage of the shooter not having to do anything except pull the trigger. This makes them still more dangerous.

Beginning with World War II, millions of soldiers got accustomed to automatic arms, including those with full-automatic fire. These people would, in some instances, hunt with full-automatic guns if it were legal and the weapons were available. Since they are not legal and are rarely available, some hunters will select the fastest-shooting guns they can get. It is an understandable matter of training and habit.

Automatics are a little more expensive than pumps, but you can still get an excellent auto cheaper than a good double. They shoot just as well as anything.

I believe that the ammunition manufacturers are especially fond of fast-shooting arms, since the shooter tends to use more cartridges. Making ammunition may pay better than making guns. Laying down a barrage is another military habit. I have seen a deer hunter fire a couple of extra shots into the brush where an animal had disappeared. Shotgunners likewise empty their guns at birds out of range.

So, really, a shotgun is a matter of choice, what one can afford, or what one gets whether or not he can afford it. Single, double, pump, or auto, all will gather the game if you do your part.

Gauges and Chokes

Since I have already made some casual references to chokes, further discussion will be brief.

There are several methods of choking guns, and I will ignore them since it is a mechanical angle well written up elsewhere.

Ordinary choking is referred to as full, modified, and cylinder. There is also skeet boring, which is not far from cylinder, and improved (i.e., tightened) cylinder as well as improved modified.

For field shooting, there is little reason for straight cylinder except when using conical slugs or round balls. (I recall one critic who said there was no reason to worry about the pattern of a cylinder-bore gun—it had no pattern!) I have one real cylinder double. The muzzle got mangled, and I sawed it off. It has rifle sights and shoots slugs like a streak. It is likewise a terrible weapon at close range with buckshot.

A full-choked gun is supposed to put at least 70 percent of its charge of shot inside a 30-inch circle at 40 yards. My old Smith will do a lot better (or worse, if the bird is too close), which makes it an extra-full.

Modified choke is proportionally less (say, 60 percent), and improved cylinder manages just enough choke to prevent blown patterns. Wads have improved marvelously, but at one time (maybe still) a wad or wads *could* be blown through the shot charge, especially if the shot is fine. Improved-cylinder boring is standard for shooting bobwhite quail, ruffed grouse, woodcock, and jacksnipe. Improved cylinder also causes less distortion if you are using buckshot, and slugs do as well, or almost as well, in improved-cylinder barrels as they do in straight-cylinder bores.

Modified choke is close enough for chukar, Hun, Western quail, pheasant, ptarmigan, dusky grouse, sage grouse, and the doves and pigeons. European red grouse could be included. For this class of game, an improved-cylinder right barrel and a modified-choke left is my choice, as previously stated.

Possibly one cannot have too much choke in a waterfowl gun. There are exceptions, if you fire only over decoys at 35 yards or less. For geese, which are easy to hit but hard to kill, full choke may never be too much.

In general, however, shooters choose too much choke rather than too little. You cannot kill anything if you do not hit it. If a bird jumps close, the farther it goes the faster it goes, so you want to get on as soon as you can. If you are too close and really on, a choke-bore gun may tear the bird to smithereens. Mercifully you often miss under those conditions.

It is something of a rule that the bigger the bore the less need for choke. For a 20-gauge or smaller, full choke may always be logical. Since choking has progressed, smaller bores have become somewhat more stylish. It is no longer legal in the United States to use a bore bigger than 10, and that is big enough, or too big, as I will shortly note. Still, in the old days of big bores, there was likely to be less choke. Few muzzleloaders were choked at all. If you were firing a 4-gauge, with 4 to 5 ounces of shot and a couple of pistol balls for luck, there was so much lead in the air that birds were in jeopardy just by the law of averages.

You are of course aware of the variable-choke devices available for all types of single-barrel guns. I have seen many in use but have not owned any and do not plan to. They are useful, but no one claims, to my knowledge, that they pattern as well as a fixed choke. If anyone so claims, I will probably still not believe him! Even so, if I had to use a pump gun or an automatic, and had only one gun, I would probably have a variable choke. But I concede that you cannot positively pick a gun for anyone else. It is too much like choosing his horses and women.

Gauges and Barrel Lengths

If no gauge but 12 existed, game would be no happier, and hunters should not be especially vexed. Arms and ammunition manufacturers are good guys. So are the wholesale and retail dispensers of their product. They largely live because of varying gun and ammunition types. At times their advertising is silly. Not as silly as cigarette and motor-car advertising, but silly enough. You can kill just about anything with just about anything, if you can point properly, and have some notion of range. It is a matter of choice, again, like the horses and women.

Twelve-gauge (or bore) means that the bore (caliber) of the gun is the same diameter as a lead ball that runs 12 to the pound. A 1-gauge, naturally, would have a bore diameter equal to the diameter of a 1-pound lead ball. A 16-gauge would have a bore the diameter of a 1-ounce ball. And so on. I may be insulting the reader's intelligence by explaining about gauges, but many well-educated people are unfamiliar with the origin of this designation of bore diameter.

Perhaps while I am insulting intelligence, it should be noted that the so-called .410 gauge has nothing to do with diameters of lead balls, so many to the pound. It is the only smooth-bore gauge that is called a gauge but is really a caliber. It means a bore diameter of .410 inch, though actually it developed from .44 caliber and is nearer to .42, but was arbitrarily named for reasons best known to those who did it. As will be noted later, if this .410 had never been devised, the loss would not be great.

There have been many gauges used through the years. The 12-gauge is most popular in all countries that are more or less Anglo-Saxon in settlement. Germanic Europe leans heavily to the 16-gauge. I feel that the 16 is an unessential bastard. It is too big to be small yet too small to be big. Still, I have worked extensively with drillings of German extraction. A drilling, of course, is a double smoothbore with a rifle barrel under the shotgun barrels. Old and new, I have five of these combination guns. All are 16-gauge. A couple of the best have barrels close to 24 inches long. With the very fine ammunition now manufactured, these smallish guns make as good patterns and kill game at long range almost as well as standard 12-gauge weapons. You will do all right with a 16. Instead of calling it a bastard, you may wish to refer to it as a compromise, or like a general-purpose horse. It is safer to make no references at all to general-purpose women!

If one would depart to something smaller than the 12-gauge, the 20 is logical. A 20 can be a beautiful little gun. You can make a little 12, or a little 16, but it may look stubby, or otherwise lack symmetry. A couple of my 16-gauge drillings are very artistic weapons, besides being small! But no little gun can be as pretty as a 20, and still be extremely effective.

My wife usually shoots a double 20 Smith, and it is the only 20 in our gun cabinets. Its left barrel is full choke, and the right is somewhat less than full, but choked plenty. It kills upland birds as well as anything at reasonable ranges. Few can lead properly if the range is longer than reasonable. The average hunter is just as effective at any kind of upland game hunting with a good 20 as he can be with anything. Since the little gun handles faster, it may sometimes be more efficient. Some years ago, I went on my biggest pheasant hunt of the year with a fine old 16 double. At the time, I did not have a 12 that was in shooting shape. I took seven birds with a total of fourteen shots, including finishing cripples. I never did better. A 20 could have done as well. I *like* biggish guns, but they are not necessarily more effective.

With the smaller gauges, you need more choke, but finer shot. You also need better pointing. A bigger gauge generally means more lead in the air. Other things being equal (often they are not) the more lead in the air, the more likely that a bird will fly into it.

Personally, I do not like the 3-inch "magnum" load for a 20-gauge. It really is a 12-gauge load, and though it will carry as far and make as good a pattern as a 12 load firing the same weight of shot, the shot-string is longer. A bird might fly through it and be missed completely. Even worse, he might be hit with too few pellets to bring him down.

By lengthening any case, you can put any reasonable (or even unreasonable) amount of shot in it, and fire it in a small-gauge gun. This is the "magnum" shotgun style. I suspect that the lengthened-case magnums *may* have gone by the peak of their popularity.

Even in this magnum area, there has been little monkeying with the efficient (if bastard) 16-gauge. But "they" have been putting 12-gauge loads in a 20-gauge, 10-gauge loads in a 12, and 8-gauge loads in the "magnum" 10.

The Smith 12 with two sets of barrels, already mentioned, is a 3-inch magnum so far as the long barrels are concerned. I have been using it since 1940. I also have a Beretta magnum 10 double, so I have omitted only the 20 in the common magnum field.

However, when I bought the old Smith, short magnum ammunition had not been developed. I needed a good *standard* 10 and only magnum 10 guns were available. They are available now, from Bernadelli in Italy and possibly elsewhere.

Now short magnum shells will do all a 12 is supposed to do. A 3-inch magnum load in a 10-gauge gun (a *standard* 10) will kill better for *me* than the same charge in a 12. The magnum 10, firing 2 ounces of shot, is an astonishing piece of ordnance. I love my magnum 10, but am not sure it has been good for anything except most interesting experiments.

The magnum 10 advertisers say their guns will kill ducks at 100 yards. I once killed a pair of mallards, flock shooting, at 110 yards. This distance was carefully calculated. I was using BB shot. It will take ducks at 80 yards consistently, with No. 2 shot, again flock shooting. However, flock shooting is bad sportsmanship, occasionally justified for research, but little else.

The trouble with the magnum 10 is that it is almost impossible to use its range efficiently. Certainly it is impossible for me to use it. I cannot calculate lead any farther than a magnum 12 or a standard 10 will kill. So what good is it? It will kill birds deader, maybe, at the 60 yards where I can (more or less) figure the lead. But the magnum 12 or a standard 10 will kill dead enough at that range. If a bird is dead, it is dead enough, and needs no more killing.

My magnum 10 is not for sale. I now have a one-power shotgun scope on it, and am still studying lead, but I probably started thirty years too late. Though any 10 is illegal in some states, it is OK in Idaho where most of my shooting is done. If it gets illegal, I will let it sit in the cabinet in honored retirement. The old magnum 12 will have to take over. It can.

I have tried breechloaders in 28 gauge that are better than the .410, but not by much. I noted that a .410 has done yeoman service for me on certain occasions, but I could have used a 20 that was almost as light,

that shot almost as light loads, and managed a shorter shot string. A
20 will do anything a smaller gauge will do, do it better, and at *very*
slightly more expense. Still, a man should have a gauge that he can shoot
best, and that he likes. He can relate his own experiences and note his
own choices. You cannot make up anyone else's mind.

Barrel lengths may be determined somewhat more arbitrarily than
gauges. Up to a certain point, more barrel length gives more shot velocity. Still, there is great human choice.

Back in the black-powder days, long barrels were stylish. Still, I knew
of an experiment that claimed to prove that you could get all the velocity a given charge had in a 12-bore with a 29-inch barrel. Bigger bores
needed a little more length, smaller gauges a little less. I saw a breech-
loading 1-gauge punt gun in Scotland that had about a 60-inch barrel.
It fired up to a pound and a half of shot.

In a 12-gauge gun, you get enough of the power in 26 inches to do
all reasonable killing. Probably 28 inches makes the best balanced length
for the relatively big 12. A gun with less than 26 inches in the barrel
looks stubby in a double, but all right in a weapon with a long breech
block. My magnum 10 Beretta is 32 inches in the barrels, and is too
long, but try and get one any shorter! You could cut it off, and have
it rechoked. That would be sort of circumcistic butchery, and rechoking
would do mayhem to that beautiful chrome barrel lining.

For certain purposes, there may be an advantage in a long line-of-
sight. "Long Tom" guns with 36-inch barrels enjoy a certain vogue.
Some excellent trap shots like 32-inch barrels. You are back to a choice.
I prefer 30-inch barrels for waterfowl, 28 for upland shooting, and 26
in the brush or the snipe marsh. They bring the game down. So do shorter
(and longer) tubes. It is again a matter of choice. Variety keeps the gun
makers eating, and their profits on shotguns have never been very big.

Summary of Shot Sizes for Game

I have touched briefly on shot dimensions while considering other
items. Some ammunition manufacturers give excellent suggestions. They
want you to get results. These instructions mostly agree with my experience well enough. But I will summarize my own views in the following
table:

Game species	Shot size	Load
Jacksnipe, woodcock	9	medium to light
Skeet	9	medium
Quail, chukar, Hun	7½ or 8	medium to heavy
Doves	7½ or 8	medium to heavy
Trap	7½ or 8	medium
Pheasant	7½ or 6	heavy
Grouse	7½ or 6	heavy
Dusky ("blue") grouse	5 is not too big	heavy
Small ducks	7½ or 8	heavy
Medium ducks	6	heavy
Large ducks	5, 3, or 4	heavy
Small geese	5, 3, or 4	heavy
Large geese	2 with 10 gauge	heavy
Turkeys	2, 3, or 4	heavy
Squirrels	6	medium to heavy
Rabbits (cottontail)	7½ or 6	medium
Fox, raccoon, bobcat	2	heavy

I have referred to BB shot, but such large shot is not important for much of anything except experiments. In regard to the above chart, I must acknowledge that some better shots than I am stick with one load, one choke, and one gun for everything, and I can think of one fellow in particular who is equally deadly on everything from doves to geese, using No. 6 in a 30-inch, full-choke pump gun. I prefer to monkey with various sizes and bores and chokes. This may have produced more profit for the ammunition makers rather than more game for me, but I shoot for fun, admitting I am something of a professional.

Muzzleloaders

In my earliest youth, some old-timers would not use a breechloader. They wanted to know what th' hell was in the gun. They could hardly criticize the handloader, but they were stubborn. They were also very efficient, if they had guns that were in good condition. The guns are still fun to shoot today, so a few words on them here may not be amiss.

I have seen muzzle-loading smoothbores in many bores from 4 to 32. The commonest have been 10, 12, 14, and 16. I own 10-, 12-, and 14-gauge muzzleloaders. Two of these guns could be choked, but I have not had it done. Any of them will kill well enough up to 35 yards. That is about the limit, except that the bigger ones do well with buckshot at 40 and even 50 yards. They are equally good with slugs or patched round balls. It can be something of a rule that you should use coarser shot in the charcoal burners. That was common practice when there was nothing but muzzleloaders, and it still holds for me. No. 6 shot is my minimum size.

Front-feeders are getting stylish because bird limits are usually so small. If a duck hunter plans a day's shoot, he may get a limit in an hour or less, with luck and good shooting. With a muzzleloader, more work and more fun will end in good enough results. The shooting is also cheap, admitting it is laborious and dirty.

The National Muzzle-Loading Rifle Association gives elaborate instructions as to front feeder techniques. There is no need to duplicate them, so my comments will be brief.

New muzzle-loading rifles are now available in both flintlock and caplock. So are new cap-and-ball revolvers. As I write, no good new smoothbores are being made so far as I can find out. These are needed, and may be a fact before this sees print. I think they will be made in either Italy or Belgium. They should be doubles, modified and full choked, and in 12 gauge with 30-inch barrels. Perhaps shorter barrels would shoot well enough, but tradition enters in.

Tradition also demands black powder, and so does safety. This is admitting muzzle jobs *could* be made for modern smokeless powder, and some, perhaps, have been so made. I have a 14-gauge Purdey caplock with Sir Joseph Whitworth steel barrels. It was a custom job, made long after front-feeders went out of style. An educated guess would put its date at 1885. Those barrels would stand any logical modern smokeless load. I do not know what sort of pot metal the breech plugs are made of. Whatever it is, it is beautifully case-hardened and engraved. I am not going to use any smokeless powder in it other than a moderate duplex load. Muzzle-loading rifles or any black-powder rifles shoot cleaner with 10 percent smokeless powder. The Lyman reloader's handbook gives excellent instructions. By the same token, up to 25 percent bulk smokeless powder is safe in any muzzleloader smoothbore that is in good condition. It adds to cleanliness, but it is harder to ignite with standard percussion caps. If you duplex Fg black with bulk smokeless, FFFFg black priming powder, perhaps a couple of grains, will help light the smokeless. That triplexing may be too complex, but I have done it, and got good, clean results. Musket caps ("top hats") will light just about anything, but I have not seen them on any shotgun except minié rifles that had been bored out to smoothbores. These were not uncommon before 1900.

Though I have seen muzzleloaders wadded with a little of everything, including gobs of newsprint, commercial wads are logical if you can get them to fit. They should be slightly oversize, such as are used for loading all-brass shells. I have these for my 10- and 12-gauge guns. My 14-gauge gun has a wad cutter in the case, and cardboard wads, hand-cut, do fine. Several cardboard wads should be packed over the powder. Only a light wad should be used over the shot. In a double gun, however, the shot for the second barrel should be held in with some solidity. Black powder revs up comparatively little breech pressure, but it kicks nobly. If the kick dislodges the wad over the shot in the second barrel, the shot drools out, and you do not have any second barrel!

I am not enough of a physical chemist to know why a big black-powder load produces violent recoil but safe breech pressure, but you may accept my word. It is possible to blow a black-powder gun with heavy loading, but to do so you will have to treble your powder charge, or perhaps go beyond that. I know of an experiment where an old single was loaded with 15 drams of FFg black and an ounce of shot. That was the accepted shot charge, but a 500 percent overload of powder. The gun was wired to a plank, and pulled off with a 30-foot string. The blast tore the gun away from the plank. It soared into the air and hit the ground 50 feet back of the researchers. It was battered but unblown. Shooting from the shoulder, one would be knocked into the middle of last week long before the charge got dangerous—that is, if big charges are approached gradually.

For muzzle-loading guns that are 10-gauge, the coarsest (Fg) powder is logical. For 12-gauge smoothbores and smaller, FFg is coarse enough. *Very* small smoothbores (gauge 34, for example), like rifles of .36 or smaller, could use FFFg well enough. Since I consider breechloader gauges smaller than 20 to be utterly unessential, muzzleloaders that small would be close to useless. The fact remains that such guns *were* made. People had to like them, and I repeat that you cannot argue with likes and dislikes.

As to charges, a fair rule would be to allow three drams of powder to the ounce of shot. My heavy 10-gauge Dickson double has a shot pouch and powder flask planned for as much as five drams and two ounces. Since it is chokeless, you have to heave a lot of shot to hit effectively at 35 yards or more. The pattern is fine, but shockingly wide. In spite of its weight, this gun really fights back with that big load. The recoil compares with my 10-gauge magnum Beretta firing standard 3½-inch shells.

I have casually referred to naked slugs and patched round balls for muzzleloader use. It may be possible to get as good accuracy with a ball as with a slug, but you need more care. The ball has weight and more power, admitting a slug is powerful enough if you can get it home. Incidentally, "rifled" slugs (I think they are all "rifled") are a delusion. There is no reason to believe that those shallow cannelures make the slug rotate like a rifle bullet. They are cast with a pitch, and that pitch adds to air friction and must reduce their velocity. Some manufacturers claim the cannelures cause the slugs to collapse better in the choke. This could be. I do not fire them in a choked barrel, so it does not matter. Personally, I have never seen any slugs without the "rifling," but if they existed, it is my guess that smooth ones would shoot as well or better in a cylinder-bored gun with rifle sights. That is the only combination that will get *good* results with slugs. You can shoot a 6-inch group at 50 yards with slugs. That is good enough field shooting to put meat in the locker.

I would not hunt big game with slugs smaller than 16 gauge. Round balls of 20 gauge or even a little smaller are all right if you can hit properly with them.

Muzzle-Loading Rifles

Though I am still writing about smoothbores, front-feeder rifles rate attention along with the black-powder shotguns of similar types.

You can get new muzzle-loading rifles, and good ones. Possibly nothing is now factory-made more accurate than the charcoal-burner slug rifles just before the Civil War. This marvelous accuracy could be factory-duplicated, but I doubt if anyone has bothered to do it. Hunting front-feeder rifles are for round balls or minié bullets, and we are concerned with hunting.

Round balls are light, and I would not recommend a muzzle job smaller than .36. That is the caliber of my Kentucky flinter. It is about a turkey rifle, but is all right for squirrels or rabbits. It is definitely too small for deer. I get best results with about 48 grains of FFFg powder.

Priming with FFFFg is an advantage. It is the finest black powder that is made, or so I believe.

I do not think big game should be shot with a round ball smaller than .45. There are exceptions. Some friends are deadly with a .42. I have a double belted-ball Purdey that is .42 in the bore and .44 in the groove belt. It is made for a hard ball, and three drams of powder. The hard ball, in a thin patch, is fitted into the grooves. The ball cannot jump or strip, and it packs a wallop. I have never hunted deer with it, but deer stalking is what it was made for.

Plains rifles, such as the famous Hawken, were very popular in .50. As I write, I am getting a plains rifle made in caliber .58, with a musket-cap nipple, and for standard Civil War minié bullets or patched round balls. The barrel is 32 inches and the stock is being made from New Zealand walnut! I plan to put an old Lyman peep sight on the tang and a leaf sight in the middle of the barrel. At 100 yards or less, it should take just about anything.

Incidentally, a sidearm is logical when hunting with a muzzle-loading rifle, and especially if the weapon is single-shot, as most are. I do not recommend pistols for hunting, though they will be briefly discussed later. Still, you may have a muzzleloader cripple, and a loaded sidearm could provide the close-in finisher. Kentucky rifle hunters and Plains rifle hunters often had no sidearm but a knife. A Bowie knife, with a blade 8½ inches long or longer, is a formidable weapon. Still, it would be a bit too close-in for finishing a bear or any big, strong animal.

The pistol I would prefer is my standard Remington New Model cap-and-ball Civil War six-shooter. I have an authentic gun of this type, as well as an Italian copy. They are supposed to be .44, but are nearer to .45. A single-shot pistol would do, but I do not have one as accurate or as strong as these old Remington types. A breech-loading sidearm would not be cricket with a front-feeding hunting rifle, and we must retain some authenticity!

—2—

Hunting Rifles

RIFLES ARE MORE complicated and come in greater variety, I scarcely need mention, than smoothbores.

The actions are not especially different, and assuming you have read my notes on shotguns, we can cover rifle types swiftly. These are:

1. Single-shots and the closely related drilling rifle barrels
2. Doubles, and the occasional Paradox muzzle rifling
3. Lever actions
4. Bolt actions
5. Pump (trombone) actions
6. "Automatic" actions (really semi-automatic actions)

Most muzzle-loading rifles were *single-shot,* and many fine single-shot breechloaders were used for hunting in the nineteenth century. At least 90 percent of the many head of big game I have shot with a rifle (and small game as well) could have been taken with a single.

The better-known (and really better) American singles were the Winchester Hi-Wall, the Sharps-Borchart, and the Remington Rolling Block. The best British action was the Farquharson, but the Martini-Henry was good enough. Now Ruger is making an improved Farquharson type that is a fine weapon indeed. A new Sharps-Borchart is also in production in Salt Lake City.

Stevens made some great .22 single-shots and equally fine big target rifles, but I do not think they matched my first three choices for strength. The Sharps Side-Hammer rifles were famous single-shots. So were Ballards, Remington-Hepburns, Bullards, and Maynards. However, I can recommend only the first three for modern hunting ammunition, with the Remington-Hepburn and Stevens No. 44½ good second choices. Personally, I prefer the Winchester Hi-Wall to all the others with the exception of the modern Ruger-Farquharson. I feel that Farquharson invented the best single-shot that ever existed. I doubt that Farquharson himself ever marketed a gun. The only rifle of this type I own was made by Greener. I will have a Ruger, if or when the exchequer can stand it.

Some horrible single-shot actions are good game killers. These include my .45–70 "trap door" Springfield and the even worse .577 Snider.

Perhaps the rifle barrels in drillings and all combination rifle-shotgun jobs should be mentioned as single rifles. They are effective enough, and my only drilling complaint is that too many were made for the rather old-fashioned 9.3×72mm German cartridge, with poisonous Berdan primers. Good drillings are shockingly expensive, and cut a small figure in modern hunting arms, but they are effective as well as interesting, and rate some attention.

Double rifles are even more expensive than drillings, and are prohibitive unless one is wealthy, or something of a professional experimenter. I own six double rifles, all bought second-hand. Of these, four are black-powder weapons that I picked up cheap. It may be advantageous to note here that any collector in any field must be alert for bargains. If he sees something for sale at a reasonable price, he reaches for the wallet. I have a double .775 (10-gauge) rifle, made by James Bott. It is an 1885 type that my son picked up for about $20 in England. I can sell it for $200. Not being a dealer, and planning to use it on an elk, I am not selling. That is, unless I have to!

However, double rifles are still being made and are most important for dangerous or very desirable game that must be taken at short range. I recently read that James Purdey, the famous London gunmakers, were stepping up sales. They make nothing except on order. Rifles sell at $3,000 or more. I have a modern Purdey double rifle that cost $280. It is a .303 deer stalker's weapon, and is a thing of beauty as well as of mechanical perfection. In the gunmaker's art, double rifles are the last word. Since many hunters have never seen one, and perhaps some do not know they exist, I can grant them little space. But they rate respect or even veneration not only from gun cranks, but from all who sport a drop of artistic blood.

Lever-action rifles were *the* American sporting weapons for some thirty-five years after the Winchester '73 was perfected. Usually not deadly accurate, they were good enough for ranges up to 200 yards, and there have been estimates that 85 percent of American game was and is taken at not over that 200 yards. Whitetail deer, the most important American big game, are rarely taken at over 100 yards. I long since lost track of my whitetail kill count, but I never took one farther away than 85 yards, and only one at over 70. I hit but lost one at around 110 yards, and have missed a couple of gun-strainers across burns or water. Most of them are shot at from 20 to 60 yards. Very often you cannot see one at 60 yards, so a lever-action will be accurate enough, to say nothing of being powerful enough.

Bolt-action rifles are the most practical all-round rifled hunting tools. I think they hold all accuracy records, and they are made in a limitless array of prices, weights, and calibers. Definitely preferred for long-range varmint shooting, they are neither less nor more appropriate for big game. If nothing but bolt actions existed, no hunter would be handicapped.

If *pumps* and *semi-automatics* are basically unnecessary (though popular indeed) in the smoothbore field, this goes double for rifles. But again, hunters who have military memories of real automatics are apt to want something that shoots fast. The arms and ammunition manufacturers may make more money on the ammo than they do on guns, so I understand, and logically favor anything that burns powder in a big way. Probably half or more of my readers use these mechanical monstrosities. If that is what they like, more power to them. This is still (more or less) a free country. As I write, Senator Kennedy and others are doing what they can to restrict free arms use. Perhaps such restrictions will be in force before this is published. Anyway, right now, you can buy anything in the shape of a long gun. If you like what I do not, so be it. I think that the pumps and semi-automatics are less safe as well as more clumsy and more complicated. In a pinch, I will shoot with anything. But I have lots of singles, doubles, levers, and bolts, and any of them will do very well for the shooting I care to do.

Rifle Manufacturers

Again, rifle makers are what you like. As luck would have it, I own 21 Winchesters, ancient and modern, and would not complain if no other

make existed. With all due respect to the other lever-action manufacturers (Savage and Marlin largely complete the picture), I especially
like Winchester lever jobs. I was raised on them. Further, when you
slam down that lever and yank it back, a fresh cartridge is chambered
and ready to go. The Winchester "thutty-thutty" carbine is now the
most famous of the lot. The only time I had to kill a grizzly bear, I
was equipped with a Winchester .30–30 with three hulls in the magazine. It was not what I would have chosen, even if I had some interest
in killing bears at all. There was an emergency, however, and that little
carbine met it head-on and cheerfully.

Among the bolt-action jobs, the Mauser types are most numerous and
eminently satisfactory. Perhaps the Springfields, U.S. 1917 Enfields, and
the pre-1964 Model 70 Winchesters are the best liked by most American
hunters. Besides these, I own bolt-action Remingtons as well as German,
Czechoslovakian, Swedish, and Spanish Mausers, and there is little
choice. For really big bolt rifles, the 1917 Enfield is less than pretty,
and inclined to be heavy. Still, it is rugged, dependable, and has been
the cheapest of any top-grade action. I have four Enfields, for the following ammunition: .300 Weatherby, .338 Winchester, .458 Winchester, and .264 Winchester. All are eminently satisfactory. Most of the
Enfields were made in Winchester, Remington, or Eddystone factories.
The Eddystone actions seem as strong as any, but are almost glass-hard.
It is difficult to drill them for scope mounts, and hard to work them
in any way. Possibly they must be spot-heated in order to drill. Made
not later than 1918, they are getting less common than they were, and
more expensive.

My experience with these rifles suggests that they are less accurate
with standard .30–06 ammunition than their cousins, the Springfields,
but they are good enough for big-game hunting. They can also be safely
rechambered for any of the short magnum .30 cartridges, that is, for
cases no longer than the .30–06 or .270. No rifle has a better safety than
the Enfield, and the bolt handle is out of the way of a scope.

Remington's 700 series, the present Model 70 Winchester, and various
other bolt rifles now have recessed bolt faces. This makes the actions
stronger, and no one claims that an action can be too strong. I have
known a couple of instances where fools should have been blown up
because they hand-loaded with big charges of pistol powder, or fired
oversize bullets. The exceptionally strong actions saved them, or possibly
neither God nor the Devil wanted them just yet. Still, an action is strong
enough when it is strong enough! I do not care to stand back of any
charge too potent for the ordinary, old fashioned, Mauser types, but the

manufacturers are truthful when they claim added strength from recessed bolt faces.

Multiple locking lugs on bolts are somewhat parallel. Standard Mauser types have only two, and they are certainly plenty for anything you should fire in them. However, some other actions have fantastic numbers of lugs; I believe present Weatherbys have nine. They claim to be the world's strongest, and I would not argue. They are made for what I believe are the world's strongest (and kickingest) cartridges. You can also argue that a cartridge can scarcely be too strong. But it can cost too much, recoil too hard, or be difficult to find.

I am not paying much attention to the pump and automatic actions, except to note that American arms manufacturers who make lever and bolt jobs also do well on pumps and automatics. I dislike them as complicated and unnecessary for taking game. If needed at all for small game or small varmints, the pump .22 has certain points, and so do the automatics. You can throw more lead at a fleeing jackrabbit, which is fun, though the jack usually escapes if you miss the first shot.

In summary, you do not need to worry about makes of rifles. All you are likely to encounter are better than their shooters, assuming proper care and adjustment.

Rifle Adjustment

Time was, in the muzzleloader days, when a gunsmith would make a rifle, and guarantee a certain group. Further, these groups were very small. Some 1858 targets still exist that many modern riflemen would be glad to duplicate. Within my memory, all but the very cheapest rifles were sold with an accompanying target test group. Rifles costing as little as nine dollars were marvelously accurate at the turn of the century. Right now, rifles are mass-produced. The barrels are as good as or possibly better than anything made in the past. Barrels steer bullets. Still, many rifles come to the retailer that (as delivered) are grossly inaccurate. These include weapons made by the best manufacturers, both at home and abroad.

Rifle inaccuracy, for a new weapon, usually results from either faulty sight adjustment, or poor barrel bedding. No matter how far the sights are off, if the shots group, the gun is basically all right. Scopes, unless attached very badly, have foolproof adjustments. Iron sights shoot higher when the rear sight is raised. Laterally, you shift a rear sight to the left if you want it to shoot farther to the left. The reverse is true for front sights, but a front sight is usually left in the middle of the barrel. Some front sights are not adjustable, beyond being able to file them lower. If a rifle just pinwheels bullets all over a barn door, you have a job for a gunsmith unless you are half gunsmith yourself.

Though "free-floating" barrels are very popular as I write, I do not especially like them. When everything is exactly right, nothing may be so accurate as a floating barrel. However, if you get some spruce needles or other junk under the fore-end, and get them wet, you might miss a barn unless you were inside it. I like my barrels bedded with plastic glass, and *tight*. I further like them held down by a barrel band, which should *not* be too tight. So rigged, and with proper scopes, my bolt-action rifles usually shoot minute-of-angle. (You are no doubt aware that that is a 2-inch group at 200 yards.) This will not win in bench-rest competition, but will manage anything in the shape of game from a head-shot grouse to an elephant. Please note my past statement that lever-action rifles do not (with occasional exceptions) shoot very well, but well enough to take game.

Sights

I remember when the vast majority of rifles were sold with open iron sights, and used with little thought of trying anything else. Tang and receiver peep sights have been available for upwards of a century. Rifle telescopes are also nothing new, but those old Creedmore scopes were almost as long as the rifle barrels, and they were plenty long.

Even worse, rear iron sights were very frequently of the buckhorn type. Though better than nothing, these are still the worst sights that have ever been invented. Even so, I know men who claim they can use nothing so well as open sights, and like these buckhorns. Further, they take game with them at short to medium ranges as well as anyone with anything. As far as I'm concerned, however, their claims are the bragging of conscientious liars who stubbornly refuse to try better sights. I try to be careful about superlatives and all-embracing statements. Still, *anyone* can shoot better with an aperture rear sight, and still better with a scope. This is as certain as the axioms in geometry.

If you must use an open rear sight, the best are flat-topped, with a small V or U. In point-blank firing, you draw the top of the front sight to the top of the notch, and hold the top of the front sight on the bottom of the bullseye, or desired spot on game—a "6 o'clock hold." I rather like bead front sights for hunting, but that is choice. I have tried everything. Further, I would not choose open sights for anything except possibly close-range shooting with double rifles. All but one of my double rifles have nothing but open sights, and they do all right. Since most of my readers never fired a double rifle and never will, this is an academic point.

Of the aperture sights, I do not mind tang peeps, but prefer them on the receiver. I also prefer a big hole, so you appear to be looking through a hoop. Small apertures are better for targeting, but even the biggest apertures made are not too big for hunting. Probably the fastest shooting can be done with a big-hole receiver sight.

If an aperture sight is better than an open sight, a scope is still better. You are looking at only one sighting point. With a good-sized field, and a low-power scope (maybe 2½×), you may be as fast with glass as you can be with any iron sights, and much more accurate.

In the high, dry West where I have lived since 1940, it is rare to encounter weather that handicaps glass sights. I own six rifles with scope sights and nothing else. Elsewhere, however, quick-detachable scopes may have their advantages, as well as hinged, swing-out mounts. I have looked many of these over, but have not used them to hunt. If I am on a late fall hunt, where scopes may be logical, two rifles make the trip. Usually the iron-sighted gun sits in the tent, but there are exceptions. Some years ago, I was on an elk hunt in the so-called Selway district of Idaho. It was unfamiliar territory to me, but two associates knew it well. I took the .300 Weatherby with a K4 scope and an iron-sighted Model 70 in .375 H. & H. The country was brushy and there was light but steady rain or snow. The Weatherby was not out of its case more than an hour. However, that big .375 took over well indeed. It connected for a one-shot kill. The range was only some 70 yards, but the elk was on the dead run, downhill.

For big game, the commonest scope size is 4×. If you plan to use a rifle on the light fringe for big game, increasing power a little is no sin. My lightweight Husqvarna in .243 is equipped with a fine old Lyman Wolverine 6× scope, and is deadly enough on deer-sized creatures. Using 100-grain Winchester Power Point bullets, or handloads with 100-grain Nosler bullets, it has stopped everything it has hit and only once a finisher was needed. However, it is slower to get on with the smaller field and more powerful lenses, and you must be right on with that light bullet, or you will cripple and not kill.

If you can have only one scoped big-game rifle, I would suggest a 4×. As in everything else, there are personal choices. If you are silly enough to be both a collector and an experimenter, some deviation can be expected. Beginning about 1952, I started hunting with a .270 Mauser, wearing a K2.5 scope belonging to my son, Colonel Barton S.

Pulling, now retired from the Air Force. It is a good custom job, and deadly accurate. I stick to 150-grain bullets, usually handloads. Deer normally collapse in their tracks, and it does all right on elk if you do not take chances. That low-power scope gives a big field, and is especially effective on running game. I once took two running deer in perhaps five seconds. I was stalking a mule deer, when a buck came out of a bed almost at my feet. It was a quiet, sunny, late-November day off of the Salmon's Middle Fork in Idaho. This deer started straight away, and I had to do some calculating to avoid a rear-end shot. It turned at about 40 yards, letting me slip a quartering bullet through the rear ribs on the off side. As I shot another deer jumped, fast, perhaps 20 yards out. It started quartering, so I could get on at once. I stopped it, but it stayed on its feet and needed a finisher. That low-power scope was just right. There was a draw within 50 yards, and just about any animal that is spooked, heads for the best cover.

At the opposite pole are scopes for varmint rifles, which should not be less than 6×. My only real varmint rifle has a Weaver K10 scope with rather coarse cross-hairs.

Right here, I might touch on scope reticles. Three types are considered all right for hunting and are a matter of choice:

1. Cross-hairs (my choice), or Dual-X cross-hairs
2. Flat-top post
3. Fine cross-hairs with a center dot, or more than one dot

You put cross-hairs dead on (or over or sideways if you are calculating by "Kentucky windage"); with the post, you devise a 6-o'clock hold. The dots are calculated on minutes of angle, and help with estimating range.

A scope worth considering if you shoot rifled slugs is a 1× for a shotgun. You can adjust it so it is "on." Under our shotgun notes, I explained that smoothbores often do not shoot where they look, and both barrels of doubles do not always look at the same spot. With a scope, you can certainly make *one* barrel shoot where you look! (I have a 1× scope on my Beretta magnum 10, and it helps calculate lead, but I have reported that these calculations leave much to be desired. I can calculate *fairly* well up to the range of my old magnum 12 Smith. Thus I am not sure that the 10 magnum, including the scope, has done much good. Probably I started 30 years too late to use a magnum 10, scope or no scope.)

As a last word on rifle scopes, one can kill, using a scope and a suitable rifle, without being a good shot, or much of any kind of a shot. If you

can see you can kill, up to a couple of hundred yards. This is the distance
for which most hunters sight their rifles to be dead on. At shorter ranges,
you aim a bit low, and it is simple. At longer ranges, you aim high,
and it is not so simple. I have a friend who has killed elk at 800 yards
with a .300 Weatherby rifle using 200-grain, handloaded Nosler bullets.
That is three or four times farther than most of us have any business
to be shooting. I have made a couple of 400-yard kills, but the animals
had run out of luck. I have been good enough, with a scope at 200 yards,
and fair at 300 with the right gun. I am at least an average shot with
better than average hunting experience. I believe in scopes, but not in
stretching luck. It results in too many cripples to be feed for coyotes,
magpies, and crows.

Rifle Ammunition

Everything has been killed with everything. I know of two moose
kills with .22 long-rifle rimfires, and that was about 1914 when the .22
long-rifle was far less potent than at present. I have personally shot big
game with the following types of cartridges: .303 British, .30–06, .45–70,
.30–30, .44–40, .300 Weatherby, .270, .375 H. & H., .338, .22 Long Rifle
rimfire (in a revolver), .38 Automatic Colt (before the time of the .38
Super Automatic), and two or three kinds of heavy 12-gauge shotgun
projectiles. I have been with hunting parties in which just about everything I have ever heard of, foreign and domestic, was hurled at wild
creatures. You cannot tell anyone what he should fire at what. He will
use what he likes, or what he has, provided (we hope) it is legal. What
he has may be the best weapon in the world for him, just because he
knows and trusts it.

Thus, all I can do is offer a few suggestions. They may be useful to
those who maintain open minds on the matter of ammunition, and possibly entertain those who already know all about it. I have had considerable experience, and have associated with men who have had as much
or more.

You will note that most of the ammunition I have personally used
for taking deer-size game and bigger was in the power class. The pistols,
the .44–40, and the shotguns were emergency weapons. This is admitting
that .44–40 rifles killed buffaloes by the thousands and all kinds of other
big stuff, including grizzly bears. Shotguns in 12 gauge have killed ele-
phants. I will write little about pistols, but I feel that they should never,
in this country, be considered suitable or even legal for big game. We

may admit further that one cartridge—the .44 magnum—was primarily a revolver round, but it is a fair big-game killer when used in a rifle.

This may be the place to state that, so far as the .44 magnum is concerned, it is a shorter-range round than the .30–30, and at close range, I doubt that it will do anything the .30–30 will not do better. The .44 magnum is simply a revved up .44–40. You may handload the .44–40 up to .44 magnum power, if you have a rifle that will stand it. Possibly the .44 magnum is better in brush than a .30–30, if the range is short.

Just as one gauge would answer well enough for *all* shotgun hunting, one caliber would do equally well for all big-game hunting, north of the Tropic of Cancer. And that may not take in enough territory. This single bullet diameter would not please everyone, including myself. But it would make do very well.

I refer to the .30 caliber, and will further venture that the .30–06 comes the closest to an all-round round that exists right now. And it has existed since 1906. The .30–30 carbine is the last word as a saddle gun, and is close to unbeatable for deer-size animals at not over 150 yards. That will manage most of them. The last members of the important .30 group are the several magnum rounds. The one I own is a Weatherby, which may be the most powerful of the lot. It may do more at very long range than anything else. I re-emphasize, you may like anything, and (within the realm of common sense) if anything suits you, that is fine. It is hard to disagree with what someone else likes, as long as it makes some sense.

Occasionally, however, someone favors something out of the horse-sense realm, such as the .30 carbine. This World War II weapon was light to lug, did not kick, and shot fast. Those characteristics made it popular. It has killed big game, but so has my .22 target revolver—all that proves is that it happened. Anyone is a fool to select such a gun for big-game shooting. In fact he is a damn fool, and you can escalate vituperatives as far as you wish, without exaggeration. Emergencies are another matter. If I were in a spot where game meat was of the essence, and nothing existed for collecting it but a .30 carbine, I would have a go at it with that carbine. But it is a horribly poor round; it was even horribly poor for the purpose for which it was made. Ballistically it is close to the .32–20 Winchester (actually a .30) that came out about 1875, if you hop it up a little by handloading. It was simply one of our government's numerous mistakes.

While I exalt the .30 caliber in several of its forms, it should be noted that it really is a bastard diameter that should not exist. For actually, above our excellent .22, there is really no reason in bullet calibers for anything except the metric system. Half millimeters work fine for everything up to eight, and then we can advance by whole millimeters. For example, our .243 is 6mm. The 6.5 is .264. The 7 is .280, and that .280 is a great all-round caliber. The 8mm is about .32, and the 9 about .36. That is enough diameter to kill anything, but I will light a torch presently for the .45.

If my comparisons with millimeters have any merit, all the .25 group, the .270, and the .30 group should not have existed! The .270 is so close to 7mm that it should evaporate, but it shows no evidence of so doing. For the last sixteen years, my .270 has taken more big game than the rest of my arsenal combined. I use it only with 150-grain bullets. Likewise, I use nothing lighter than 180-grain slugs for the .30–06 and the .300, and stick to 200-grain bullets for anything bigger than deer. Sadly, some hunters demand 150-grain bullets for the .30–30, and (sadder yet) the 150-grain weight has been most popular for the .30–06 and its excellent .308 associate. Truly, these lighter bullets start faster, but by the time you get out far enough for the velocity to do some good, the 180-grain ammo has caught up. At this point I suppose I should observe that right now, shooters are running wild on light bullets and speed. It is a delusion, and a reaction is due. (Newton's Third Law applies to just about everything.)

Everyone can profit by studying ballistics tables, but these must still be taken with a pinch of salt. Seemingly, bullets with the most footpounds of muzzle energy should be the best killers. They are not. Weight, diameters, sectional densities, and what-have-you also enter the picture. You must have either expansion or diameter to put an animal down and keep him there. A straight blow, or concussion, does not usually do it. The shooter's shoulder gets almost as much shock as the game gets from the bullet. The weight of the gun lessens this shock, and there is some scattering of the gun butt's wallop. Projectiles kill, very largely, by doing simple tissue damage.

With these very fast, light, expanding slugs, there have been some studies made of hydraulic shock. An English hunter named Baden-Powell reported on this in the *American Rifleman,* some years past. The bullet pressures body fluids, largely blood, and brain capillaries burst, resulting in a "stroke." The animal goes down and stays. I am enough of an anatomist to agree with this principle. It definitely appears to have been operative when I have shot mule deer with the .270 at medium ranges.

In general, one must consider what happens to the game rather than what appears in the tables. A .45–70, with a 405-grain bullet, will usually make a cleaner kill at close range than a hot, light charge with twice the listed energy. Further, big, heavy, slow bullets are usually fatal in situations where the fast bullet does not even get close (in damage) to its intended victim. As a specific example, I was hunting elk, some years ago, in Idaho, near the Bitterroot Mountains boundary of Montana. I took the .300 Weatherby. The country is largely open, but there are some wooded or brushy creek bottoms. My rifle, with a K4 scope, was loaded with rather fast 180-grain bullets, but presumably I had some hulls charged with 200-grain slugs. No one in the party saw even an elk track. They were higher than we could get them out, hunting on foot within a couple of miles of our truck. But I was only a half-mile from camp when I saw a fat little forkhorn buck, standing in brush, 60 to 70 yards away. He was squarely broadside and knew I was around, but was not worried especially. I drew carefully behind his left elbow, and squeezed off a shot. Some twigs flew, but the deer did not stir. I slid in another round, and aimed for the same spot. The bullet again blew up in the brush, but a twig or jacket fragment may have stung. The deer jumped and spun around, without traveling 10 feet. He was quartering, and in a worse spot to do meat damage, but my scope suggested that there was a small hole through the brush, back of the animal's right elbow. I slipped a slug through that hole, and that was that. A weak .45–70 or even a .44–40 would have crashed through the brush and killed with the first shot. I once took a whitetail, late in the season, in an aspen thicket, with a .45–70. That big bullet cut down a couple of trees the size of broom handles, but was not deflected, and still went through the deer. It jumped but soon fell dead. A .30–06 with a 220-grain soft-point bullet might also have been effective but none of my really hot rifles would have gone past the first little aspen. The foot-pounds of power may be ample, but you have to get them on the target, and *inside the animal*, rather deep, if you want it to go down and stay down.

In brush, a .45–70, with a modern steel barrel, and revved up to start a 405-grain bullet at perhaps 1,800 foot-seconds, is *the* brush rifle. A .375 H. & H. with a 300-grain bullet will do as well. The now obsolete .348 with heaviest lead, or a .338 will also do well. The '86 Winchester is perhaps my favorite for brush hunting with a .45–70 load. One is not easy to come by. If you have one, you should treasure it. (I have four and none is for sale! Two fire the .45–70 ammunition, and one of these has a modern steel barrel that will manage heavy landloads.)

A whole book could be filled with the pros and cons of rifle ammunition. Later, when I discuss taking individual species, the stoppers for each particular species will get some attention. In general you should use what you like, assuming it is legal, but if you are in doubt between two calibers, take the bigger one! In a specific caliber, if you wonder which bullet weight is best, take the heavier. You can be certain that the animals you shoot do not read the ballistics tables. Big, slow bullets bring game down, and do not destroy meat or ruin trophies. I have much respect for "hot" rifles. My arsenal includes a .264 magnum Winchester, and they do not grow them much hotter. You could kill an elephant with it, if you put the right bullet in the right spot. But I'd sure hate to have my life depend on it.

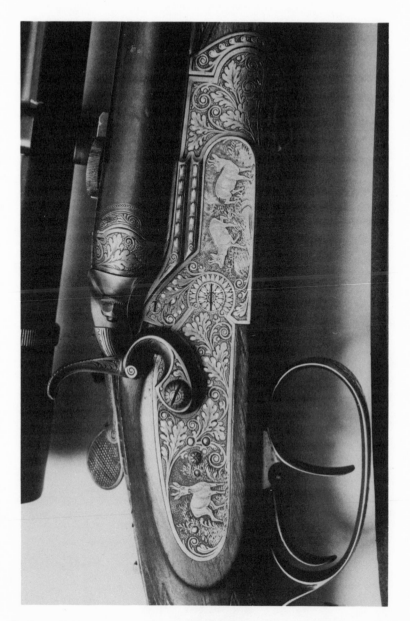

For the gun fanciers among my readers, the following pages will provide a look at a few special pets in my collection. To begin with, here is a close-up of the engraving on my hammer drilling by Robert Mahrholdt, of Innsbruck, Austria. (You will find the whole gun on the next page.) Superlatives are always dangerous, but if the Mahrholdts are not the world's best engravers, they are good enough for me. I acquired this fine piece some fifteen years ago—luckily, for I could not afford it at today's prices!

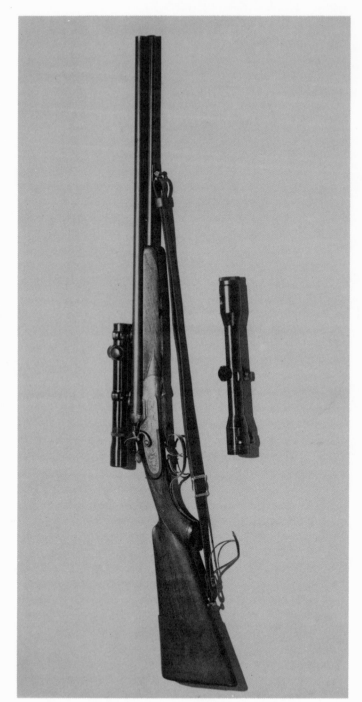

My Mahrholdt drilling, a very fine one for my money. The shotgun tubes are 16-gauge, choked full and improved cylinder, and the rifle barrel is chambered for the 6.5 × 57 Rimmed. The scopes are 4× and 1×, and the whole works came in a good oak case.

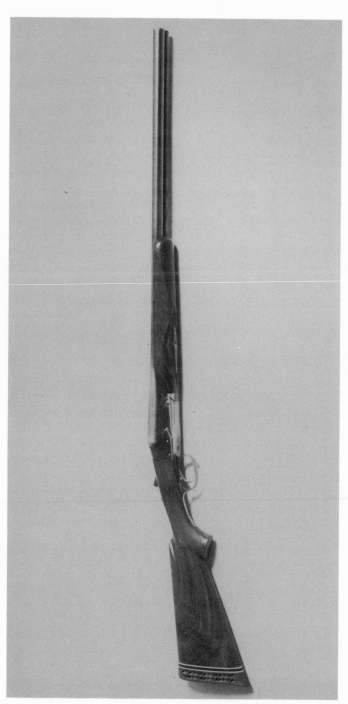

My favorite upland gun, a 12-gauge Winchester Model 21. Barrels are 28-inch, improved cylinder and modified choke. I don't especially like those white spacers under the recoil pad, but they were there when I bought the gun secondhand, and can wait until the pad oxidizes and must be replaced.

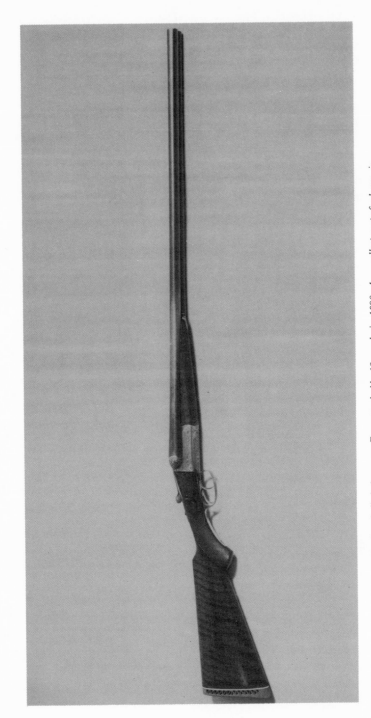

My "regular" duck gun, a Francotte double 12, made in 1890. An excellent waterfowl gun in situations in which heavier ordnance is unnecessary. Both barrels are full-choke, and the weight is about 8 pounds, about right for the 1 1/2-ounce short magnum loads I prefer.

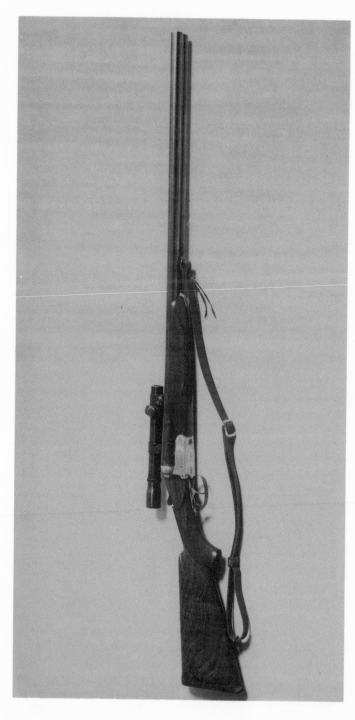

My long-range wildfowling gun, a 10-gauge magnum Beretta fitted with a 1× scope. I find the scope an advantage in calculating leads for long-range waterfowl shots. With both eyes open and after a bit of practice, the shooter is not appreciably slowed, while all-round accuracy is improved.

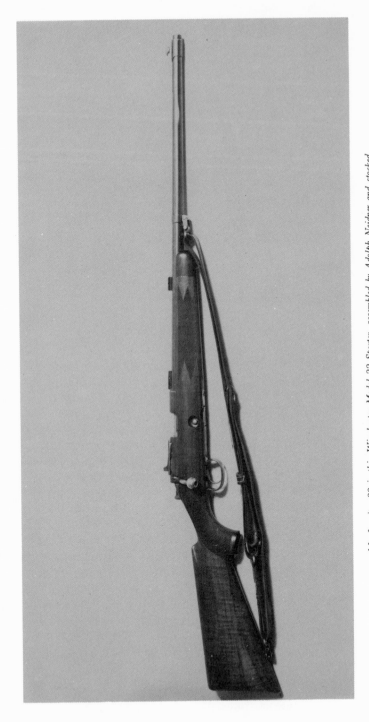

My favorite .22 is this Winchester Model 22 Sporter, assembled by Adolph Neidner and stocked by Tom Shelhamer. The butt plate and receiver sight are by Neidner. Though a sporter, this little beauty fires 50-foot indoor "possibles" when fitted with a target scope.

My most useful big game rifle. The action is a "liberated" Mauser, with a Johnson Automatic barrel; caliber .270 Winchester, always loaded with 150-grain bullets. The scope is a 2.5×, which is ideal for running muleys. Though primarily for deer-sized game, the .270 can manage pretty much of anything if you are aware of its limitations.

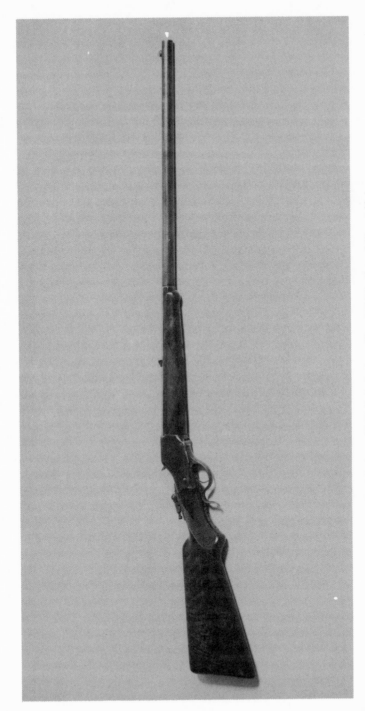

An old pet, a fine Winchester Hi Wall single shot, caliber .405 Winchester. I like outside hammers, and the Hi Wall is my favorite single-shot action. This is a very deadly weapon, limited by sights to about 150 yards, for the .405 is just a short- to medium-range killer with any sights.

—3—

General Principles

Since small game is usually taken with a shotgun, and we discussed shotguns first, it seems logical to consider the harvesting of small game first. However, there are a few points, like mathematical axioms, that apply to hunting big game as well as small game, and they will be considered here. I am using the term "hunting" to mean the pursuit of game. The British refer to "hunting" as chasing with horses and hounds. Going after small stuff on foot is "shooting." In the U.S., sometimes we may hunt and not find anything to shoot! Anyway, you know what I mean. I do not want to seem too ignorant if some of our British friends happen to peruse this book.

With few exceptions, hunters should rarely hurry. Occasionally one has to chase a crippled pheasant, tear after a fast dog, or otherwise make haste, and physical condition is most important. Still, few of my readers would be able to run down very many species that they would shoot. I ran the two-mile during my University track-team days and for much of my long life have been faster on my feet than the average. Still, I can find few reasons for speed. You see more if you take it easy. "Walking up" birds, you may often walk by one rapidly, but he will fly if you stand near him. This is true no matter what you may be hunting. There are exceptions, but "go slow" is a pretty general rule.

Spooked game generally runs (or flies) uphill. Spooked squirrels run *up* trees. Thus it is wise to try to get higher than the game. (Not the squirrels!) Inexperienced saps may chase the game to you. Again there are exceptions. If you follow a deer track to the top of a hill, when you jump him, he is going to run down—there is no other place to run! Birds are less consistent, but they are *inclined* to fly uphill if there is any uphill.

Experienced hunters acquire a certain amount of animal psychology. They know where game should be. Still, if the game is heavily hunted, and the hunters are all rather skilled, you may have to go into reverse. In that case, the game will have been chased out of where it should be. You then have to go where it *is*, even if it should not be there. I have thus achieved success with big game several times, by hunting like a sap!

Admitting that a poorly trained dog may be worse than none, a good dog will quadruple the fun of hunting. Just watching a good dog work is nothing short of marvelous. His sense of smell is something we cannot guess at. It is as amazing a natural phenomenon as the eyes of a falcon. (Which reminds me: Hawking is a neglected type of hunting. It will remain neglected until hunters are educated about not shooting hawks.) Even a pooch of low degree will stir up game. Since there are whole libraries written about hunting dogs, my touch will be light indeed, but I emphasize that anyone who has never shot over dogs has never really hunted.

A hunter on a horse does not frighten game as much as one afoot. Fences may be a nuisance, but a good horse is a fine adjunct to a fast dog. And if cover is high, you can see over it and spot the dog (especially a white dog) on a point. The field-trial judges do not ride without good reasons. Since I have been West, I have known hunters who would not even hunt prairie dogs without a mount. One never walks unless he is "ketching up a hoss," or going to the parking lot. Further, horses (or horse critters in general) have noses that approach the canine's in sensitivity. During my federal biologist days, I rode a smart mule named Madame for several years. I was largely concerned with bighorn sheep. Working upwind, Madame could smell sheep for at least a quarter-mile, and around complicated crags. Of course, any sort of sheep are a bit aromatic.

Horses often like to hunt. You should start training them when young.

After a little practice, they know just what you are trying to do. They do not really mind shooting, but shooting from the saddle, right over their ears, is poor policy. Generally you will slide off and ground-hobble the horse. If you shoot from his back, I suggest you always swing his near side toward the target—that is, if you are right-handed. For from-the-saddle shooting, a handgun is the handiest for training. But if you are right-handed, you should shoot it cross-handed, or left-handed. Then the horse will get accustomed to game on the left when you shoot with a rifle or scattergun. With a fast horse and open ground, it is exciting indeed to go after a muley deer. You can win too, at times. You will not win over an antelope, though they have been run down with two relays of riders. You can also run down a coyote on a lake with glare ice. The horse must be properly shod. I respect coyotes. They should rarely be trapped and never poisoned. But run on the ice, they are fair game indeed. It is also fair to run them with dogs.

Parallel to the horse, a man in a canoe is also more a part of the landscape (or waterscape) than one afoot. Apparently it is legal everywhere to shoot from a canoe, or a rowboat. The rowboat is less handy; you can sneak in a canoe. Aluminum and plastic canoes are in style now, and I have one of each. But I also have an old canvas-covered, cedar-framed canoe that is quieter. Canoes are neglected hunting tools in certain areas, especially the Rocky Mountain West where I now live. But *I* do not neglect them! I will go into more detail about them in discussing specific game.

I have known many professional guides and outfitters who could scarcely believe that all mammals except man are colorblind. Deer, and all other big game, see color like a black-and-white photograph, or perhaps like dusk and dawn. Black on a light background is conspicuous; white on a dark landscape is the same. These days there is considerable popularity for iridescent caps and shirts, but I mistrust many of these since they may reflect the sun. The material should be soft, like some sort of flannel. Of course, red is accepted as poorer protection than yellow or orange. I would not worry about shooting another hunter if he was wearing a deerskin coat and horns on his head. People, in my eyes, just do not look like legal game. Still, bright big-game hunting clothes are logical. In the soft fabrics, I can see orange maybe a little better than yellow or red. Any of them will do, but stick to soft, light-absorbing fabrics. They can be seen well enough by man, and are less visible to game.

Birds have the best eyes in the world. Maybe the unshootable hawks, eagles, vultures, and owls have the best eyes of the birds. (Just possibly, a duck hawk can see a mouse move a mile away.) And birds know plenty about color. So you better be camouflaged when bird hunting if being seen makes any difference. In hunting upland game over dogs, your red shirt is inconsequential. When you are walking around, the birds see you anyway. While hunting whitetails, wearing red, I have had ruffed grouse thumbing their beaks at me all over the woods. I was not interested in them, and they sort of liked to be shot anyway. However, when waterfowl hunting, or when waiting for driven pheasants from ambush, inconspicuous dress is important. The army's camouflage cloth is rather hard to beat.

There have been arguments about tobacco smoke scaring game. Birds have a poor sense of smell, so we may forget them. I do not smoke. I have never known guides who approved of their clients smoking when doing close-up shooting, or stalking. Contrarily, we have all known instances where game came right upwind into tobacco smoke. But all big-game animals have good noses, and when you hunt them legally, they usually have the advantage. There is no reason to give them any more advantage than is necessary. I believe there is some advantage in not smoking in the actual big-game field, but the proof substantiating this belief is very sketchy.

In suggesting that one move slowly (with certain exceptions) there is the assumption that it is a good idea to be quiet. Noises do not scare some game at certain times. Mallards are among the wiliest game birds. A shot will sometimes bail them up at a distance of a mile. Still, canoe-jumping on a creek, we have killed mallards. Around a point, not 50 yards from the first victims, we jumped more. If a duck is afraid of anything he should especially fear gunfire. Apparently it pays to be quiet. Watch a foraging fox for an example. But proof about noise spooking game is inclined to be contradictory. I will continue to be sneaky. You might do likewise until there is further proof.

This brief spate of general principles may well end by emphasizing the advantages of experience. I have noted that perhaps one cannot become a successful hunter by reading about it. As stated, the best hunters I have known *couldn't* read. However, if I did not believe that writing about it would be useful, I would not be writing. Reading *can* save time in speeding certain knowledge. Those unread hunters I admire had verbal training and had observed their skilled elders from the time they could toddle.

If a hunter is skilled, by experience and/or observation, he makes the logical move when there is a choice. If he must walk around a pond, he walks on the side his judgment tells him is the best for game. It is the same if he is circling a burn or a butte. If there are two hunters, they split. They usually should be spread out some anyway. After a hunter has hunted enough, and particularly some sleuthy creatures like whitetail deer, he learns certain things. He does not know exactly how he learned, or what he learned. Of course, one can never beat dumb luck—I will cite some examples later—but training can be an adjunct to luck. It may involve the use of certain senses not too widely understood.

Writers lacking biological training refer to a "sixth sense" without trying to define it. There may be fifteen senses, or even more. After the well-known five, the senses of direction, balance, and rhythm may be the easiest to accept. A sense of danger is clear to some people. We do not all have all of these senses to any great degree. Man's sense of smell is rudimentary at best.

All senses can be trained, and I would be the last to criticize the "extrasensory perception" that has been studied and written up on the scientific fringe. Still a fringe, it undoubtedly exists. And there is nothing fringy about instincts and reactions ahead of thought. They all enter hunting. You can acquire some of them, no matter what your age, background, or previous condition of servitude. Some brilliant psychologist, if also a skilled hunter, might write something in this area that would be of use. Or he might not. All I can do is point out the existence of these important little things that you learn by experience. Uneducated primitives learned by precept, example, instinct, and necessity. Poor hunters died—it was that simple. But there is nothing simple about this long paragraph. If you get to be a good hunter, in spite (possibly) of being well read, you will (as possibly) get what I am driving at. And *probably* you will never be as good a hunter as an illiterate Eskimo or Swampy Cree. After all, it is your luxury and his necessity.

—4—

Waterfowl

WHOLE LIBRARIES OF BOOKS have been written on waterfowling. Since it is far more complicated than other bird shooting, I attack it first. Market hunting is well within my memory, and you are aware that professionals did things differently and (usually) better than run-of-the-mill shooters.

Since the problem involves biggish and *very* big birds, I will discuss them separately, considering the commonest first.

Duck shooting, if you will recall some earlier suggestions, may be more successful with specialized guns. Though ducks have been and can be taken with smaller gauges, there is little reason for anything less than the common 12. Further, my experience proves that for me, there is nothing a 12-gauge will do that a 10 will not do better. A magnum 12, loaded with 1⅝ ounces of shot, kills fewer birds for me than a standard 10 with the same charge of lead. At least two thousand ducks have been killed by bow-gunners in canoes I have steered during the last twenty-one seasons, as I write, and these shooters do not disagree. A number have used both my 10-gauges and my magnum 12 Smith. Of course a standard 12, especially when full-choked and firing short magnum shells loaded with 1½ ounces of shot, does well enough.

I further repeat that a duck gun can scarcely be over-choked. I note that hunters in general are inclined to favor too much rather than too little choke, but that is not true as to ducks. Further, with biggish bores and potent charges, the shooter gets less punishment if his gun is not light. Eight pounds is little enough for a 12. A standard 10 needs another pound of iron. And 30 inches does fine as a barrel length. You rarely hike long distances when ducking. Of course, if you do, a lighter weapon is logical, if you have it.

Incidentally, many women shoot ducks. One of the best I have hunted with uses an over-and-under 12 of man size. My wife shoots her 20 Smith double and does all right. Remember, little guns suggest little shot. No. 6 is big enough for a little gun. The majority of the damsels can manage a 12 if the fit is right, and the recoil may not bother them. My wife's 20 is a standard and not a magnum, but the heaviest standard loads are desirable for ducks. With such, I have known her to blast all afternoon with no shoulder damage. Sometimes she has not damaged the ducks much either, but more often she has.

There are three commonly recognized systems for taking ducks, and several combinations among these methods. These are (1) shooting over decoys; (2) pass shooting; and (3) jump shooting. Since the decoy method is the deadliest—*if* the birds will "come in," as often they will not—I will discuss it first.

Ducking over Decoys

Presumably you are aware that along big waters, both fresh and salt, decoy shooting *is* duck shooting. The club boys go to the clubhouse or go home if the birds do not fly. Truly enough, along these big waters, there may be big winds. Rough weather stirs the ducks. Inland, decoying is most undependable. I have hunted waterfowl in ten states and two provinces, all north, and decoying did not often work well except in the Mississippi marshes between Minnesota and Wisconsin. During the last twenty-two years in Idaho, there has usually been a ninety-day season. Probably I have not hunted waterfowl more than twenty of those days, and if decoying was really good two or three times, that was average.

Thus, though decoying is ancient and time-honored, ducks have got to fly and come in if one would limit. Frequently you cannot do much about it.

All sorts of instructions have been given as to types of decoys and
the way they should be set out. Since live decoys have long been outlawed, I will ignore them, but I have seen live birds, and especially
"English callers," that really brought in the game.

Using something less than a million blocks, a gigantic "S" or a big
"fish hook" have been widely advocated. There is little doubt that if
a dozen decoys are good, a hundred are better. The duck species and
the locality definitely enter the picture. On the Mississippi, during the
late scaup migration, experienced gunners favored a big spread of
blocks. The hurrying migrants rarely circled and came in seriously, but
they swung over, hesitated, slowed, and gave the hunters a chance to
fire a broadside before whooping on. Before the victims were collected
(often there was a current), another flock might hurtle by. A limit (then
ten) was often a short enough matter for a good shot. No. 6 shot was
standard for that type of shooting, though I knew duck hunters who
stuck to heavy 7½ charges and even size 8, over decoys, of course.

The big spreads, at the clubs, are usually put out by a couple of gillies,
and these same gillies gather the shot ducks, and pick up the decoys.
Incidentally, there should be and usually are retrieving dogs. For late,
rough, cold water, Chesapeake retrievers and curly-haired water spaniels are unbeatable. Among the scores of good retrievers I have seen
work in cold water, the Chesapeake could be my choice, admitting he
is no lap dog when it comes to handling. The curly spaniel is as tough,
but usually not so big and strong. I recall one that weighed 85 pounds
when trained down hard, and assure you that he was big and strong
enough.

In mentioning these canine preferences, I must hasten to say that the
Labradors are close to the top. Their hair is not quite so waterproof
as that of the first-mentioned breeds, but they stand cold with little
discomfort. Further, they handle well, and are good pals. Black Labs
are the commonest, and are sort of conspicuous in a duck marsh. Yellow
Labs are not far from dead sedge color, and are almost as inconspicuous
as the Chessies, which truly enough do not look like much of anything.
There are arguments about waterfowl being afraid of dogs, and I have
heard that if an old mallard has a dog to ogle, he pays less attention
to a man. Still, an old mallard does not miss much, and the less there
is for him to see, the better. This is admitting that motion is what he
seems to notice first.

The golden retrievers are hard to beat early in the season, and they
courageously battle ice water. So do springer spaniels and Brittanies.
But the hair of these breeds is less dense and less oily. They feel the

cold badly, and may get arthritic—or something—before they are through their normal prime of life.

As to real retriever efficiency, training or instinct or both mean far more than breed. I knew of an English bulldog that was second to none as a duck dog. A big English red cocker likewise. And within days of the time I write, I was out with a friend who has a doggie that is definitely half beagle. Only God knows what the other half is, but he will hunt and retrieve anything, and cheerfully swims for Christmas recess ducks in very coolish Idaho.

Getting back to those decoy spreads of various fancy forms, I am dead sure that the ducks could not care less. Please recall that I do not deny the advantages of a big spread. Usually, however, if birds give thought to coming in, a dozen blocks will do fine. The species vary in their acceptance of decoys. In Idaho, greenwing teal especially like decoys. We rarely shoot them, and I have seen a greenwing drake light among the blocks and stay there with little fright while we were shooting mallards right over him. With four guns going, and after various cadavers had sploshed down and I launched a canoe to retrieve them, he reluctantly took off. Coots sometimes swim around the block spread, and perhaps help the hunters. We do not want them usually, and dumb as they are, they know it.

It is most important to know the range from the blind to the decoys, and just where and when you should fire. If birds plan to light, just as they drop their "landing gear" and set their wings is the time to throw lead. And I repeat the advantages of smallish shot. If birds swing and circle, showing interest but not planning to land, you have pretty much pass shooting, at anything up to sky-busting range. That changes the picture. A double man, and lacking the advantages of the third shot in a repeater, I often take two guns into the blind. Legally, one gun cannot be loaded with more than three shells, but you can have two guns or a dozen legitimately enough. If you have them. I have!

Going back to this second gun, it is always an advantage for finishing cripples. Nor can cripple-shot be too fine, down to skeet loads. I knew about cripple trouble since the days of yore, but frequently had no shot charges finer than 7½, which are generally good enough. However, when we moved to Idaho in 1948, I had two or three boxes of old hulls loaded with No. 9 shot. I had used them for Wilson snipe and woodcock in Minnesota, and had them in Nevada for six years where there were few enough ducks and fewer snipe. Snipe are not very important in Idaho either, but did those little shot ever rake in cripples!

Peculiarly, no one seems to know why a duck in the water is so hard to stop. One hears about "sitting ducks," and the apparent ease of taking them. This is true enough if they are sitting on the shore, or you are on a high bluff above them, but in the water, tain't so. A winged bird comes down and begins to swim like fury. You fire with your regular charge. He is squarely in the middle of the pattern, and blithely continues to swim. I have seen a duck withstand four such blasts. If the cripple is in a pattern of fine shot, he is raked in the head, and that is that. A scientific study of this escape phenomenon should be of interest. Not that it would help any in killing! We know what to do, but I would like to know what happens. I do know, further, that the coarser the shot the safer the cripple. No. 6 will get them maybe half the time. With No. 4 (my choice for late mallards), you might as well try to kill a moose by throwing bricks. I would wildly guess that the big shot skip some on the water's surface, thus missing the duck's body and either missing his head and neck, or the skipping pellets are so slowed that they are not lethal. I have considered this situation for well over a half-century and questioned dozens of experienced hunters, including some old-time market gunners. All have had similar experiences.

Incidentally, some of those market hunters used very fine shot in very big guns for all shooting. They flock-shot when they could, had a smaller gun or guns for cripples, and if a lot of badly injured birds flew away, they did not worry especially. My father knew a market gunner who brought down twenty-eight ducks with one shot from a 4-gauge muzzle-loader. The charge was 5 ounces of No. 8 shot over 15 drams of Fg black powder. Though the gun weighed 18 pounds, it was said to have fought back some. I happen to have known one old-timer who used such a weapon for geese. He was the late Dr. Philip Cox, well-known Canadian biologist, who was very old but a faculty colleague when I taught at the University of New Brunswick in "Down East" Canada, 1919–1924. For long goose shots, he used BB shot plus a few .31 pistol balls, or all pistol balls! The pattern had to be pretty wide, but one of those balls would stop a goose, the charges were tremendous, and he aimed where the birds were thickest. These shoulder-fired guns were of course pipsqueaks compared to swivel or punt guns. I have mentioned one of the latter in a previous chapter. A breechloader, it weighed some 70 pounds, and fired a pound and a half of shot, usually BB. The punt had to be light and free to recoil. Otherwise the gun would smash out of its base and commit all sorts of havoc. It took something of an artilleryman to handle it. Just possibly a handful of these guns are still in use on the Scottish coast or among "The Isles."

An important adjunct to the duck shooter's decoys is of course a call—and the ability to use it! Most duck calls seem to copy the quack of the female mallard. Individually, she may be the noisiest of all ducks, though old-squaws collectively make a bigger fuss. Since mallards are perhaps the smartest ducks, it stands to reason that the other species may know it. If mallards are there, why not join them? Definitely, other ducks often come to a caller squawking like a mallard.

Squawking needs practice. My hearing has sadly deteriorated, but I am often aware of a hunter trying to sound like a duck, but only sounding like a hunter. Ducks' ears are not in the class with their remarkable eyes, but they are pretty good. If I size up the calls with my bad ears, what is logical regarding the ducks? You have guessed it, unless the ducks are very young, very dumb, or both. Further, mallards are rarely dumb; the dumb ones do not last long, and the survivors learn fast.

So an orthodox duck call is useful, but sometimes an unbelievably unorthodox device is better.

During my varied duck-shooting life, I have met several callers who just called with their mouths. They varied from perfect mallard imitations to sounds that bore no resemblance to any duck language I had heard. Further, when my hearing was 20 percent better than average, I heard and remembered most of the duck sounds. One chap held his nose and squeaked a sort of "Eeny, eeny, eeny." Another shouted "Peely, peely, peely, peely." And so on. The ducks responded cheerfully. When I tried it, they emulated Lady MacBeth when she told her guests: "Stay not on the order of your going, but get the hell out," or words to that effect. At any rate, they made like those guests and sure got out. My caller friend was not talking duck, so far as I could tell. But the ducks thought he was, and we thus got results. I have also heard callers who sounded the mallard alarm note, which is the easiest to imitate. If I cannot call ducks, I can guarantee to scare them. The mallard's feeding note is the most efficient. You can get onto it if you hang around the swamp long enough.

A last and obvious suggestion to the decoy hunter (and any other duck hunter) is to keep out of sight. Peek through cover—do not stick your head over it—and be still. Like other rules, however, there seem to be exceptions. All experienced duck hunters have had birds almost knock their hats off when picking up decoys minutes after the official closing of shooting. Nor were these dumb ducks, but mallards and their first cousins, the blacks that are rare in the West except as stragglers. Perhaps the ducks can tell time, and know law-abiding hunters when they see them. Definitely, they can read refuge boundary signs! Sometimes they read them better than the hunters! But further than these examples, there are holes in duck intelligence that may largely be influenced by the weather. Again I am thinking of mallards and blacks, because if you can outwit them, you have solved most duck-shooting problems. Canvasbacks are sometimes almost up to the mallard I.Q., and *their* cousins, the desirable redheads, are far down among the flunk-outs. In cold, windy weather, when ducks are really moving and inclined to decoy, we have all seen them fly right into our gun muzzles when we were picking up kills or were out of the blinds for any reasons. If they are in the right mood, *ducks will decoy*. A slight crouch, to break the human silhouette, and ducks may come in so close you can see the whites of their eyes. If any! And with or without decoys, if ducks decide to light in a certain spot, they will light, hunter or no hunter. Late season, late afternoon, wind, and food supply a bit short—that is the time to make hay with smart ducks.

Pass Shooting

If decoy shooting is the easiest ducking, pass shooting is the hardest. Possibly it is the most difficult of *all* scattergun shooting, admitting passing doves are tough enough, though under sky-busting range.

If a big gun is a general advantage in waterfowling, you may double the dose for the passers. Often when decoying with poor or no success, passers will come by or over, and give you some shots. Judging lead is of the essence, and pass shooters may be the ammunition makers' best friends. I have seen passers fired at when they were at twice to three times normal killing distance. These sky busters are also friends of the ducks, but arch enemies of hunters who are out to bag a few birds. Especially the more desirable species. Mallards are so smug I especially enjoy proving to them that humans have something on the ball.

In general, ducks in certain places have certain flight patterns. In the West, they frequently rest at night on big pieces of water, but fly to grain fields and then fly back. You cannot tell exactly when a given bunch of ducks is hungry, admitting mallards are hungry most of the time. Or thirsty. Thus they move around to work up more appetite or sweat up more thirst. If there are a lot of birds, you can generally figure some flights and get some shooting. The call may influence them to swing in. The carefully camouflaged doggie can make the difference between success and dismal failure. If the shots are long, many of the birds that fall are only winged. They can run like rabbits and hide like mice. The doggie has speed as well as a nose that is totally beyond human understanding.

It may be trite to mention that in water-to-field shooting, you only get field-feeding ducks. The puddlers. Since these include the mallards, blacks, pintails, teals, widgeons (baldpate is more exact for the American bird), and gadwalls, they take in considerable territory. The diving feeders (I am not saying mallards do not dive!) may also be sky-bombed under certain conditions. They uneasily move from place to place, even when they will not decoy. Canvasbacks, redheads, the scaups (bluebills), and ringnecks are of course the diving birds hunters are after.

Pass shooting, like decoy shooting, may be from a blind. If the blind is elaborate and comfortable, it makes for the laziest of all hunting. If two are in the same blind, one can watch for birds while the other thinks. Or perhaps reads. It just could be illuminating to read about duck shooting while doing it, or trying to! A real good blind provides a windbreak, and late in the season, an oil stove or other type of heater.

Duck Jumping

You will have noted that I believe decoy shooting is complicated enough, but easy enough shooting if the birds come in. The theory of pass shooting is indeed simple but the shooting is difficult. Jumpers are easier to stop than passers, because they may be close. Still, you shoot when a jumper is accelerating while decoyed birds are often taken when putting on the brakes. Besides, jump shooting is rather hard physical work.

Most simply, you walk-up ducks on small creeks or springs. If you know their favorite stopping spots, you stalk those spots. I have often crept or crawled 50 yards to reach a puddle where ducks were, or I hoped they were. Just as they start is the time to get on their tails. This type of jumping mostly involves the puddle ducks, and mallards get up and get going fast. There has to be some cover, and the hunter must know his territory. Some of the best jump shooting on foot I have ever had is within a dozen miles of my home in Pocatello, Idaho. It is around the so-called Jimmy Drink Springs on the Fort Hall Indian Reservation. Palefaces can get a reservation permit for a reasonable fee. If conditions are right (often they are not) and especially late in the season, I can leave home at two p.m. and have my half-dozen mallard limit before sundown. Sometimes you do not have to do much walking-up. Sometimes you do.

I could hammer this old Smith portable for hours (though I am better with the same Smith's old guns) with examples of mallard jumping. I was raised on a farm in Dutchess County, New York, and some of our land included a marshy tract called the Owl Swamp. Mallards and mallards only stopped on occasion. There and over a little round pond in one of our pasture fields, I clobbered my first ducks. One bagged bird indicated a successful hunt. I do not recall ever getting more than two. My father once took three mallards in a short edge-of-the-evening hunt, and that was a record.

Since this is written largely for instruction, reminiscences of jump ducking over ten states and two provinces would not be especially important. But the generalizations are important. You must study the terrain and sometimes crawl as well as walk. An unobtrusive dog that will crawl at your heels when so ordered is decidedly helpful. A rangy dog is a curse. Nor is an especially big gun important for this type of jumping. There is no need for going to a gauge smaller than 12, and tight choking is still no handicap. My favorite foot-jumping tool is a beautiful old Francotte that (believe it or not) was built in 1890. It is not small, weighing 8 pounds, with fully choked 30-inch barrels. I usually fire it with short-magnum shells, charged with 1½ ounces of shot, No. 6 to 4 depending on the conditions. Of course there are some 7½ finishers in one pocket. I might add that this ancient Francotte (a year my senior!) has barrels of very fancy Krupp-type steel. It lacks nothing common to modern guns except a single trigger. One trigger is an advantage in foot-jump shooting, as it is actually upland-type gunning. My much lighter Model 21 has taken many ducks when I was pheasant hunting but in lowland where mallards might be jumped or where there was the occasional passer.

Canoe Jumping

Among certain of my Western associates, I am charged with inventing canoe jumping. Truly, in the Snake River bottomlands, I *did* get it started about 1949. But Quebec experiences going back to 1914 rate all the responsibility. Time was that in much of Canada, when smallish boats were being considered, discussion was confined to what kind of a canoe. There were of course exceptions, such as the lumberman's pointer ("bateau"), but even it was often paddled. I used a canoe as light as 39 pounds and 14 feet long. I have also handled a freight canoe 22 feet long that lugged 5,000 pounds. Yeah, 2½ tons! Two men could move it, but they did not buck much wind or current nor make fast time. Canadian hunters "jumped" all sorts of game from a canoe. Or "potted" it, which certainly indicates shooting success. Ducks were included, as well as moose and polar bears.

Under the right conditions, duck-jumping from a canoe is deadly. A small crooked river, or equally crooked creek, is the most logical water course for this sport. Poling through tules ("tules" is good Western lingo for any sort of emergent marsh vegetation) is another satisfactory condition, and certain species of water birds may sometimes be taken in any open water if the hunters have both skill and luck.

As to equipment, a little of everything has been used. I prefer a beamy 18-foot canoe with no keel, or if the craft be aluminum, only the little rounded shoe keel essential for holding it together. A metal boat of any kind is noisy, and a metalbound plastic canoe is similarly inclined. I own both as I write, but a standard canvas-covered, cedar-lined craft is really preferable. It needs care, however, and protection from the weather, if it would survive year after year. Special camouflage painting, or white paint for a snowy environment, is an advantage. Paddles may also have some camouflage under certain conditions, and so well may the hunters. If you are out on a creek (pronounced "crick"), however, and moving, a duck that is in sight will spot you. He is less likely to spook if the device does not seem to be human. His ego is such that if it is not human it is harmless, and thus he may be in the bag before he has learned about being jumped from a canoe.

Logically, a steersman paddles (he may use a duckbill pole in tules) and the bow gunner shoots. As logically, they swap places at intervals. They also land and walk across points in likely places, so as to get two broadsides on the game. This is desirable only when working upstream, unless the current is most sluggish. We work some fast creeks and the duck cadavers will end as crow bait unless you get below them soon after they fall. Further, if the shore cover is heavy, you had best not fire unless the duck will come down in the creek. Landing on shore, a mallard with a spark of life will run and hide if there is anything to hide in. Here a canoe dog is valuable indeed. A small dog does not need much special training. A bigger one must learn to keep quiet unless he has other instructions. A smart dog learns with a relatively few hours of instruction. For fourteen years I had a big Irish setter named Jim. He became a fine canoe dog, even though I never taught him to paddle! If a situation was especially exciting, he might tremble so the tremors could be felt by the paddler, but otherwise he did not move. A wiggling dog is especially troublesome if the gunner has to concentrate carefully on a cripple. Sometimes a close-up bird must have its head shot off, and stability is important. In fact, stability is a part of good canoeing, no matter if the craft is relatively large and steady.

Further, the bow gunner should usually have both guns. The steers-

man's gun should not be loaded if he has it within reach. If both guns
are pointing over the bow, you are safe enough. Further, one gun can
be charged with jumping loads, and the other used as the fine-shot
finisher. Crippling is the bane and the waste of waterfowling. We lose
some in spite of all precautions. With great care, losses can be kept
low.

Usually the gunner as well as the paddler should kneel. The prayer-
bone position gives the one more flexibility, the other more power. Both
enjoy better balance through a lowered center of gravity.

Since we have been in Idaho, I have had the misfortune of having
to do much of the paddling. I can scarcely hit ducks by just aiming the
canoe, but to my credit as a paddler, please note I was barred from
an amateur race in 1914 because those managing it allowed I was a
professional. Having given canoeing much attention during the fifty-six
subsequent years, I should be pretty good by now. Conversely, I have
never been more than so-so as a scattergun shot. Nor have I trained
many canoeists to be as good as I am myself. Some, but not many.
Further, it is as much fun to paddle during jump-shooting as it is to
shoot. There are far more good wing shots than there are good canoeists.
Nor am I likely to run out of enthusiastic gunners!

The techniques of this canoe jump-shooting are simple and obvious.
You sneak close to points. Ducks out in the open creek usually take
off, but one or two who think they are smart will stay put, and you
get a shot. Occasionally one is really smart, and hangs tough until you
are actually past him. He then has it made, as the gunner cannot turn
around. The paddler of course aligns the canoe to help the gunner, but
naturally he cannot turn the boat around in time to catch a mallard
galloping off into the wild blue.

Going downstream, the bow gunner just shoots unless his partner
needs help in turning to find a cripple, or some similar contingency.
Going upstream, if there is much of a current, the gunner paddles, but
as he comes up to a point, he drops the blade. He *literally* drops the
paddle if it is tied with heavy cord. (Unless it is tied, you sometimes
have to chase a paddle.) I occasionally jump shoot alone by canoe. If
the birds jump close, I can drop a paddle, grab a gun, and perhaps make
a hit. Unfortunately, there is nothing to steady the canoe or keep it in
proper alignment with the current during the shot, so the lone-wolf
method is to be avoided.

When birds decoy badly, sometimes strategy works out with two
crews. One gets down the creek and puts out some blocks. The other
runs the creek and not only gets some jumpers but razzles the ducks.
Some fly near the decoys. Since they are up anyway, and perhaps plan

to stop, why not stop where there are already some ducks? This plan sometimes does all right and both crews will limit out. For this system to work well, at least one of the crews must know the terrain.

I emphasize that a paddler has to do quite a bit of work when he moves upstream, and upstream shooting just may be the more efficient. One of my favorite jumping trips is on Spring Creek in the Indian reservation I have mentioned. The creek splits, going around a slim island, possibly seven miles in length. You slip down one branch, and up the other. Two limits are not unusual, and sometimes you can choose your duck species.

It is essential to add a bit on open-water jumping, especially when going downwind in a fairly stiff breeze. If the crew is camouflaged so as to not look very human, and the paddler sculls, keeping his slightly moving hands more or less behind the gunner, it is sometimes possible to paddle within range of ducks. Rarely will they be mallards, but redheads and even canvasbacks may thus be taken. You may ride right over ruddys and buffleheads, though we rarely want them, for it is difficult to make them fly. When training an inexperienced shot, drifting for coots is sporty shooting and good practice. The coots usually get up against the wind, and fly back. They are easy to bring down, and size 7½ shot or even 8 is coarse enough. Still, under the conditions I describe, they are also easy to miss. I rank them low on the gastronomic scale, but some think they are as good eating as ducks. My wife cooks them using a "Hasenpfeffer" recipe that is really for Pennsylvania Dutch rabbits. One meal of coots, however, does me for a year, and if I miss it, the loss is less than tragic. Perhaps I should explain that the coots I refer to are members of the rail family, and are also called mudhens. On Cape Cod, where "coot stew" is (or certainly used to be) stylish, the "sea coots" involved are ducks of the scoter group. Perhaps any sort of scoters. I can get along fine without this viand too, even if a skilled coot-stew cook puts a little of everything in reason (or possibly out of reason) in the stew, but very little coot. My principal dislike for these concoctions is that about every sort of on-the-fringe meat is highly flavored with onions. I put onions and the whole *Allium* genus at the bottom of the totem pole. I cheerfully eat ants, snakes, muskrats, and similar "small deer" not commonly found on the old Delmonico's menus. Still, anyone may be forgiven one pet food hate. Onions and all their ilk are mine.

Goose Shooting

In general, goose hunting may be divided somewhat like duck hunting.

There are differences largely because most geese (certainly Canadas) are smarter, and there are vast differences in their likes and dislikes.

Since I favor 10-gauge guns for most duck shooting, it would be illogical to suggest anything smaller for geese. Canada honkers (both the greater and lesser species, if such exist) are our only important geese near my Idaho residence. When really after geese, I use my magnum 10 gun. I have elaborated on its being more gun than I can use to the limit of its efficiency, but I have it and it kills geese admirably. I do not lug it far. Definitely, admitting just about anything *may* kill just about anything, any gun smaller than 12-gauge is sorta small. I once saw two geese killed with two shots from a 20-gauge loaded with No. 6 shot. A shooter I hunted with at Tule Lake shot geese with No. 6 shot in a Remington over-and-under trap gun. He was a fine trap shot, and he pretended the head of a goose was a clay bird or maybe a dove. He could hit same at 40 yards, and the bird should fall. Usually it did!

All of that may be illuminating, and it may not. In any event we must admit our big geese are the hardest to kill of any North American game bird. Whistling swans are legal in a few spots and they are bigger, but also dumber. Turkeys are tremendous and have terrific vitality, but their feathers are lighter than geese, their wing bones not so tough, and their flesh less dense. Sandhill cranes have been occasionally legal, and they need considerable killing. At Tule Lake, where I shot a goose about any time I chose to eat one, *the* gun was a 10-gauge and No. 2 shot. Fairly close or over decoys (not more than 40 yards), my 12-gauge with No. 4 shot did the best. When primarily duck hunting, using No. 5 shot, I took a honker or two that died right in the air. The ranges were about 35 yards. The somewhat smaller white-fronted geese ("specklebellies") needed nothing smaller than No. 3 shot, but this size is hard to get and I did not use more than a box or two. I shot a few lesser snows, but they are about a stand-off with the "specks," and blues farther East, and any of the brant. Over decoys, No. 4 shot is hard to beat for any of these medium-sized birds. The greater snows, usually in the Northeast, are almost as big as Canadas, and almost as hard to bring down.

The surest way to bring a goose down is to hit it in the head or neck vertebrae. (The theory of the dove.) It will likewise come down with a broken wing. If it is only one wing, the slant is considerable. If its feet are OK it can run. And how! On land, that is where the dog comes in. On water, go after it with the canoe. I have had some disgusting experiences losing geese in heavy cover.

A goose call is valuable, and I am better at honking than I am at squawking. Further, though hiding is important indeed, geese that have decided to come in over decoys may be very dumb. We have dropped birds on their first close swing, and had the survivors come back for another shot. Within weeks of the time I am writing, I got a couple of careless honkers. We were waiting for some to fly out from an American Falls Reservoir bay across open ground. I was on absolutely open wheat stubble, camouflaged by a white parka. There was a couple of inches of snow. My mittens and gun were anything but white. Naturally, I sat as small as I could. A flock swung by, and each barrel took a goose. I doubt if they paid me any attention until I raised the gun to fire. Their flare just slowed them. They were against the wind, and I did not lead much.

My elaborate suggestions on duck shooting apply equally to geese, admitting you are less likely to jump them. Occasionally we jump a goose when duck hunting on creeks—usually a loner. But one type of goose jumping is deadly indeed if you can sneak with a canoe in fog. Some years ago, there was an especially foggy period in December. The weather was cold. Geese were concentrated in a piece of open water where our small Portneuf River flows into the American Falls Reservoir. Following their honking, I sometimes sculled the canoe within 20 yards. A good bow gunner (really, he did not have to be good!) could make hay. We usually had limits in an hour or so. Any sap can get a goose as he takes off at close range. If no game bird is harder to kill, certainly none is so easy to hit under those conditions.

Further, fog or no fog, a canoe can scare geese up, and they may decoy where otherwise they sit glumly for hours. Recently, we saw several thousand sitting on ice. They were there at daybreak. Most of them were still there at two p.m. We were expecting them to fly out, and be in line with the flight of some. Those that flew went elsewhere. We could not razzle them off of that ice. It was too thin for walking. Had they been in the water, I would have had them out, maybe for some shooting. Maybe not. There would at least have been some sort of action to break the monotony.

Once in a great while, especially in cold, windy weather, a goose will let you get a 10-gauge magnum shot at him in open water. At 100 yards, with a magnum 10 gun, as many as three BB shot may hit a goose-sized target. Those big shot drill deep. If you wing the bird, of course you can catch him with two paddlers. It may take a bit of chasing, but I have never had one escape unless he took to the ice and made off on foot. That is again a dog situation, if the ice is safe for a dog. Fortunately, I have never seen a dog lost under these conditions, but occasionally it happens. It is pretty tough to have a dog get in a hole through the

ice, and be able to do nothing. I risked my own life a couple of times
getting my old setter Jim, already mentioned, out of icy water. Once
I saved him only because he had been taught to grab a branch with
his teeth. I cut a long alder bush, and crawled close enough so he could
reach it. This smart animal (with certain dumb streaks) was absolutely
fearless about falling through the ice. He paddled around with absurd
nonchalance waiting for me to drag him out. He did not try to get out
on the ice. I have seen curly water spaniels that could flop out on ice
as easily as an otter or a seal. Incidentally, though I have never fallen
through the ice, for many winters my regular field work subjected me
to run certain ice risks. Usually I carried an ash pole, about six feet long,
with a steel pike-and-hook on the business end. You could try the ice
with the pike. The hook was there to pull out with if you fell in. If
I were to fall in a small hole, the pole, if carried properly, would keep
me from going clear under. Less effective but lighter are a couple of
hand-pikes, like two big shoemaker's awls. They were imported from
Norway, I dimly recall. They could be carried in two breast pockets,
and connected by maybe three feet of heavy set-line. With one in each
hand, you could claw your way out of a hole. Hand-making such devices
is not hard.

My last goose-shooting suggestion is to not expect too much. I live
in a good goose area. One hunter I know recently set a record (for him
or anyone else that I recall). He hunted eleven times and got his limit
of two honkers each trip. He and his neighbors were eating geese madly
to stay within the limit. Very experienced, with the best equipment and
a fine dog, he is also very patient, which I am not. After I lie around
for a couple of hours in the mud, snow, or ice, I get out of there and
hunt ducks or hie on home. I have looked over some beautiful blinds,
mentioned above, partly underground, out of the wind, and heated when
desirable. I have not had the luck to use one. That is the way to hunt
geese in my book, especially in cold weather. If you are sufficiently
dedicated, you will manage such a device. I am a dedicated enough
hunter, but lack the singleness of purpose that is essential if one would
clobber honkers in a big way.

—5—

Upland Game

THE RUFFED GROUSE (*please* do not call him "ruffled"!) has been called the king of American game birds. Unless it was ambushed doves, ruffs were the first game birds I shot in my youth, not that I ever got many. Actually, I was grown up and taking the dumber ones with a pistol before the ruffed-grouse population suffered much from my clumsy hands. Ruffs are among the tamest birds when undisturbed. I have shot hundreds for meat. I once got six that were sitting in a little yellow birch tree, just as the sun was setting. I took them with six rounds, fired from an old Stevens Off-Hand single-shot .22 pistol. You must shoot the bottom bird first; if you start with the top one, he tumbles through the rest and they fly. Back in 1914 in Quebec, I saw a young man fire thirteen rounds at a grouse not over 15 feet away. It never stirred. He could not shoot, and the little .380 automatic he was firing never won any Wimbledon matches. He allowed that the damn bird was stuffed and the bullets were slipping right through it! There were three of us, but there was a consensus that if any creature weathered thirteen shots, it should be saved for a breeder. Like Poe's raven, it "still is sitting" for all I know.

In heavily hunted coverts, however, ruffed grouse get smart. They lie until you all but step on them, and get out like a thunderbolt. They are usually in brush, in dampish ground. Since much of the East is dampish, they may be in any woods, anywhere. I am rather sure that they drink every day, though there may be exceptions when they are eating juicy berries or green Dutch clover.

One of the best upland game hunters I have ever known (the late Harry Chestnut of Fredericton, New Brunswick) always used No. 7 shot for ruffs. If he was expecting shots at either grouse or woodcock, he loaded with No. 8 pellets. His gun was a double with 25-inch barrels, and no choke whatever.

No. 7 shot is rare in the U.S. so far as commercial loading goes. You will do all right with No. 7½. In thick brush, I have used No. 6, but can scarcely prove any advantages. There is nothing wrong with improved-cylinder boring. Nothing wrong with a skeet gun either. I always use doubles for everything. If you use any sort of a single, remember that any choking heavier than improved cylinder is a handicap. Further, for anything except meat-hunting dumb birds, I prefer a 12-gauge gun. It should be light, using field loads with as little as 1 ounce of shot. You need to get as short a shot string as possible, and start your swing fast. Few ruffs are shot at a longer range than 25 yards. Dogs help. A white dog that you can see in the brush is especially important if it is one of the pointing breeds. A close-working spaniel also has his advantages. Though not pointers, with the single exception of the Brittany, they get "birdy" when on birds and you can learn to be ready for the rise. A retriever is especially useful, as a winged grouse will run like fury and hide in nothing. Unless knocked cold, the bird's chances of getting away are indeed numerous.

As to finding grouse, remember that they like to eat, and early morning or late afternoon is the time to get them near the food supply. Naturally, their fall feeding habits are all we need to consider here. They live on buds or catkins during the winter. In early spring, they "graze" on such stuff as Dutch clover and wild strawberry leaves. Come shooting season, if you are among the beechnut ridges, and it is a beechnut year, that is the place. It is especially the place if a stream or a spring is handy. Everything that can get at them goes for beechnuts. Including humans! Unfortunately, every five years is as often as you can depend on beechnuts, so this is a long shot.

Berries come next. Viburnum ("nanny") berries rate high. So do the fifty-seven species of hawthorns (thorn apples). So are any of the wild cherries and any of the gooseberries and currants if their fruits are still hanging on. If you spot the food before hunting, it will be easier to make hay. Further, grouse drum in the fall. Drumming is supposed to be a breeding activity, but ruffs are dumb except when educated by hunters. If you hang around the woods at dusk and hear drummers, come the open season, you may find them. They are quite local in habit. There may be some seasonal drift for food, but generally if they are here today, they will be here next week.

Perhaps I should note that ruffed grouse are known as partridges—or "pa'tridges"—in much of the northeastern range. In the mountain South, some call them pheasants, or some corruption of that name. I have heard them called willow grouse (or partridge) in the West. Also birch partridge in both Canada and the West. Fool hen is also a common name where they have not been educated. They are noble, charming creatures everywhere, and right tasty on the table.

My last remark on the ruffs is that they are cyclic—the most cyclic of all grouse, perhaps, and all grouse are cyclic. Maybe all *animals* are cyclic, up to and including man. The ruff cycle is short enough to be very noticeable. It is more or less coincident with the cycles of the varying hare (snowshoe rabbit). When they go up they really go up. When they are down, they all but disappear. Part II of this book, on game management, is the place to consider cycles, but they must be touched on here, as ruffed grouse are cyclic indeed.

Spruce grouse (fool hens) are associates of the ruffs, where there is spruce, and the fool hens have not been exterminated. They are the first bird to go where man has completely taken over. I do not consider them game birds at all, and they should be on songbird lists everywhere. I shot a few, forty years ago or longer. Young broilers are not bad eating. Fully grown specimens taste sprucy. They live on spruce buds, or sometimes young spruce needles, for much of their lives, and certainly all winter.

The cocks are very beautiful birds. Dark bluish-brown with a red "wattle" over the eye, they do not look so dumb, but they are easy to catch in a landing net, and I have caught them in my hands a couple of times. When so caught, and released, they may not fly ten feet. They are fair skulkers, sitting on a spruce branch near the trunk. But unlike the ruffs, they never learn.

Spruce grouse may be blood brothers to the Franklin's grouse of the West. There is an open season on the latter in Idaho, but I have never shot one. Few hunt them. Exactly like spruce grouse, and just as ignorant, I have seen them miles from spruce trees. Their food, therefore, has to differ. Probably you will never throw shot, or even a rock, at either species, if they *are* separate species. But they are ornamental, interesting, and supposed to be game. They are thus worth a couple of paragraphs.

As to the other grouse, note that the heath hens (Eastern prairie chickens) are no more. The last one (an old cock) died on the island of Martha's Vineyard many years ago. From study skins in the University of Michigan museum, the heath hen and the Midwestern prairie chicken or pinnated grouse look alike. Maybe ornithological taxonomists can tell the differences. All taxonomists are fine people, and have to live, but I find their specialty rather dull.

As to hunting *prairie chickens,* there are or have been open seasons. In Wisconsin, thirty-five years ago, I found that a few pinnated grouse were shot on the Moqua Ranger District of the Chequamegon National Forest. It was quite legal. They were mixed with sharptail grouse. If a party took twenty-five grouse perhaps three would be prairie chickens. The sharptails go for more open ground than ruffs, but sometimes they are both in brush or aspen thickets. Pinnated grouse are even more open-country creatures, but they may be in the same flocks as sharptails. If you have an opportunity to shoot them, the following sharptail instructions will do well enough.

Sharptails are a lot bigger than ruffs, are more likely to be in flocks, and are harder to kill. Usually (by no means always) out of the brush, taking them resembles pheasant shooting. I manage them best with one barrel that is modified choke or tighter. And I like that tighter barrel loaded with a heavy charge of No. 6 shot. Of course a dog is an advantage. (When is a good dog *not* an advantage?)

Sage grouse, exclusively Far Western birds, are the biggest grouse of the Western continent. Except for the rare capercaillie (capercailzie) of Europe, he seems to be the biggest grouse in the world.

Peculiarly, sage chickens are remarkably easy to stop. At one time, I hunted them for several seasons when they were rather numerous. Far bigger than pheasants, they start slowly, and it is easy to over-lead. If one jumps close in, you need little lead or swing. Draw a little high on the tail if it is going away. Aim at its beak if it is swinging. Passers that are really started can travel! A passer at 50 yards suggests the magnum waterfowl gun with 1⅝ ounces of No. 5 shot. Lead one at least 10 feet, and he *may* fly into it.

Since I had the opportunities and the ordnance, I experimented with sage-grouse guns and ammunition. I took them with equal ease with bores 10, 12, 16, and 20. I used shot sizes 4, 5, 6, 7½, and 9. I have seen them shot with a .410. I did not have one. There is little pattern difference between a .410 with 3-inch shells and a standard 20-gauge. The 20 has a shot-string advantage.

Thus monkeying more with these gigantic birds than any others I have hunted, I proved to myself only what the old-timers told me, and I had no reason to doubt them. Still, there is small reason to fight airplanes with pepper, and a 12-gauge with No. 6 shot is the logical combination.

Further, we rarely lost a sage chick with or without a dog. They are poor skulkers when winged. The bag limit is *very* small. Dumb birds, they know enough to get outa there. They often fly for miles. Maybe other hunters will chase them back. The shooting may be rather crazy, but don't pass it up if there is a chance to try it.

The *dusky* (blue grouse) is also a Westerner. A very striking bird, it is another fool hen when undisturbed, but when hunted, it learns fast. A creature of the high country, it is not usually hunted heavily as such. Westerners in the four states in which I have hunted do not take any grouse very seriously. In Idaho, the grouse season opens along with bighorn shooting. With a full-curled ram around the corner, grouse are small potatoes. A rifle, firing .22 Short cartridges, would be the auxiliary weapon. These blues are great birds on the table.

When or if you do hunt them, please respect their lead-carrying capacity. A sage grouse is the easiest to stop of any big bird I know about. The dusky is totally in reverse. He will fly away if his wings still work, even if he is otherwise a sieve. Any of the big ducks are rugged shot-toters, but they are nothing compared to a dusky. You do best with a 12-gauge gun loaded with short magnum hulls. No. 6 is big enough shot, though I know hunters who stick to 5 or even 4. The birds are big, and not hard to hit unless the cover is thick. Being truthful (except when lying seems ethical) I admit having potted them sitting most of the time. Usually I wanted to eat chicken, and usually a .410 was the weapon. If the birds are youngish, and at the top (or bottom) of the fool-hen scale, I might line up heads and scrape two or even three birds off a Douglas fir limb. Sporting, what? Knocking their heads off with a .270 is more fun.

I have only seen one dog work on blue grouse. He was a small fuzzy-faced sheep dog who belonged to Dan O'Connor, the well-known outfitter of the Salmon's Middle Fork. This doggie was named Pooch, and he would hunt anything from cougars to rattlesnakes. This would include chasing grouse up trees and barking, or retrieving cripples. As to cripples, even a greyhound could help chase them. Seriously, a big spaniel of springer or Brittany type should be of much help. A big spaniel is OK for *any* grouse.

I doubt that a tenth of my readers will ever hunt blue grouse, so perhaps I have devoted too much space to them.

Ptarmigan are the only other American grouse that I have not considered. And ptarmigan hunters may be almost as rare as dusky grouse hunters.

There is no ptarmigan open season in the U.S.A. so far as I know, except in Alaska. We have rock ptarmigan high up in all northern Rocky Mountain states. I never heard of any being shot. I have hunted (certainly "collected") "willow" ptarmigan on the east coast of Hudson's Bay. Though I was concerned primarily with their skins, the meat was not ignored. It is *very* good. They are rather big grouse, and as dumb as the dumbest, unless it be the spruce-grouse group. You are unlikely to take them unless you are hunting arctic waterfowl, or big game, or fishing possibly, and want chicken for the pot. If you would give them a sporting chance, and have a wing-shooting tool, they will fly if you pelt them with rocks. Perhaps there are regular ptarmigan hunts in Canada and Alaska. I have not happened to know about them.

While we are dealing with the gallinaceous birds, we must now give some space to the true partridges and quail.

The *bobwhite* seems to have always been called a quail, and so be it. Technically, I consider it a partridge, the only native North American member of that group of scratching chicks.

Imported to most places where it can thrive (and some where it cannot) the bobwhite's natural range was from southern New York south to the Gulf, and west into the prairie states. At one time it may have been most prosperous in Georgia.

Except for the rare opportunity, bobwhites need a dog, the various pointers being the favorites. You flush a covey, get a bird or two (you hope), and then go after singles. Cylinder bores, or skeet guns, are logical for quail, but I find that my Winchester 21, with improved-cylinder and modified-choke barrels, does all right. No. 7½ or 8 shot is good enough. My father hand-loaded for quail with No. 10 shot. His gun was a bit too big, heavy, and over-choked for these birds, but he got a lot of quail, not to mention woodcock and jacksnipe, with that old gun and those fine shot.

The principal thing to remember on a covey rise is to shoot at a single bird and not aim at the whole covey. You just might hit more than one bird, but usually if you blast through a covey, nothing falls. So one bird is the objective, and if that one is out on the periphery where nothing else can be dusted, that is an advantage. Frequently, big quail coveys do not all get up on the same tenth of a second; they may take off in two or three waves. This gives a fine opportunity for the leisurely second shot. Incidentally, I doubt if anyone knows who gives the signal that flushes a covey. Wheeling flocks of any birds on the wing are equally hard to understand. They behave with greater precision than can be achieved in the most meticulous military drill. But no winged sergeant barks the order. (In fact, it is hard to imagine a sergeant with wings!)

Hunting *Hungarian and chukar partridges* should closely follow bob-white methods, since they are all partridges, but this is not exactly true. These imports thus far are the only successful imported U.S. upland game birds, with the exception of Chinese pheasants. Most of my "Hun" shooting has been incidental while I was after pheasants. I recall at least one instance in Montana when I took a Hun with one barrel and a pheasant with the other. Chukars are not so different in that I have taken some while shooting sage grouse in Idaho.

Heavy loads of No. 7½ shot in a 12-gauge gun are my choice for both of these bigger partridges. Straight skeet boring may be a bit too short range for either Huns or chukars, and I prefer improved-cylinder and modified tubes. Chukars are always in or near rocks, and are not embarrassed by flying a mile across a canyon. When you get them up, you'd better take what you can and try to get others up. Following is generally futile in my experience. I have known them to fly across a canyon, and be chased back by other hunters, but that is a rare break. Since my chukar shooting has been limited to the last twenty years, and largely in Nevada and Idaho, I am aware that others will know much more about them. They run like rabbits and are flying fools. And they are hard to hunt, except incidentally.

Huns, like chukars, can manage a dry, nonagricultural range. Though I have taken Huns in perfect pheasant cover, I am familiar with them many miles from where a pheasant would show his face. Huns do not take as long flights as chukars, but longer than bobwhites. You can follow them, but sometimes they take off when far out of range, irrespective of whether or not there is a dog to round them up. A Brittany spaniel happens to be the best Hun doggie I have seen in action. Like the chukars, Huns are hard to hunt, but not *as* hard.

Perhaps I should now proceed to the real quail. All are Western or Southwestern, and I have only hunted three species: Gambel's, valley (or California), and mountain.

Gambel's and valley quail are just about identical in size and color, except Gambel's quail have big black belly spots.

All these birds are hard enough to hunt, though Gambel's can be "ground-sluiced," if one is hungry and not fussy about methods. I have shot a considerable number of Gambel's limits in Nevada, but it involved a lot of footwork, sweat, and shells. Gambel's quail are the runningest birds that exist, short, perhaps of the ostriches and their ilk. I had a

fine Irish setter named Jim who would hunt just about anything unless
he got temperamental, but he was always temperamental with Gambel's
quail. My old Nevada friend the late Frank (Butch) Allen slaughtered
them as they ran up pebbly washes. He wanted shot that were No. 6
or bigger, and well-choked barrels. Running uphill, the shot would ricochet and kill birds above the real line of fire. When Butch was with
other hunters, he claimed that they did most of the shooting, but he
took most of the birds! A marathon runner, assisted, possibly, by retrieving greyhounds, might be a good combination. Though desert birds,
Gambel's quail demand water, so you will find them near springs.

Dogs are less puzzled by *valley* ("California") and *mountain quail*.
But do not be surprised to find the names are misleading. You may find
mountain quail when hunting chukars, and it is no mistake to stay with
7½ shot. I have found both of these birds in rough, nonagricultural
terrain. Any of the setters can learn to hunt them. Pointers may be a
bit fast. At my age, I am pretty much a spaniel man, and the close-working, smart-pointing Brittany is hard to beat. It is a relatively new breed
in my experience, and rates all the fame it has enjoyed.

I have not hunted either the *scaled quail* or *Mearn's quail* of the dry
Southwest. Reports from hunters suggest that the scaled (blue) quail are
the hardest to kill of any of the quail or true partridge group. The
heaviest No. 7½ charges will stop them, and a dog is essential unless
you stumble on them. Mearn's quail may be in the same area. They are
little, but may well be taken with the same 7½ charges.

Pheasants, where they thrive, are the most commonly hunted upland
birds. Big, tops on the table, and game birds par excellence, their popularity is indeed understandable. They were the first exotic game birds
to get a U.S. foothold, and only one species (plus a few hybrids) have
really made it. I refer, of course, to the Mongolian ringneck, or Chinese
pheasant. In Part II of this volume, I will briefly touch on some other
import efforts.

In the United States, pheasants do fairly well where it is not too cold
or not too hot, and actually, cold may not limit them much if the food
supply is right. They make it in Montana over into the Alberta wheat
country, and the winters there can get cold enough. South Dakota may
be the best pheasant state, but surrounding Jerome in southern Idaho
is good enough. They make it in the ranching areas of northern Nevada,
but attempts to introduce them in the general vicinity of Las Vegas were
unsuccessful, the last I heard. The food was available, so perhaps they
just did not like the climate. I do not like it either! In general, I do
not care to spend a summer where pheasants cannot tolerate the climate.

They do all right through the farming areas in the Midwest and southern New York, southern New England, and down to the Missouri and Virginia boundaries. Where the better pheasant shooting peters out, the better bobwhite hunting begins.

Though big, strong birds, pheasants are not hard to kill if hit squarely at the proper range. However, being big, they often seem closer than they are. Some of my friends take them easily with 20-gauge guns. They use 1-ounce loads of 7½ shot, however, which might answer as well in a bigger bore. I usually stick to my Winchester 21 double, with 7½ shot in one barrel and 6 in the other. The finer shot in the improved-cylinder barrel takes most of the birds. Express loads with 1¼-ounce charges are not too big; remember, my philosophy suggests that the more lead in the air, the more likelihood of a fowl flying into it, though even a 28-gauge in the right hands can take pheasants very well. Late in the season, or when I know them to be flushing wild, or when I am expecting passing shots, I have used my old Smith magnum 12, with 1⅝-ounce charges. Occasionally (especially in Montana) I took pheasants while hunting ducks, just as I have done the reverse in Idaho, and I have done all right with No. 4 shot.

The last word, naturally, is to have dogs round up the birds. We have hunted with friends near Jerome who have two fine Brittanys. Trailing a bird, when the scent gets hot, one swings wide and cuts off the retreat. I have seen them holding a bird, their noses not eighteen inches apart. Get two or more guns strategically located before the cock rises, and chicken in the pot is most predictable. I have seen four shots fired under these conditions without a feather being ruffled, but that is unusual. Presumably the hunters had been missing church and not paying their tithes, while the bird was living right in all respects. No decent shot, with proper equipment, should ever miss a pheasant that is close-up-and-away.

Most pheasants are young, and some are foolish during the first hours, or certainly the first minutes, of the open season. They learn fast, however, and are hard to get up within range without a dog to corner them, or without some sort of a barrier. Sometimes you can drive them toward a plowed field or any open ground. Then they will squat and rise when you get near them. I have known a half-dozen birds to be close to such a barrier and refuse to get up unless literally kicked out. A good dog will keep after them until all are up. I have shot a rising bird, and had another within six feet still lie doggo. You may almost step on one and he will not rise if you walk by rapidly. Stand still, within a few feet, and he cannot manage the suspense. When approaching a barrier, where birds almost certainly are, one can scarcely move too slowly. But if a dog is holding, it is logical to get over there. Birds will hold for a dog when a man that close would certainly spook them out. That is an angle of bird psychology I do not understand, though the reason is hardly important if the fact is known. A good dog is simply the arch enemy (or possibly long-range friend) of all upland birds. And his speed makes him doubly important when hunting pheasants that would much sooner run than fly, but can make good time at either kind of locomotion. Incidentally, a pheasant can also swim well. I know of at least one instance where a big cock swam across a canal when there was a good bridge within a hundred feet. He could have run or flown. He simply chose to swim.

Pheasants, like mallards, demand certain outguessing. Along the Milk River, near Fort Peck, Montana, there is a fringe of almost impenetrable brush. It includes a mass of wild roses, and rose berries are good pheasant food. When hunted, they learn to hop across this smallish, slow stream, keeping below the hunter's vision except in rare instances. With a party of four guns, preferably two dogs, and a canoe, we managed to take limits, using a man on each side of the river taking pains to be noisy, the canoe with a steersman and a gunner sneaked midstream. When the birds hopped, they were right in front of the gunner. Most fell in the water and were easily retrieved. The few that slanted ashore were usually picked up. Only a quarter of the party got any shooting, so swapping roles was essential. Those birds were very smug and arrogant, but they certainly looked surprised to see a hunter in a canoe where only a stray duck or muskrat was expected. Smart birds learn to outguess hunters eventually, but you can get some while they are learning. We did not use this canoe strategy more than two or three times a season, but always got birds when we tried it. As truly as there are many ways of killing a cat besides choking her with butter, there are many ways of outwitting game. Especially pheasants. Everything depends on conditions.

Like everything else, pheasants have to eat and like it. They especially like corn. Thus cornfields or cornfield margins are hard to beat as pheasant prospects. They also eat all sorts of field grains, including beans and peas. Tall wheat stubble, where cut with a header-type harvester, often produces birds. They can run indefinitely, however, and unless they are cut off by a dog, you may have to chase them to some sort of a barrier to get a shot. Montana and Idaho wheat fields may be big! Dumb birds may get up at close range the first day of shooting, but the survivors take up cross-country running. A half-dozen hunters, drifting toward each other, may get results, but driven pheasants, like driven whitetail deer, invent strategies undeveloped by either generals or football coaches. End runs are common. Refusing to fly when a hunter passes within inches is another. Dogs get confused when there is too much scent. Hens squat while cocks run, or vice versa. While you are putting up hens you do not want, the cocks may run far out of reach. The birds have the advantage. Still, if they are reasonably numerous, one occasionally makes a mistake, or is outfoxed by the hunter or the hunter's dog. As in bobwhite hunting, that dog may be the bridge between failure and a limit, once the uneducated, opening-of-the-season birds have been cleaned up. I cannot overemphasize the importance of a dog.

Wild turkeys are the last gallinaceous birds whose hunting I will discuss. They were too good on the table and lived in too delicate an environment to survive well under the savage pursuit and lack of management that existed for centuries. There are several species, or possibly subspecies (if there is any such thing), of turkeys. Certainly there are two vastly different turkey groups so far as habits go.

In my native southern New York and contiguous New England, turkeys had been exterminated by flintlock weapons. So had whitetail deer. Now they are coming back.

Though turkey shooting may be legal with either a smoothbore gun, a rifle, or both, smoothbore guns loaded as for geese are the most logical turkey killers. Relatively recently, Arizona permitted turkey shooting only with a rifle. My Kentucky .36 flintlock could be the sportiest and most authentic turkey tool that exists!

Still, though I prefer 10-gauge goose guns, that may be too much bore or too much weight, unless you are waiting in a blind. A 12-gauge, charged with short magnum loads of 1½ ounces of shot, No. 4 in one barrel, No. 2 in the other, is my turkey choice. A 12-gauge drilling (they are hard to come by) with a low-power rifle charge is the perfect turkey gun. The rifle barrel bore is not important, but the cartridges should be handloaded, with slow-moving, cast bullets. This rifle barrel (or any turkey rifle) should be sighted to be "on" at about 100 yards. Cast bullets can do accurate shooting, and moderate loads will not tear up the game. Calibers of .25 to .30 are logical enough. I have a 16-gauge drilling with a .25–35 rifle barrel that will do, though the bore is smallish. A bullet bigger than .30 is no handicap if it is slow enough to not hamburger the bird.

A turkey is not as hard to kill as a goose, but hard enough. If you get a shot, you should plan on a dead bird. Few turkey hunters pass up a sitting shot. If a rifle is used, the target had best be quiet. With a scattergun, a starting turkey is not a difficult shot. A turkey usually runs like Billy O just before taking to the air. A pheasant sometimes acts similarly; but a turkey, if he chooses, can jump almost like a mallard. Usually he does not so choose. In fact, he does not choose to fly at all without a good reason, such as crossing a river or flying up to a roost. Turkeys are running creatures. Their flying speed is sensational once they get going, but they are not built for long flights. And come the river crossing, they can swim well if they must.

Turkeys are hunted by several different methods. Calling gobblers in the spring is one of them. It is the most sporting, in some ways, and is conservationally unbeatable under the proper restrictions. This means that too many gobblers must not be taken.

Turkeys are among the most polygamous or perhaps most promiscuous birds. I am not sure that a desirable sex disparity has been worked out. One to twelve is ample for domestic turkeys, but a domestic tom does not have to travel in order to handle his harem. Like pheasants, male turkeys fight, and the fewer there are, the less chances for wasting time in combat. Definitely, it is good management to take some toms during the spring breeding season without risking infertile eggs. (More on this in Part II of this book.)

Whether or not a squirrel hunter can be successful if he makes a noise like a nut, the turkey shooter can definitely win if he can sound like a hen turkey. This first involves getting a turkey call. The box type, made of dry juniper, is time-honored and has my recommendation, but anything that the hunter can use to make turkey sounds will do. Some hunters do well with their own built-in caller!

As in calling ducks, practice and skill are essential. If you hang around a farm where some tame turkeys are being raised, you can swiftly get on to hen-turkey talk. We raised turkeys on a small scale during my farm youth, and I had very good ears. But it is one thing to know good turkey calls, and another to duplicate them. Turkeys—or anything—spot poor calling very swiftly.

After learning to call, the next item is to not over-do it. The call is supposed to come from a wistful hen, and hen turkeys are somewhat coy. If they get really wistful, they take considerable pains not to show it. If they call, and a gobbler answers in arrogant challenge to any other tom in the vicinity, the hen may not say a word for several minutes. She relies on the tom having a good sense of direction. He should be drifting her way. But eventually she will call again to pinpoint her location. She may not move much. This is to the advantage of the shooter who is making like a turkey hen.

Always remember that calling too much may result in no shot. The hen is interested in calling a mate, but refuses to be too interested. If the gobbler does not come at her call, she figures the hell with him. Moreover, the gobbler also figures that if the hen is too anxious, the hell with her—there are other hens—and perhaps "she" is a hunter! Turkeys are among the wiliest of birds, quite possibly the smartest in North America, and if they hadn't been, all of them would have been exterminated.

Though not as good as spring calling, fall calling also has its points. Turkeys are gregarious and sociable creatures, and you may locate a turkey roost. This takes a little doing, but please note we are discussing America's rarest game bird. If you find a roost, you will have to get your turkey when he flies up at dusk or flies out at dawn. They are early risers.

Of course you can still hunt in the proper environment where there are some turkeys. For the Eastern and Southern birds, an abundance of "mast" food suggests the best hunting areas. Beechnuts, acorns, chestnuts (try to find some!), and anything of that nature attracts turkeys. Of course they eat almost anything, animal or vegetable. Grasshoppers are great turkey food. Or any of the grains. Their diet resembles the pheasant diet, and ornithologically, they are closer to pheasants than any other commonly known birds. You may still hunt the proper ridges, near the proper springs, and root out a dumb turkey.

In the West, the Merriam's turkey is an equally omnivorous feeder, but he chooses to live in a Western yellow pine type. Since this tree (*Pinus ponderosa*) is the most widely spread Western conifer (or Western tree), the environment could extend from far into Canada to well into Mexico. The facts are that Merriam's turkeys are being beautifully distributed, and within a decade, any careful hunter may well have a chance to get one of these magnificent birds. They are doing well in Idaho, better than I hoped for when they were introduced. Ponderosa pine does not grow everywhere, and I do not know why Merriam's turkeys insist on living with these trees, but the fact remains. In the forseeable future, there will be turkey shooting wherever good state fish and game departments manage them in good *Pinus ponderosa* forests.

—6—

Doves and Marsh-Fringe Birds

I HAVE COVERED upland bird shooting rather fully, excepting the dove tribe and the shorebird fringe that now include only woodcock and jacksnipe (Wilson's snipe).

Many shore birds were legal game in my early youth. All are good eating, and all can be "potshot." Only the two species are now legal, and taking them is restricted enough.

Woodcock shooting may be the sportiest if not the hardest gunning that exists. First you must find a flight that is in. Tomorrow it may be gone. Next week it *will* be gone, though a specific covert may enjoy two or more flights. Very likely you will find woodcock when hunting ruffed grouse, or even squirrels and rabbits. Alder swamps is where they feed, but I have often found them on ridges above the swamps. They do not like open timber, or open ground of any kind. They are bushy indeed.

Woodcock are exclusively Eastern birds, except for the very occasional straggler. I have not seen one in thirty years of field observation in the West. In fact they have not been common in the Lake States.

There was a short open season in both Minnesota and Wisconsin in the thirties and I took a few in both states, but some old Wisconsin hunters did not know what they were until I explained. The best woodcock shooting I have had was perhaps in New Brunswick, not far from Fredericton, but they are all over the East in suitable places. They nest widely too. As a small boy before 1900, I was familiar with their nesting "song" around a swamp on our Dutchess County, New York, farm.

A woodcock gun should be light and fast, and have not *more* than improved-cylinder choke, or no choke. A skeet gun is ideal, and I prefer a 12-gauge solely because of my belief that you do best with a short shot-string and considerable lead in the air. Of course I prefer a double because I prefer a double for anything. Barrels 26 inches long are either long enough or too long. Few would consider a gun exclusively for woodcock, but 24 inches would be fine. And the shot should be skeet shot, No. 9. I have taken "timberdoodles" with 7½ shot charges when loaded for grouse, but they are less certain. No bird is easier to kill, if you can hit him.

Few woodcock are hit at ranges of 25 yards or more. You rarely *see* one farther away than that. You must get some at 15 yards or even closer if you get them at all. Often they go out at your feet. If you can get one in the open, he is not hard to hit, but that situation is rare. He twists through the brush, and you get the gun up and pray as you point.

Woodcock may leave the least scent of any American game bird, but a shot bird bleeds and gives your spaniel a chance. A woodcock dog should work close. Of course if a real flight is in you can burn a lot of powder and limit out. Woodcock rarely fly over 50 yards, though on a cloudy day, late in the fall, I have seen one or two that got tired of being pushed around! They rose perhaps 100 feet in the air and headed South.

Jacksnipe are near relatives of woodcock, but live in the open on or near marshy ground. I have seen a few in all of the five Western states I have hunted. There is a brief open season in Idaho, but I have never shot one there, or fired at one so far as I can recall. They are on the duck-shooting fringes. These Western snipe seem to be wild as well as scarce, and few bother with them. For good jack shooting they should be numerous. I have taken some all over the East where I hunted. The only areas where I hunted them seriously was in the Mississippi bottoms, where I occasionally took a limit of ten.

The No. 9 shot preference holds for snipe even as for woodcock. And skeet bores are also desirable. Long shots at jacks *are* possible, though I usually miss them! A jack usually gives off with a sort of "eep" just as he starts. The bang of the gun should follow the "eep" swiftly indeed. Snipe fly low and straight for a few yards. Then their dodging flight is fantastic. You try to aim where the bird will be, but the jack usually zigs as the gun zags, and the ammunition manufacturers' profits soar. When duck shooting in the Midwest, I often carried a few jack charges, and hit the odd bird with a choke-bored gun. But this was rare. I love to shoot (at) them, and they should continue to be important enough if management can maintain enough habitat to produce them in harvestable numbers.

Again, a retrieving, close-working dog is valuable in snipe shooting. If there are enough birds to be worth hunting, it is easy enough to get them up, but if they fall in mucky margins, a retriever is important. Like their woodcock cousins, they give the dog very little scent, but good retrievers find dead birds very well.

Doves and their ilk are the last important upland game birds I will discuss; in Part II I will also discuss some very important and peculiar dove problems.

The common mourning dove is North America's most numerous game bird. He is found in perhaps all states to some extent, but is on the songbird list in too many.

In my considerable experience, doves are the hardest game birds to hit. Further, for such tiny creatures, their lead-lugging capacity is remarkable. If a dove shooter brings back half as many pounds (or ounces!) of doves as he expends in ammunition, he is doing well. I brag of once dropping five doves with five consecutive shots. I only did it once, and have known very few dove shots who consistently did that well. If I get my ten doves with a box of shells, it is good shooting for me or most of the rest of us. Doves, whatever their other characteristics, are the ammunition manufacturer's best game friends.

Hunters argue more about dove guns and ammunition than about other game killers. At least the arguments are more persuasive. I have done my best dove shooting with the Model 21 Winchester that I regard so highly for upland game, choked improved cylinder and modified. I stick to No. 7½ shot, in 1⅛ to 1¼-ounce field loads or their handload equivalent.

The best dove shot I have ever seen in action, however, used No. 6 shot in a 20-gauge double. He averaged two kills for every three shots. Another almost as deadly dove killer shoots a full-choke 12-gauge pump-action trap gun, and No. 8 shot. And you can go on from there. I do as well with No. 8 shot as with 7½, but I definitely did worse when using No. 9 skeet shot.

I know less about white-winged doves, the little ground doves, and band-tailed pigeons. Few will bother with ground doves when or if they become legal. Whitewings are about parallel to mourners, and the band-tails drop all right to 7½ shot in field loads.

Doves are largely shot from ambush. They are heavy drinkers, and in the dry West, the way to take them is to hide near a well as they come in to drink. When numerous, they may fly wildly and be taken when passing any sort of a stand. Though they often veer away from a hunter, often they do not. Doves are fast, tough, instinctive dodgers, and all-round sporty birds, but they are dumb.

It is most important to get in your mourning-dove shooting when they are available. The Idaho dove season opens on September 1 and lasts fifteen to twenty days. But one cold snap and they are gone. If this snap should come before September 1, the season has ended before it started. The situation is similar in southern Nevada. Most doves do not like cold weather. A few will hang around until December. We do not know where the majority go. We certainly know where they are not. No doves cuts down the ammo and gasoline bills, and does not affect the meat supply very much, but just possibly dove shooting is my favorite bird shooting. One of the reasons for this is that when doves are numerous, one gets a chance to shoot!

Possibly I should not wind up the suggestions on upland bird shooting without a brief reference to cranes. In 1969 there were open seasons on cranes in parts of Texas, New Mexico, Alaska, Saskatchewan, Colorado, Oklahoma, and possibly portions of other states or provinces. Of course the very rare whooping cranes are fully protected and are on the endangered bird list. There is likewise little or no shooting of the greater sandhill cranes. Only lesser sandhills or little browns are usually legal thus far, nor are little browns especially little.

Cranes are taken as passers from their roosting lakes, much like geese, and heavy loads of No. 4 shot in choked guns are the crane tools. Possibly I would use No. 2 shot in a 10-gauge. I have been around breeding sandhills quite a bit in both Wyoming and Idaho but have thus far had no chance to hunt them.

"Plains turkeys" were once very important game birds and are coming back where a habitat still exists. My educated guess is that greater sandhills will be legal birds within a few years as well as the smaller species. The whoopers will continue to be "songbirds" if they survive at all. Though further discussion belongs in Part II, I will predict that they are going to make it. Trumpeter swans were touch-and-go thirty years back, but are now believed to be out of the woods. It will be 1975 before whooping-crane conditions can show a safe trend. By then, some reversal may have finished them, or so reduced them that they will go out like passenger pigeons and heath hens.

At the risk of more intelligence insults, perhaps it should be noted that cranes are in their own bird group and have no American relatives. They are cousins of the Old World bustards and excellent on the table as well as being canny game birds. Their approach to extermination was caused solely by neglect.

Though their voices are gooselike (but less musical than the honker's "song") they are not related to the true waterfowl. Neither are they related to the herons that are often called "blue cranes." Great blue herons are about the same in wing spread, and have much the same color, as the greater sandhill, but herons fly with the neck in an S, the heron beak is much longer, the body is much lighter, and on into the night. Crane necks, in flight, are straight out, like geese or swans, and swan length.

Though cranes breed in low ground, and often roost standing in shallow water, they are not exactly aquatic birds. I have even heard a rumor that their underfeathers absorb water and that they will drown if forced to swim any appreciable distance. This I doubt. Only once have I seen a crane light in deep water and swim. This was in August 1951 or 1952, in the Squirrel Meadows of Wyoming, just east of the Yellowstone Park boundary. The bird was young, and not afraid of me, or possibly he thought I was only a harmless extension of my horse. The lake he lit in was not large. Possibly he was tired and had to light. He swam all right, and I kept my binoculars on him until he swam behind some tules. I am under the impression that a swimming crane could not take off from the water, but he swims well enough. Better than a pheasant or a turkey, and neither of these definitely upland creatures is unhandy in the water.

—7—

Varmints

YOU ARE DOUBTLESS aware that definitions of "varmints" often differ with geography, just as an action that is legal on one side of a state line may be a crime on the other. My discussion of varmints deals largely with creatures that are not protected by law, and that are either injurious or, at best, useless from the viewpoint of the human majority. Though much varmint shooting is done with a shotgun, like the gamebirds we have been dealing with, varmints may be hunted with anything, and the real "varminter" is usually considered to be a small-caliber, flat-shooting, scope-sighted rifle. Hence this chapter will deal with every type of weapon.

I will deal only lightly with varmint-shooting ethics here, because this important and controversial subject is elaborated on at some length in Part II of this volume. I would like to emphasize, however, that certain varmints of my youth—notably the raptorial birds—are now protected in most states.

In Idaho, we still have eight species of unprotected birds, several of which cause little argument. The house (English) sparrow, European starling, and magpie are nuisances or definitely destructive. Kingfishers, pelicans, and ravens are not protected, and I feel sure that they are harmless as well as very interesting. Crows vary according to localities. They can be destructive indeed unless legislated against carefully. I admit them to my varmint list, and feel that few sports equal crow shooting. Cormorants are also unprotected, and I am not sure whether they belong with their pelican cousins or not. Protected gulls are sometimes a nuisance. Protected blue herons, to my certain knowledge, have literally cleaned some brook trout headwaters when they established a heronry right over the stream. Protected blackbirds can also be destructive, and you can go on into mammal and reptile arguments. The specific creatures I list for varmint shooting are pretty well accepted as such by both scientists and the shooting fraternity. But both law and conscience enter the picture; when in doubt, don't shoot. That is an axiom that is difficult to refute. One may respect the Kentucky sheriff who shot first and then served his warrant, but *his* game could shoot back; the mammals and birdies cannot.

In addition to satisfying the urge for shooting, varmints are valuable for giving the hunter practice. Here in Idaho, during an upturn of the blacktail jackrabbit cycle, I have fired at them with as many as a thousand rounds during a winter, this with the Ackley version of the .220 Winchester Swift rifle. It weighed thirteen pounds and sported a K10 scope. I wore the barrel out with perhaps three thousand rounds. After that type of winter shooting, one does not miss many head of big game the next fall when shooting with a 2½× or 4× scope. Further, some wheat-rancher friends have lost as much as 15 percent of their crops because of rabbit damage. Our shooting gave them some protection, and it is easier to get permission to shoot pheasants on private lands if you have saved the owner some $1,000 from rabbit depredation.

As to varmint rifles for jackrabbits, woodchucks or rock chucks, sitting crows, and up to coyotes, a "hot" .22 is my choice. The one I now use is a .22–.243. It is a wildcat, but the ammunition is easy to make from standard .243 cases, and I have a .243. Further, a local gunsmith friend rather specializes in making the .22–.243, and especially for loadings with 63-grain bullets.

I had this rifle put together shortly before the .22–.250 round was standardized. It would also have a worn-out barrel by now, but the rabbit cycle turned down and its use has been limited. If picking a new one now, I would choose the .22–.250. It is partially a matter of choice, but the .222 is perhaps the *slowest* round that is logical in the open country shooting we do here in Idaho. Contrarily, the .222 might be the *most* powerful cartridge I would consider were I back on the New York farm where I was raised. A .22 rimfire may be varmint rifle enough in some areas. And if one would combine a varmint rifle with a deer rifle, the various 6mm rounds such as the .243 Winchester and the 6mm Remington are most satisfactory. The 6mm cases should use 75-grain bullets (for varmints, of course). My .243 does not really like bullets lighter than 100-grain. It is light but marvelously accurate with the heavier lead and a 6× scope. Since you need all the accuracy you can get for jackrabbits, and need the 100-grain weight for any sort of big game, I stay with 100-grain spitzers.

Further, with the hot .22 rounds, the common error is too light bullets. The old .220, now rather obsolete, was close to the flattest-shooting factory round that was ever devised. However, the factories loaded with 48-grain bullets. At close range, I have known them to collapse in a few inches of dry grass, to say nothing of a sagebrush twig of pencil size. And in our local winds, they blow all over hell's half acre. I use 63-grain bullets exclusively. They do not travel quite so flat as lighter slugs, but buck wind and brush better. If you hold right (a bipod is an advantage) you can hit at 200 yards, and a bunny or a rock chuck is not plumb safe at twice that distance.

My present rifle weighs the same as its predecessor—too much. But it shoots! And the Mountain Men who operated right where I write used caplocks that weighed 12 pounds. If I get so beat that I can no longer shoot this vast piece of ordnance, I struggle back to the truck and call it a day. Still, including the 10× scope (a 6× is really minimum), a 10-pound rifle is plenty of iron. This weight in mine sneaked up. I bought the action, barrel, and stock separately, and inherited the scope. When it was assembled, I could scarcely throw it away. Further, when the barrel burns out, it will be rebored and possibly cut off some and turned down. My used-up .220 barrel is now a .338 magnum and a killer. My favorite reborer allows that shooting until a barrel wears out refines the steel through continuous heating and cooling. It is thus more accurate when properly rebored. He has proved that it certainly loses nothing. Muzzleloaders were sometimes rebored two or three times until the barrels were on the point of leaking! Or made into shotguns. History can repeat.

Considerable has been written about varmint-shooting techniques, especially as concerned with crows. I will not suggest many tips, as a hunter can usually work things out. Conditions vary. Jackrabbits sometimes sit around, anxious to be shot. Again, they run like crazy. Two parties, drifting toward each other, frequently improve shooting, as a jack (and even a deer) inclines toward a single-track mind. He is getting away from something and is blown up by something in front that he did not reckon with. And varmints can be called and shot from ambush. Or crows may come to a simulated owl. One should be ingenious.

When I was stationed in Montana, we got a start on coyote hunting with hounds and horses. I was transferred and got less of it than I wished. The plan was to prowl the truck trails with a crate of dogs and the horses in pickups or trailers. When a coyote was spotted, we unloaded pronto. You could get to a hot trail fast and the chase was on. A couple of trail hounds and several borzois were standard equipment. I violently object to poisoning coyotes (or even ground squirrels) if it can be avoided. Trapping coyotes is also a last resort, to say nothing of being very difficult. Hunting them is another matter. The horses and hounds may be the most sporting method. Another is to run a coyote on a frozen lake (with snow for traction) using a pickup truck. The driver—if he can manage—swings alongside the quarry some 40 yards away if his gunner is using a smoothbore. As gunner, I preferred my 12-gauge magnum Smith with standard No. 2 goose loads. As you are going the same speed as the coyote, you do not lead, but draw on the animal's head. If the ice and covering snow are a bit bumpy, a miss is not unusual. Nor is it exceptional for the coyote to get ashore on ground too rough for chasing. Somewhat contrarily, I have shot a few coyotes when motoring on ice with a .22 rifle. A rear-end shot is then the easiest. If the aim is correct, you have a kill. If you aim low, the ricochet may kill just as well if the essential snow is light.

A last and equally sporting method of taking coyotes is on glare lake ice with a sharp-shod horse and a .22 pistol. The horse can turn and the coyote skids. With luck, you just might get so close you could lean over and catch him by the scruff of the neck! Which is a bit more sporting than I will risk. With any of these methods, you do not always skin the coyote.

Again I will perhaps insult the reader's intelligence to note that the ice should be carefully checked before any of this lake chasing is attempted. An average rider on a half-ton of horse thunders rather heavily. And a speeding pickup sliding through a springhole could result in a very sticky situation. Such accidents have occurred in Montana, off the Missouri, right where I did this type of coyote hunting.

Perhaps I should emphasize here that it is easy to teach a smart horse to hunt. All those I have thus used had long stock-horse ancestry, but this may not be a requisite. A stock horse or a polo horse would, however, be my first choice. I first tried horse-hunting, again in Montana, about

1941. I owned a little cayuse named Smoky, and started shooting off his back with a .22 handgun. There were plenty of jackrabbits, the big whitetails that turn pretty much all white in the winter. My greatest sport was one spring when the snow left suddenly and the rabbits were still white! Smoky would spot one, seemingly hidden in the sage, at 200 yards or more. With pricked ears, he would jog, then sneakingly walk, to some 30 feet on the rabbit's left. He watched intently as I shot, scarcely breathing. If the rabbit was crippled, but could still run, he was after it as soon as he got the word. He could outrun a healthy rabbit (it takes a little doing), but of course the rabbit dodged as soon as the horse got too close. I have tried shooting rabbits on the run, but never hit one from the saddle. I am sure that I could have managed to thus kill a buffalo, with a handgun considerably more potent than a .22, but a jack going all-out was (and is) beyond my skill as either a rider or a shooter.

This Smoky would hunt anything and loved it. Nor was he afraid of anything except barbed wire and rattlesnakes. If he stepped on any sort of wire, or a snake buzzed, he would bolt. If the snake was close, and to one side, he could bolt sideways. He never slid from under me and left me on top of the snake, but several times it was close. His faithfulness and devotion were as extensive as his intelligence, but when a rattler was involved, he was concerned with only one form of action—to get outa there, and fast.

Repeating my inference that a rimfire .22 was a fair-enough varmint weapon in relatively well-populated farm country, it may be noted that I have ample personal experience for proof.

I think it was at Christmas in 1903 that my Uncle Ben gave me my first gun. It was a .22 Stevens "Crack Shot" that cost about $3.50. The 20-inch barrel was as soft as cow dung, and the sights were horrific, but it was plenty accurate up to perhaps 60 yards. I had to be sleuthy to get a woodchuck, since this very vital animal will rarely be kept out of his hole by an ordinary .22 blast—the head or vertebrae have to be hit—but occasionally I made it. Really, most of my early woodchuck victims were chased into stone walls by my dog. I got him as a puppy when I was eight and he had the unusual name of Rover. He was a magnificent brown-black creature, with a white necktie. Half black Newfoundland (I believe) and definitely half Irish setter, he hunted anything from quail up (or down). One late summer, for several weeks, he cornered a woodchuck every weekday, and two on Sunday. I was only a club hunter until about age ten, when I managed to borrow guns. Still, Rover and I got game. Once we took a raccoon that weighed 16 pounds.

I could barely lug it home, and got a dollar for the skin. It was big game and big money!

Getting away from digression, I re-emphasize that a little rifle demands good hunting. Possibly I worked harder at hunting when I was twelve than I ever have since. My rifle was soon augmented with a single 12-gauge shotgun, but earlier I used a double-hammer job that I could barely cock or let the hammers down on. I could *not* hold it up for conventional shooting. And the black-powder recoil was punishing in spite of the 8 pounds, 3 ounces of weight. I still have it, if anyone would check. I still have the little Stevens too, but the bore has deteriorated to skeetergun condition. Years ago I polished out as much of the lands as were left, so it shoots .22 dust-shot charges respectably. I should have it actually smoothbored and choked, but have simply not bothered. Skeeter clay shooting has its points, but I have not had much occasion to shoot "small deer" with .22 charges.

When crow shooting with a smoothbore, a combination of sneaking, ambush, calling, and baiting may be called on for maximum results. The baiting may have had the least general attention, but when practicable, it can produce amazing results. It now can be of certain interest to read about, but the existing opportunities are limited.

During the days of farm-horse power, the occasional used-up dobbin had to be killed. As far back as I can remember, a rendering company would take any useless big animal off the owner's hands, but shooting and skinning a horse was standard. Doing this in the winter was also standard. There was time to do the skinning since other work did not press, and the carcass was often left where ambush crow shooting was possible. During Christmas recess, until I left the farm at age twenty-one, I usually knew where there was a horse carcass for crow shooting, or a beef skull behind the cow barn. Crows, when hungry, will work on the last smidgin of meat, or even hang around skeletons hoping that some long-ago-consumed flesh may be reincarnated.

Any sort of wing shooting is of some practice value for important shooting. Crows that jump from bait are easy to hit. So are incomers that approximate decoying ducks. Crows pitching in the wind, however, are very sporty targets—not like pitching doves or passing ducks, but good fun. Any gun is a crow gun, but the 12-gauges are logical, and so are heavy charges of fine shot. I have used anything that was left over and convenient, but when handloading for crows, No. 7½ for one barrel and 6 for the other are my choices. And one will use up the finer charges fastest.

While still discussing varmint shooting, it would be careless indeed not to mention rats. Common rats, of course, that were imported a long time ago. Some economic biologists consider rats to be the most destructive vertebrate animals known to science. Likewise, they are the most dangerous of the disease-carrying vertebrates. The term "varmint," presumably a corruption of "vermin," applies to rats if it applies to anything.

Traveled and schooled until I was aged forty-nine, I had assumed that rats had reached all parts of the U.S. However, they had missed most of Montana when we moved away from that magnificent state in 1942, and they are not in much or any of Idaho as I write. Rats make interesting shooting indeed around city dumps, or what-have-you, and are a species of "game" we can well spare. They are widely distributed, however, and most of my readers can find some easier than they can locate more desirable targets. Truly enough, shooting is too slow a rat-reduction method to have more than incidental importance. Poisoning, trapping, cats, dogs, clubs, and pitchforks all entered the picture on our New York farm, but we always shot some. Hogpen rats, in that area, had furnished shooting sport for a very long time. It may still be in style.

My oldest report on this hogpen ratting was told by my grandfather, the late William H. Pulling, of Wappingers Falls, New York. He was past seventy when he described it, and still had a scar, high on his right forehead, as a memento. Born in 1828, he was perhaps ten at the time of this incident. At that time they lived near a hamlet called Shenandoah in the township of East Fishkill, not far from the Connecticut "frontier."

There were lots of rats lurking around the hogpen. Grandfather had access to a flintlock "horse pistol." It was big, and probably smooth-bored. He knew how to fire it, and had plenty of powder, but no shot. He found an old piece of lead pipe, however, flattened it, cut it into "shoestrings," and then diced it into little more or less cubical slugs. It was standard procedure, when loading any muzzleloader, to put in plenty of fodder. This grandfather did. In retrospect, he had little recollection as to probable drams and ounces, except the certainty that there were too many. He baited the rats with a train of cornmeal, just outside the pen, but near a strategic exit hole. He was in ambush perhaps 30 feet from the closest end of the bait train. When he fired, rat fragments were widely spread over the immediate landscape, but for the time being he was unaware of that desirable fact. The recoil had blasted the pistol against the side of his head, and he was out cold. Whatever part of the pistol had hit his head (presumably the cock) had cut it to the bone. His later rat killing was effective enough with half the original charge.

One of the places where both my son and I shot rats was the city dump outside Winona, Minnesota. From just before sundown to dark was the best time to shoot. The rats laid low all day but perhaps hunted food all night. We shot with .22 rimfire rifles, or pistols if we felt sporting and wanted handgun practice. Though rats are usually smart enough creatures, when hungry they may come out again in a few minutes after a shot. Baiting, like the method Grandfather used, and blasting with a scattergun and fine shot, is the best way to clobber rats, and the sporting angle is hardly significant with such low-lived beasties. Still, such shooting is of no practice value either, so I suggest .22 Short cartridges, especially when firing a rifle. Shorts make little noise in any moderately long barrel. Out at perhaps 25 yards, the rats may scarcely know what is happening and may give you two or even three shots before taking to cover. The roar of a big shotgun creates more panic, suggesting that the lightest .410 charges are desirable. Though I am inclined to look down my nose at any .410, I will not cut that nose off to spite the rest of my face, nor discount usefulness when it is obvious.

Another less varminty semi-domesticated creature providing sporty enough shooting is "tame" pigeons, where they are convenient. Very few of the birds descended from the European rock doves belong to anyone or are considered property. Frequently they are found around barns or feed lots, and the owners, though considering the pigeons a nuisance, expect gunners to ask for permission to shoot, and demand certain care. Wing shooting is logical, though I have also shot them with a very accurate .22, going for their heads. Amazingly enough, I have shot a lot of pigeons around our house in Pocatello. I used a .410 H. & R. Handy Gun chambered for the short cartridges. I am a Bannock County Deputy Sheriff and an *ex officio* State Conservation Officer, and could thus get municipal police authority to shoot within the city limits. That 8-inch barrel would only manage a pigeon within some 15 yards, but happily that very small charge did no damage to the roofs of either my own or the neighbor's houses. I was just clobbering pigeons to get rid of them—no wing shooting.

You thus fit the shooting to the situation. Usually you can manage wing shooting with any upland game gun and 7½ shot. Further, the birds are excellent on the table, despite the fact that they are often serious disease carriers (fortunately, you do not eat them raw!). Of course, they are cute and a tourist attraction in some places. I have not seen the thousands that add to the fame of St. Peter's in Rome, but I *have* been properly "bombed" by the Trafalgar Square birds—an umbrella is recommended. They will eat out of your hand or your mouth, and go into reasonably loose pockets, looking for food. I did not ask if the London authorities had any control over them, or if they panhandled until they died of old age. It seemed to me that a few goshawks could have been imported to balance the environment, but such a move might result in public clamor.

I occasionally knock off a magpie when hunting doves, or blast one with the hot .22 during jackrabbit shooting. Restricted to the West, at moderate elevations, magpies are smart nuisances. They understand shotgun range unless you are quiet and somewhat camouflaged. At 100 yards they are bold enough and can be exploded if you aim carefully. Though big eaters, they are largely feathers, and very small targets.

Both English sparrows and European starlings are in the varmint category, and I recommend shooting them whether or not they furnish much practice. Interestingly enough, both are good to eat, and fat starlings have been table birds in Europe since the days of yore. Just possibly the "four and twenty blackbirds, baked in a pie" were starlings. The true British blackbird is a thrush, almost identical to the U.S. robin, excepting the color. (A female blackbird appears to be a very dull-feathered robin.) I have been in some amusing bull sessions with educated English, speculating on the well-known jingle. The consensus favored starlings as the pie ingredient, but the singing when the pie was opened continues to be a mystery. In any event, with these very small creatures, you need fine shot. No. 10 is all right, though even finer pellets are no mistake. If you are not a handloader, and can find nothing finer than No. 9 skeet loads in the market, they will do. Choke helps if the shot is a bit coarse for this specialized shooting.

Though possibly they would be more appropriate in Part II of this volume, since varmints and their reduction are in mind, I will risk a few remarks about these bird-varmints and their influence on desirable small species. It must be emphasized that I am paying little attention to "dicky birds" in general. I can identify most of them, and do this easiest if there is a good book with colored cuts in my pack. And I know their economic situations as groups. (Definitely, none of the warblers or swallows will eat up your wheat fields!) Still, if I miss out on spotting the species of some wee sparrow or a still wee-er wren, it does not worry me much.

During my farmboy days, a big orchard was behind the house, a dozen Norway spruces were included among the shade trees, and the ancient barns were a fine habitat for swallows. We had an amazing number of small birds. One summer, around the dooryard and in a small patch of nearby woods, I recall identifying sixteen sparrow species and thirty-two different warblers. I spotted almost everything that existed in that area. And around the house, we controlled the nesters rather simply.

The spruces made the finest nesting sites. Every spring there was competition. If we had let them fight it out, the spruces would have been dominated by grackles, bluejays, and English sparrows. Though the sparrows were smallish, they were scrappers, and held their own. But we entered the scene with the old 12-gauge double, and plenty of shells loaded with No. 10 shot. Couple of days and the surviving would-be boss birds gave up and left. Even then, I believe, the beautiful jays were protected, but we shot them anyway. They will eat eggs and even nestlings if they can overcome the rival birds, and it takes a fighter to chase any species of jay. Red squirrels are also nest destroyers and were intolerable where the nesting was so intense as it was among those spruces. We simply managed the situation. I am not *absolutely* sure we were right, as I claim no special dicky-bird knowledge. Still, no one seemed critical and everyone liked our birds. I still believe it was sound procedure.

Further, just possibly this is the place to mention something about housecats and birds, admitting that cats (and dogs) can get on the varmint list if they make any real effort.

Because of the rat and mouse situation, we always had a number of cats around the barns. My mother also kept some housecats, and one, with the unusual name of Tabby, was a great hunter, a fantastic breeder, and an all-around character.

I emphasize that we had a lot of cats and the most remarkable assortment of small birds I have seen anywhere. This does not suggest that I am carrying any torch for *Felis domestica* and his (or her) association with birds. Feral cats, or any uncontrolled cats, are usually a menace to birds and an especial danger to nestlings. Town cats, in particular, should be licensed and controlled. Feral cats belong on the varmint list, and rate routine varmint treatment. Still, they may not be as dangerous as they are described as being.

Just possibly our bird and cat situation was the result of careful culling. Cats are smart and get on to survival methods. We raised too many and had to dispose of several litters a year. Our chickens were handled rather crudely, and we raised some 150 each year, hen-hatched, and broods kept in individual coops. Chicken-killing cats were intolerable. A cat must not even look wistful in the presence of young chicks. The alternative was a .22 slug through the head or the head rendered totally *absent* by a 12-gauge blast. Our cats learned to ignore chicks, and how.

This seemed to carry over to wild birds, but some were caught, especially swallows. If we saw a cat with a bird, we took it away and chastized it. This old Tabby brought in varied game for her kittens as soon as their eyes were open. It included mice, rats, squirrels, rabbits, snakes, and once a weasel! No birds. Yes, cats are smart and Tabby was a feline genius. She lived long and serenely. Probably she caught and ate birds, but she took pains not to get apprehended. I thus suggest that cats may be educated. Or culled. The indoctrination calibers should run from .22 up. The philosophy: "Conform or perish." The speed: *"Tout de suite!"*

More could easily be included about varmint shooting, but I may already have overdone it.

—8—
Deer

WHITETAIL DEER HAVE had more volumes devoted to their pursuit than any half-dozen other American game species combined. They are, of course, more important than any other hoofed wild animals. Their muley cousins are close seconds.

My own whitetail shooting, though considerable, has conspicuously failed to cover their tremendous range. I have hunted them in New Hampshire, New Brunswick, Michigan, Wisconsin, and Minnesota. Though I have observed them extensively in a dozen other states and two other provinces, conditions have restricted my hunting.

Earlier gun discussion suggests that remarks on deer weapons should be brief. Whitetails have been taken with about everything that burns powder. Flintlock riflemen using peashooters as small as .31 killed successfully, though the .36 round ball was probably the favorite Eastern pioneer caliber. For muzzleloaders, I would prohibit shooting deer with balls smaller than .42. Limiting to .45 would be even better.

Carbine .30–30 rifles (.30 Winchester) are the most numerous deer guns that have ever existed. They are all right with 170-grain bullets.

Possibly the .30-calibers in higher power, and the .303 in Canada, come next in popularity. I used the .30–06 extensively, with no slugs lighter than 180 grains. Possibly 220-grain bullets are better, or 215 in the case of the .303 British. Short-range shooting is the rule. Across burns or over water are usually the only long-range opportunities. Always using iron sights, I have missed a couple of long-range shots. I have missed some short-range brush shots too, when the animals were going all-out.

Actually, the best whitetail deer gun I have used was a .45–70 Winchester. An '86 model, with shotgun butt, 22-inch barrel of nickel steel, and half magazine. I let it get away from me, but have one now that is a copy. My replica came out a bit heavy, but it is a killer. It has a modern barrel, of course, and can be loaded to make a 405-grain bullet skip right along.

Other excellent whitetail rounds are the somewhat obsolete .348 with slugs of 200 grains or bigger and the peculiarly neglected .358, with the same bullet weight restrictions. The .444 Marlin is a fine deer round, but the existing bullets are too light. They should weigh at least 300 grains. Brush-cutting ability is important.

Only shotguns are legal in many deer areas. Slugs should be 16 gauge or bigger. For the best accuracy, the gun should be cylinder bore (which does not mean improved cylinder), and the gun should have rifle sights. A big-holed receiver sight and a big bead front (ivory or gold) are the fastest for me, and speed is important, since whitetail bucks rarely stand around waiting to be shot. I have taken deer with both round balls and 00 buckshot and ordinary shotgun sights. They always killed, too, but such shooting was under 40 yards.

In general, a big chunk of slow-slogging lead is best. I got one late-season buck with a .45–70 that cut several aspens of broom-handle size before it reached the animal, but the deer did not take many jumps.

In my earlier remarks, it was noted that spooked game often travels uphill. That goes double for whitetails, if there is any uphill.

Whitetails are local creatures. They drift some, and if it is late and snowy, they drift toward yards. When jumped, however, they rarely run out of the country. I have started a buck that I was sure was the same animal, on the same acre of woods, for the third time before I got a shot. He liked that patch of brush too well for his own good!

There are only three ways of hunting Northern whitetails that are reasonably distinct, and they may sometimes be combined by two or more hunters.

Still-hunting is my favorite method if there is room (not many hunters) and a tracking snow. You cannot still-hunt in dry, noisy woods because you cannot avoid a racket. Snow is quiet. Get a buck going right after daylight in new snow, and if you are a good hunter, he should be down by three p.m. You go slowly and watch ahead and both sides. Your best chance is when he backtracks to watch you from the side and you catch him at it. It takes practice, luck, or both. You may have to take a running shot, but avoid it if you can.

Waiting on a stand is deadly when the season opens and there are many hunters. In a tree with sixty yards of visibility all around is my choice, if such a spot exists. Deer have runways, and they are easy to find. I have taken a deer soon after daylight on the opening day by waiting in the right place. The animals tear around. A whistle or a bleat often makes a deer stop, and they seldom look for danger in a tree!

Driving may be the best system of all, if one of the hunters really knows the country and there is a fairly big party. Once in Minnesota, on the Superior National Forest, eight of us got eight deer by noon of the third day. We were properly laid out—three "hunters" and five "dogs" to drive. As soon as a "hunter" made his kill, he was a "dog" to the end of the hunt. I was always a "dog" on that little hunt. On the first drive of the first day, I was on one end of the line, and a fine buck attempted an end run. We were in fairly open timber, and he stopped to figure me out at about 60 yards. It was his last error! And I never got on a stand.

Occasionally, on a drive, deer will break back on the dead run. "Dogs" must not fire ahead because it could endanger "hunters," but after passing the drivers, deer make the most of existing cover. I never hit one of these line-busting deer, or recall that one was hit during my shooting experience, but I have stopped two or three of the end-runners when I was a flank driver. They were sneaking and the shots were easy.

If one wrote a volume or a library on whitetail hunting, I doubt if more basic theory than this would need explanation. Whitetails are playful and I really believe that trophy bucks like to play games. They are smart or they would never have become trophy bucks. Every buck learns about hunters whenever he is hunted. Naturally, the hunter learns about deer, and a dumb hunter has some advantage (but only that) over a smart deer. The deer are tamest during the first hour of shooting. Also, during that hour, the hunters may be the wildest!

However, whitetails vary in distribution throughout their vast range, and also vary in size, going down to the tiny Key deer off Florida. There are a lot of so-called subspecies, and possibly one different species, the Arizona whitetail. This is also a brushy creature, but suggests a long-range rifle, in the .270 group, perhaps, with a 4× scope. Iron sights are good enough (or the *best*) in the thick, wet Northern forests. The swampy

Southeast deer run small, and a rifle in the .44–40 class, or a shotgun, has range enough. In fact, a .44–40 has range enough for almost anything if you are close enough and can shoot.

Preseason reconnaissance always has its advantages, and this is especially true for whitetail hunters. Even for a hunter who knows his territory, the axiom holds. Behavior varies from season to season on the same square mile.

One amusing proof of the value of early observation happened out of Duluth, Minnesota, before we moved West.

A young businessman was transferred to Duluth in the spring or early summer. He was a rifleman with considerable training, but had never hunted deer. He and his small family, with certain friends, went on weekend picnic parties to a park area not a dozen miles from Duluth. They saw deer frequently, and he found that it was open to shooting, but no one hunted there. It was not worthwhile. Everyone drove to the real woods, 100 miles or more away.

This chap was busy, but he managed to be free for opening day. It was snowy, and he decided not to use his fine big new car. So he arranged to get a taxi driver to take him out, and also arranged for him to come back at sundown. Confident, he gave the driver a waterproof tarp so that the deer would not get the taxi bloody.

This was a tremendous joke to all his friends, and even to the taxi driver, who was collecting a good enough fee. He asked several associates to go with him, but all politely declined.

You have probably guessed the result. When the driver arrived at sundown, the hunter had just dragged in a good buck. He had not seen another hunter and had had a choice of shots. Other hunters went to the same place the next day and saw nothing. It was a lucky situation for this green hunter, but he had some intelligence. I could cite several such instances of admitted luck where the hunters made hay when the weather was good. In fact I have been in on a couple of such hunts myself. There is nothing like a little luck!

We can sum it up by stating that whitetails are very interesting animals who like to play games. I will cheerfully play with them, and sometimes I win. Deer are my favorite quarry so far as *any* hunting goes, and I prefer whitetails (just a bit) over the muleys.

Mule-Deer Hunting

My mule-deer hunting has been rather extensive in Montana, Nevada, and Idaho. Of course Montana and Idaho both have whitetails, and I have seen them much during closed seasons, but have thrown no lead their way. Incidentally, in Nevada, I knew old-timers who had hunted deer they called desert fantails. None had been known for a quarter-century when we went to the Desert Game Range in 1942. These fantails, from the reports, could hardly have been a myth. They must have been some variation of the Arizona whitetails. Of course myths are plausible. I know Nevadans who claim to have shot ibex, and ibex have been in the game lists—certainly in Nevada, and possibly in Idaho. These animals may have been bighorn ewes. Whatever they were, they were *not* ibex. In Arizona there have been authentic reports of wild camels during my life. Probably these camels (dromedaries) are now all dead, but seeing one now would not be too surprising. If I ever saw a wild ibex, however, I would never again drink my customary libation before dinner!

Mule-deer hunting is usually vastly different than hunting whitetails. Muleys *can* be bushy indeed, but they do not mind open country, and a scoped rifle is logical. I have taken upwards of thirty-five in Idaho, three-quarters of them with a .270 on which a K2.5 scope is mounted. A 4× scope could be better, and I have used such for muleys on both a .338 and a .300 Weatherby. Brush-hunting elk with iron sights on a .375 H. & H., Old Model 70, I incidentally took some muleys. That .375 with 300-grain slugs will drop about anything, and it will kill even forkhorn deer dead without mutilating meat.

While I have never taken a whitetail at over 85 yards, I have managed a couple of muleys at 350 or a bit more. I have also jumped some under my feet and had them down in from 15 to 40 yards.

Muleys will run for miles and perhaps not come back for a week or longer. Brush driving is just as successful as for whitetails. So is a stand; even with only one hunting companion, I have put him on a stand and driven deer (sometimes a number of them) to him in a couple of hours.

In the Salmon's Middle Fork, where I have been on some seventeen hunts, there is little competition for deer. The favored game is elk, or bighorns early in the season. In open ground, we have seen as many as thirty deer within a half-hour after sunrise. Some may be a mile or more away. You look them over carefully with glasses, and plan a stalk. Tie your horse, get in a draw, and possibly sneak for an hour to get within shot. Sometimes they move and you have to start fresh; sometimes you sneak onto deer while on this stalk and get one (even two) and forget the original plan. (It is a two-deer area.) There, I take meat deer, as I have long since lost a personal interest in trophies. And if it is easy, I get two in the same general area the same day, to facilitate packing.

A good pack animal will bring in both carcasses if they are smallish and for meat. The biggest one I ever helped pack out weighed 260 pounds hog-dressed, and it took a good horse to lug him. This was in Nevada's Ruby Mountains.

Possibly here is the place to mention a few things about deer weights.

Maximum sizes for whitetails and muleys are not very different, the muleys averaging a little bigger. Whitetails seem to get bigger the farther north you go. But whitetails are small in Arizona and Texas and *tiny* in the Everglades. On the Florida Keys they are tiniest of all. Similarly, Columbian blacktails—which are only a variation of mule deer as I recognize them—are small animals.

You hear all sorts of deer-weight stories. Few get weighed just as they fall. Hog-dressed (bled and gutted) is the commonly recognized condition for hunters to consider weights. The biggest mule deer I ever saw weighed was this 260-pounder already mentioned. The biggest one I ever took weighed 226. I know of one that weighed 307. Bigger weights than that I take with a pinch of salt unless the verification is very definite. A muley that hog-dresses over 200 is a big deer.

I never shot a whitetail that went much over 180, but I know of one that weighed 217, and I saw one in a Canadian Pacific baggage car that I am sure weighed over 250. On checking stations, I have weighed many hundreds of deer, and one gets to be good at estimating weights. A whitetail is a monster if over 200, big at 180, and a pretty good deer at 160. I like my meat deer to be fat little chaps, hog-dressing 115 or less. Incidentally, some very big, very old bucks are also very fat and excellent on the table. The most active bucks, with the biggest antlers, are likely to be skinny and gamy. Small does and spike bucks (whitetail) or forkhorns (muleys) average the best eating.

Trimming the scent glands off a deer's legs as soon as he is down is good policy. And using a different knife for gutting is equally wise. A small amount of deer musk does meat no good!

Getting back to guns, the best muley weapon could be the 6.5 to 7mm calibers, such as the .270 Winchester, the .280 Remington, and that general group. The .243 Winchester, 6mm Remington, and .264 Winchester are all right, but need more precise pointing and plenty of scope power. Possibly the all-around .30–06 and the iron-sighted .30–30 carbine kill more muleys than any other calibers. Local hunters usually have one rifle each, and use what they have. And the muley rifles of the 7mm type I prefer will do all right on elk. There are some elk in much mule-deer territory. You can get some close shots, but you should be prepared to kill at 200 to 300 yards. The rifles should be sighted to be on at 200 yards. You may ignore elevation at lesser range with these long-range rifles if you aim at the middle of the animal. Those fast bullets should be kept out of the good meat areas if you *want* any meat. Head and neck shots are deadly, but if you are winded by climbing, or eighty-one last fall as I was (or both), that type of precision is difficult unless you are close. Like whitetails, mule deer have been taken with about every type of musket that exists. This situation will continue. But the scoped rifle with a fast bullet has advantages. One friend, who is not much of a hunter, borrowed my .270 for a little hunt on which he was a guest. He had never fired a scoped rifle, and being a science Ph.D., asked some questions. He swiftly discovered that to kill you just put the cross hairs on the spot you wanted to hit. He declined to take any practice shots and took a deer with one shot. He allowed that with that type of gun, no one needed to be a good shot. All that was required was reasonably normal eyesight. His views were rather sound!

Though that is enough on our ordinary deer, there are three other groups in the true deer family that are important game. Locally, what we call elk are the most important of these. They should be renamed wapiti, but I will not further elaborate in this part of the book.

Elk are big, strong, intelligent animals, with beautiful trophy heads, good hides for "buckskin," and excellent meat, granted that old bulls are not always topflight as they appear on the mahogany.

Like all other big animals, elk have been killed with just about everything. I once killed one with a .22-rimfire single-action revolver. It was an emergency situation, of course, and the animal was not healthy, though possibly as hard or even harder to stop than if it *had* been in perfect condition. Further, the shooting had to be done with the animal at a fast trot, driven downhill. I got off five shots at ranges of 50 to 75 feet. This proved nothing except that an elk *can* be stopped with a .22-rimfire pistol. It does not suggest that such a weapon is logical for elk or even for woodchucks.

Probably the universal .30–06 with 180-grain bullets is the lightest charge that could be recommended for taking elk. Some of the hunters that travel 2,000 miles to hunt in the Salmon's Middle Fork bring rifles in the .270 class. I was "in" on one hunt where three elk were dropped with four shots from .270 rifles. The very-long-range 7mm Remington magnum charges, with 175-grain bullets, take elk well indeed at any range you can possibly hit them. However, if you are really hunting *elk*, it is no error to depart *up* from the .30–06 to the magnum .30 class or heavier. Among these, my choice is the extremely powerful .300 Weatherby. That is the .30 magnum that I have, admitting that my barrel is worn out and in the gun shop awaiting a new one. For bushy elk or in the snow, an iron-sighted bigger caliber gets the call as I see it. Among these, I hardly see how the .375 with 270-grain bullets can be bettered. I plan to take an elk with a .58 muzzleloader "plains" rifle, firing 480-grain minié bullets, but have not yet managed it. To do so, I must get to 100 yards and have my elk reasonably quiet.

I re-emphasize that elk are big and strong, and popguns are not their medicine. If you occasionally get one with a popgun, it proves nothing.

Horse transportation goes with elk hunting the way ham goes with eggs. Once in a blue moon you may get a pick-up truck or some sort of a car close enough to an elk carcass to get it out, so it *is* possible. (Or you could camp alongside the meat and eat it—that definitely has occurred with Indians and moose, so it would work for elk.) But truck trails rarely go into elk country. If they do, the elk are not likely to last long. So you'd better start leaning on equine critters for lugging meat. You will manage that too, with sufficient dedication. Even though I am poor, I continue to own a couple of old mountain horses, just as I manage to own some good double guns. My horses are now in the custody of an outfitter, so I do not feed them.

The Middle Fork hunters who operate with an outfitter vary from millionaires to working stiffs who save their money for several years to manage just one trip. After that trip, they work like fury to manage another as soon as they can. Possibly their families starve, but I am inclined to doubt if such trips cause either privation or divorce. Undeniably, however, an elk hunt usually runs to time, expense, and a spot of hard work. Furthermore, outfitters' camps are luxurious in view of distances, weather, and rough terrain, but something less than a topnotch resort hotel.

It is fifty-fifty or better that you will *not* get an elk unless you get guidance from an outfitter, saddle and pack stock, or help of some sort from people who know the country. And there are open country elk, mountain elk, and forest elk. Without a guide, you will do better in the forest, such as in the Selway country of Idaho, than in the Middle Fork. On moderate snow, if you are hunting *above* a usable truck trail, it is not hard to drag carcasses to that trail. Some years ago, three faculty associates and I got three elk under such conditions. We might have managed the fourth but my ¾-ton pick-up had a big enough load. We were all operating out of the same vehicle, our camp gear was for zero weather, and we did not try for the extra animal. That is the only time I have helped in a successful elk hunt with no horseflesh.

In the woods and especially on snow, you hunt elk just as you hunt deer. Usually you still-hunt, though elk are such wanderers that following a track is questionable policy unless it is very fresh. Further, if both the hunters and the elk are numerous, the animals "mill," and patience on a stand frequently pays off.

In open mountain country, you generally ride and ride and ride. Finally your glasses pick up a band of elk. Then you tie up and stalk. Prayer may help, if you have been living right and the elk have not! Results suggest that the animals are the more righteous, but occasionally you connect with either a sinner or a moron.

With or without a mess of meat, elk hunters have fun as well as stiff muscles and saddle galls. Usually there are deer even when the elk do not bite. Usually there is excellent food, and I have never heard of anyone freezing to death on a late hunt, or even catching cold. There is no one to catch it from!

Thus, elk are great game animals when you get them, and possess a considerable number of advantages even when you do not. They advance sporting traits that are indeed hard to beat.

American moose, the world's largest member of the deer family, and possibly larger than any known prehistoric deer, parallel elk as truly great game. There is a further parallel in that if you do not bag a moose, you are likely to get a deer. (However, moose do thrive in some parts of Canada where deer are scarce or absent.) In both Canada and Alaska you may combine hunts for both moose and caribou. And moose are among the most magnificent creatures that live, or ever have lived.

My suggestions regarding elk guns also apply to moose. Back in 1924, *Forest and Stream* published an article that I wrote called "Successful Moose Loads" if I recall correctly. My data went back as far as 1914, so it is evident that I have given some thought to moose ammunition for an appreciable period.

At that time, I considered the .405 Winchester to be the best moose weapon. If you have one and proper fodder for it (I have), you may take it to the Canadian bush without any misgivings. Moose are usually taken at iron-sight range—that is, at 100 yards or less. Across burns or across water, there could be longer shots. Contrarily, if you spot a moose at long range he is unlikely to know it, and if you have any skill as a stalker, you can get closer. Moose are not very bright, and demand meticulous protection if hunting pressures are at all severe. That is the reason that they have been largely exterminated in much of their U.S. range below Alaska. Of course Canada is still lightly populated and much is inaccessible, considering its vast size. However, air travel has opened it up dangerously in spots. But again I am trespassing on management, the subject of Part II.

Some of the most successful moose hunters I have known used .30–06 rifles with 180-grain slugs, or the .303 British with the formerly common 215-grain bullets. I have not been around Canadian moose hunters for some time, but I do not recall ever seeing one with a scoped rifle. Both the ranges and the weather do not suggest scopes in the bush.

There are at least three types of American moose. The taxonomists, rightly or wrongly, call them separate species. They are the Eastern moose, the Western or Shiras moose, and the Alaskan moose. That is enough separation for now.

Idaho moose are on high ground that is close to mountainous. The climate is usually dry and a scoped rifle is usable. A hunter must draw for a moose permit and pay a special fee. I got a permit in 1949 and the moose was taken with a .30–06 and 180-grain bullets. It was good enough, and most of my friends in Idaho who have drawn permits have used similar weapons. There have been no long-range shots. In the Canadian bush I would take either the iron-sighted .405 or the .375 H. & H. In Alaska I would use my iron-sighted .375 and 300-grain bullets, or the .338 with a 4× scope and 250-grain slugs or thereabouts. Possibly I would choose the .300 Weatherby over the .338. It is a toss-up. That combination would take care of any game in Alaska (or out of it).

When hunting Western moose, we "cased" the country carefully and just mooched around until we found a suitable bull. Most of my friends who got permits have taken moose. I have not been in Alaska, but reports suggest that they get them by similar mooching around. In eastern Canada, we often hunted them by canoe, and portage, early in the season. In New Brunswick we were inclined to shoot both deer and moose late in the season so it would be easy to take care of the meat. The lakes were usually frozen solid. You then hunted moose just as you hunted whitetail deer.

Moose meat is excellent, certainly the best of the American deer family, if my own taste can be used as a criterion. Even old bulls are tops at the table. The rarely legal spikebulls, cows, and calves are simply out of sight, if you have a chance to pick up a quarter, as I have occasionally. Good heads, though they take up a tremendous lot of room, are among the most striking trophies, and moose hides produce the heaviest and strongest "buckskin." And moose hunting, especially off of Canadian lakes, may be the most unique experience a rifleman will ever know.

Hunting "deer" should not be concluded without brief references to caribou. There is no caribou season in any state except Alaska, and no caribou hunting worth more than casual mention. We have a few in Idaho that are gradually spilling into the corners of Washington and

Montana. If you have a slant toward U.S. geography, that will suggest that they are largely in the narrow Panhandle. Formerly they were in Minnesota and possibly all the Great Lakes states. They were also in Maine and on west through the upper Adirondacks. They were once fairly abundant in much of eastern Canada but have been exterminated through some of their range. Or perhaps they migrated. I saw one in New Brunswick in the summer of 1920, and consultation with the guides who worked their best-known ranges suggested that that was the only one left! In New Brunswick, I have seen old caribou trails worn 6 inches deep on solid granite ridges. That suggested a lot of walking.

If you do get a chance (or make one) to hunt caribou, please note that you are dealing with (possibly) the dumbest of the deer, and also with one of the most beautiful and majestic of that tremendous family of game animals.

Caribou guns are deer guns, admitting caribou are rather big. But the .270/7mm class of rifles is big enough. Naturally, they can be taken with something bigger, and since they are likely to be in the same habitat as the great Alaskan brown bear, bear guns often gather them in.

You are most unlikely to hunt caribou without a professional guide or someone with intimate local knowledge. So again, you mooch around to get a shot, or take a shot when you would prefer a shot at a moose or a brownie.

Caribou *may* be brought back to shootable numbers in their former ranges. This will come in Idaho and the contiguous states, I am rather sure, if politics do not disrupt the progress that is now developing. That is, if anyone would hunt that unbelievably rough terrain where they live. I have not seen them, but I have looked over the mountains of the Canadian boundary to some extent, and 75 percent of the land looks totally unhuntable. (Not that the Middle Fork is much more hospitable; but it enjoys more river and creek bottoms, and "benches.") Maine and Minnesota are better possibilities and are huntable.

Caribou have beautiful heads, and their skins make the finest gloves and shirts of anything that is Indian-tannable. I put their meat, however, very low on the totem pole. Some Indians have pretty much lived on them. So have some Eskimos and the closely related Lapps who herd the closely related reindeer. (Please do not confuse who is closely related to whom.) Caribou meat does not taste really bad, but it does not taste like much of anything. This is not surprising, since the animals live on "caribou moss," or lichen, most of the time and it does not taste like much of anything either. Reindeer meat has been sold commercially to some extent, and there may be tasty ways to cook it. My experiences

could be too limited or unfortunate. If you get one, I am simply suggesting that you not expect too much of the meat. I will cheerfully try it
again, given the opportunity, hoping there is something better in the
grub sack if caribou steaks continue to taste as I recall them.

—9—

Antelope, Sheep, and Goats

THOUGH THE OTHER hoofed creatures besides deer include some of the most important trophies, hunting them is not usually so intricate, nor are the methods especially varied.

Antelope (as we call them) are the least important, in my view. Charming animals, we have raised some on bottles, and personally I can scarcely consider them game. My wife is broad-minded indeed, but if I lugged an antelope cadaver home, my reception might be frigid! They have never been extensively domesticated because they would be only ornaments, but they can be tamed very easily. They will ride in a car, eat off of the kitchen stove, and lie on the back porch like (or with) the ranch dog. Good heads make beautiful mounts, and that about covers it, as far as shooting sport goes. The skins are pretty much worthless when tanned and the meat is most variable. Antelope winter largely on sagebrush, and cheerfully eat sage any time. If "fattened" on blue grama or alfalfa, the meat is good. However, if they have been living on sage they are very sagey, and you may have my share of their meat. Incidentally, they are *not* antelope. Lewis and Clark called them "goats" and those fellows were pretty fair taxonomists as well as expert geographers. They are close to goats, but have no known living relatives anywhere. They are a single species, in a single genus, and in their own one-species family. They run with any gait that exists and some that are purely their own. And they can travel! Even a rabbit-sized fawn can stay up with momma before he is dry behind the ears.

If you choose to collect one of these near-pets, you may need a long-range rifle. I would use my light .243 with the 6× Wolverine scope if I ever went after one, as presumably I will not. Of course you can take them with anything you can hit them with. Weighing some 100 pounds on the hoof, they are the smallest American hoofed animals except maybe Key deer and javelinas. They are very easy to kill.

So you ride around until you see a band and then put on a stalk. Or you may hide in the sage and wave a white handkerchief on a stick. Antelope are curious, and not very bright. Of course if the hunting pressure is high, the animals run, occasionally stop, and run again, like mad. The best time to get one is right after daylight on opening day. If you have slept out on the range, with your loaded rifle handy, you may pot one without getting out of your bedroll. It has been done.

"Goats" are called goats (Rocky Mountain goats, of course) but are closer to being antelope even as the antelope are closer to being goats. But Rocky Mountain goats *do* look somewhat like goats. At least they have beards!

Goats are as interesting, as beautiful, and almost as dumb as antelope. You get them with scope-sighted deer rifles. Almost pure white, they are visible for miles against the dark fall rocks.

In goat country, you climb until you see a goat and then stalk him, unless one pops up from somewhere while you are stalking. The Idaho laws require you to take out the meat, but fortunately do not require you to eat it! Goats produce the worst meat of any game mammal I have tried. Some antelope meat is good, but if any goat meat is good, I have thus far missed it.

Once you have spotted your goat, with decent care you will get a shot. They are no harder to kill than deer, if as hard. But take great care to make a clean kill. It is tragically common for a struggling, mortally wounded goat to topple off a cliff or even a big ledge, and break its horns. If the breaks are clean and you pick up all the pieces, your taxidermist may glue them together and end up with a perfect trophy head, but again, he may not. Making a wall "rug" may be the most effective goat trophy, and there are few that are finer.

Perhaps it should be emphasized that a goat is built like a diminutive bison, with most of his not-very-great weight far to the front. This makes him easy to topple over a ledge. Still, there is power in his hindquarters; in fact, there is power everywhere, as he is the greatest hoofed North American climber. He might even climb well enough to compete with the chamois, or any other hoofed creature anywhere. His climbing is slow poetry in motion, just as the running antelope is poetry at a faster tempo. Though I cheerfully make suggestions as to the "harvest" of each of these animals, I will leave this harvesting to other hunters' guns. Antelope could progress to nuisance numbers but goats never will. They are legitimate trophies, but I prefer them alive.

Bighorn sheep are second only to goats as climbers and are also unbelievably beautiful and graceful animals. Possibly they are the most coveted of any American trophy. A full-curl bighorn head on the den wall is something.

Their management is complicated, but the instructions for taking one are simple.

Like goats, you first have to find your ram. Unlike a prize billy, your ram is very smart. They are trusting enough when on a refuge and unhunted. During six years on the Desert Game Range in Nevada, I knew some of them by their first names, and they knew me and my mule, Madame, equally well. But they learn fast. I was instructed to collect three specific sheep for chromosome studies. The first one was simple murder, but the second highly suspicious and the third demanded very careful stalking. Probably none in that area had been shot at for twenty years or more.

Bighorns have good eyes, possibly the best among North American game, though antelope eyes are good indeed and all the deer tribe are far from blind. But bighorns are inclined to look down rather than up. True enough, they are frequently so high that down is the only direction there is anything but sky to see. For all that, you must get above them if you can, but not on the skyline. If your glasses can help you spot a suitable ram, the stalk must be painstaking indeed. It may be your only chance during a hunt. And you may make two or three hunts over two or three years and longer to get a good shot at a good bighorn. I am sure that the average full-curl Idaho bighorn costs his collector $2,000 in cash plus the most heart-breaking climbing he ever endured. There is occasional first-trip luck. It is balanced by hunters who hunt and hunt and *hunt,* and never see a good head. Law determines the sizes of the horns. When sighting sheep, if one in ten is legal and one in twenty is really good, you are up to the average.

Though sheep are taken at all sorts of distances, you should be prepared for a long shot when you cannot get a close one. My favorite mule-deer rifle, the .270 with the K2.5 scope, would be my favorite sheep rifle if I again have occasion to take a sheep, as presumably I will not. This is admitting that I am used to it, and that for a long shot, a 4× scope would be better. I always use 150-grain bullets in the .270. I might add that I have never had any real complaint about any brand or make of bullets, though possibly the Nosler partitioned bullets or the very similar Germanic H-mantled ones will outkill any of the others. Among the common factory-loaded jobs, it is a tossup between Winchester's Power-Point and Remington's Core-Lokt bullets. I have used everything that has been advertised. All are fine if you put them where you should. If you only knock off a leg, or paunch-shoot an animal, it will generally run. I *have* noted that, though the Winchester Silvertip bullet is indeed a stopper on *big* animals, it does not expand properly on the smaller ones unless you hit the heaviest bones. And I avoid hitting *any* bones if I can. Ribs are hopefully the biggest, excepting the occasional head or neck shot. Naturally you hit what you can, and nothing brings an animal down so totally as smashing both shoulders.

Returning specifically to sheep, you do not want to tear up your trophy's head or neck. A good taxidermist is a genius as well as an artist, but you should give him all the breaks you can manage without breaking bones. A middle to high lung shot is my favorite to finish *any* animal, but you cannot always get that sort of hold.

Incidentally, mountain mutton is excellent meat, but an old trophy ram will have passed his best meat years. In contrast, old buck deer (*very* old ones, whose antlers have started back toward heavy spike condition) have sometimes quit competition and make excellent meat. Old rams with their more or less continuously developing horns are fighters almost to the end. Sometimes when they have seriously deteriorated as breeders, they continue to garner huge harems and beat the stuffing out of fine young rams who have everything except that massive head. Ram shoulders and necks have to develop in order to lug the head, and old animals who may be physically slowed still have egos and courage to match their horns. Considering the meticulous rules under which bighorns fight, the veterans usually win. If bighorn rams live so long that they die of old age (an associate on the Desert Game Range saw one die with nothing else wrong with him, so far as we could discover) it is possible that their horns may slough off at the base and lose diameter. I have seen *very* old specimens with badly worn teeth who apparently had thus deteriorated. They should have been collected and hung on the wall a bit earlier.

Lastly, whether or not you have the patience to continue your reading into Part II and its discussion of management, perhaps it should be noted here that a Rocky Mountain bighorn sheep *is* a sheep! An antelope is a sort of goat and a goat is a sort of antelope, but a bighorn is a sheep and a noble one. He is smaller than the Asiatic *Ovis poli* or *Ovis argalli* (if there is any real difference between these giants) but his horns are prettier and he is big enough.

The white Alaskan Dall sheep may be even prettier than the bighorn, and is definitely a separate species. There are no essential differences in hunting methods for any American wild sheep. Some minor differences are inevitable, naturally, according to the region concerned.

Before passing by the hoofed animals, the *peccary* or *javelina* rates a little hunting attention. He is considered to be a pig, but is not very closely related to the real hogs, such as our domestic animals and the foreign wild game hogs of the Old World. His snout is hoggish, however, his feet likewise, though the dew-claws are different, and his hair is bristly. His range is pretty much restricted to parts of Texas, Arizona, and New Mexico, but it might be spread. I do not know that they ever weigh even 50 pounds on the hoof, admitting that my weight checks are sketchy. They are definitely small animals.

Peccaries have razor-sharp canine teeth and will fight if cornered. (Most animals will, except rabbits, and I have been clawed by rabbits' hind feet.) Still, the pugnacity of peccaries has been exaggerated. I doubt if our little collared peccary, no matter how large his herd, has ever attacked anyone. There is another species, deeper into Old Mexico, that is reputed to be dangerous. I have not had a chance to study it. The real wild hogs, some of which have been imported for sport hunting, are another matter. Big boars have killed both horses and men. Our son shot some in Germany, but I know too little about them to give advice that would be worth anything.

Some peccary shooting may be at reasonably long range. Your problem is to select a charge that will kill the animal but not blow it to smithereens. A head of a good "boar" is an interesting mount, and there is nothing wrong with peccary pork if it has not been run to death or is not from too old an animal. These are meat axioms that apply well enough to anything.

For brush shooting, or any sort of close ambush shooting, my peccary gun is a .44–40 or .44 Winchester, if you choose. A .38–40 or even a .32–20 should answer. Possibly the new .44 magnum would be a bit hot unless handloaded down to about .44–40 power. For long range, the 6mm jobs, among which the .243 Winchester may be the best known, should fill the bill. Of course, 100-grain bullets are standard for this type of shooting. My .270 is all right if loaded with cast bullets, and that K2.5 scope is unbeatable for fast shooting. But the shot would have to be very well placed (assuming the standard hot charge was used) if one hoped to put meat in the smokehouse.

Peccaries are rooters, and locating their feeding areas is easy enough. They are also lively travelers. This is admitting that their habitat is rarely cold and they may do plenty of resting in the shade.

When hunting them, after locating their general travel routes, you may drive them with a party, sit in ambush, or still-hunt. There is considerable choice according to conditions. Definitely keep in mind that these little piggies are intelligent and will give you a run for your money.

—10—

Carnivorous Game

PLEASE NOTE THAT this chapter title might be subject to argument, depending on one's definition of carnivorous game. The same arguments might arise in connection with the chapter on varmint shooting. It may be sufficient to explain that the specific animals I am considering are game as I see them. What others call them does not alter the shooting problems, though management may be a horse of a different color.

The bears may be the first animals one would think of as carnivorous game. They belong to the order Carnivora unless the taxonomists have recently been monkeying with them. You are aware that that suggests being meat eaters, which is partially true, but actually all the bears are inclined to be omnivorous. They will eat just about anything, like hogs, humans, rats, raccoons, and opossums. The most omnivorous American bear is of course the black bear, in its milder habitat. It will eat considerable vegetable food because it is more available. Contrarily, the polar bear, during much of the year, has no vegetation to feed on, so it eats meat or it does not eat.

Black bears may well be taken with deer rifles. And best, perhaps, with the deer rifles recommended for deer in the typical deer-bear habitat. In Eastern whitetail country, a bear shot will usually be as close or closer than a deer shot, so a scope is likely to be a nuisance. In the dry West, the ranges can be longer and there would be little trouble from rain or snow.

I do not like to kill bears, nor have I killed any except through duty as a Yellowstone Park ranger. In that capacity I had to kill seven, and I hit one that should have stopped but did not. I have every reason to believe that it was dead within a minute or two, but it ran furiously and we never found it. A crippled bear is serious enough anyway, and especially serious in a heavily populated area like Yellowstone Park. However, we were in a remote area where the guests were specialized and relatively few. I was worried, but no damage was done and I did not have to bury that bear!

All but one of these Yellowstone bears were killed with my wife's .30–30 carbine, with iron sights and commercial 170-grain bullets. That class of rifle is good enough, just as it is good enough for deer in thick cover. As to the cripple that got away, it was one of those things. It should not have happened, least of all to me, but it did. It has happened two or three times deer hunting too, and it could happen again. Obviously I did something that was not quite right, but still do not know what it was.

Black bears average larger than deer, are somewhat harder to kill, and some are very, *very* big, but I insist that deer rifles will handle them. Where anything is hit is far more important than what it is hit with.

In most states, bear trapping is outlawed, and possibly the majority are taken incidentally while hunting something else. There are no restrictions in many places against chasing them with hounds, and I recommend it. Actual bear hunters are the most skilled bear hunters. If the dogs tree a cub, the best policy is to call them off and look for a better bear. This is admitting that a cub cooks into a very tasty type of roast pig!

Further, bears enjoy eating carrion, hence any sort of a carcass may be worth watching. This is true whether or not you choose to shoot the feeder, as usually I would not. Still, you could be interested.

Further, late in the season you may find a fresh bear track and follow it in the snow. They have thus been taken when run out of (presumably) temporary "hibernation" under a windfall. Bears do not really hibernate, though we call it that. I have thus followed a couple, largely to see what they would do. They led me a merry chase and I did not come up with them, but I added to my bear knowledge.

Black bears are also driven, like deer. I have known some Adirondackers who did it successfully. Usually some deer were incidentally driven too, but the "hunters" on stand had to wait for the bears. They usually do not range very far ahead of the drivers.

Bears have poor eyes, but good hearing and a keen sense of smell. They are also intelligent, often too intelligent for their own good. Unfortunately, their good I.Q. is marred by a crude ruthlessness that sometimes makes bears become troublesome even when they are not ruined by tourists, as they are in Yellowstone. A National Park needs some bears, but they are often terrific nuisances. This is especially true where it is not practicable to barrel-trap them and lug them to another ranger's territory!

Perhaps it should be noted that bear meat varies widely in edibility. Young bears are invariably good eating. Big ones vary from excellent to horrific. Probably this is the result of what they have been eating. In the fall, which is the only time you should be taking them, they are always fat. The meat texture resembles pork, but it is as dark as beef, or darker. A smoked bear ham, by the way, could easily be mistaken for a hog ham, and a good one does not suffer by comparison.

Besides the black bears the U.S. has few indeed except in Alaska. There has been a very limited grizzly season in Montana, but I do not expect the season to last, whether or not the animals hold their own. Grizzlies are mean. Once widely distributed, they are now gone almost everywhere in the contiguous states, except a very few in and around Yellowstone Park and Glacier Park. They may be exterminated even in these areas in the foreseeable future.

If you get a chance to take a grizzly in Canada or Alaska, you should have an elk gun. One of the bears I had to kill off Shoshone Lake was a grizzly, and I had nothing to do it with but that little .30–30 carbine. The grizzly died, but I was worried. Grizzlies are tough, fearless, and definitely the only dangerous wild mammal in this country except possibly the few (if any) jaguars that may exist north of the Rio Grande. (The jaguar is not remotely in the grizzly class, but he can be a rough pussy and he *has* attacked people.) So a .30–06 is the lightest gun I would consider for grizzly shooting, and if there was reason to kill another (as I trust there will not be) I would choose my iron-sighted .405 or .375. If there was likelihood that the shot would be at glass-sight range, I would use the .338 and 4× scope. Naturally the .375 will do more out a bit than the .338, and possibly the .375 should have a scope with quick-detachable mounts, but mine does not. Not that I would worry about a grizzly if I had my .30–06, a .348, .45–70, or .358 and half a dozen other guns including a double 12 smoothbore with a couple of slugs. There is always the chance that you will do something the least bit wrong, and a crippled grizzly only needs one paw swipe to wipe out a puny human. Grizzlies have made unprovoked attacks on people in the parks, and killed them. These attacks are rare, but old Ephraim should be given plenty of room unless you have the equipment for stopping him.

Polar bears in North America are and have always been restricted to Canada and Alaska, plus Greenland and Iceland, if you consider these great islands. I have never shot one and never will, and I question whether shooting them is now ethical anywhere. My views on their management will be carefully stated later.

I was more or less in on the deaths of four polars in 1937 on the east coast of Hudson's Bay. I handled the skins and helped clean the skulls.

Polars have killed people, perhaps premeditatedly (as if a human was a sort of upright seal); but they are far less savage than grizzlies, though as big or bigger, and with plenty of potential for doing damage.

Whereas grizzly meat is poor, though there is evidence that early-day Mountain Men ate them extensively, northern natives definitely like polar meat. We tried two of them. One, an old female, was inedible unless you were in the last stages of starvation, a condition all too common in the North. A big young male, however, was excellent, and we ate on it as long as we could keep it (it was summer). We did not try the other two, but the natives or their dogs did. They also saved every ounce of fat, which totaled hundreds of pounds.

If you go after a polar, as I trust you never will, grizzly ammunition will do, and a long-range shot with a scoped rifle would be logical. Peculiarly, the natives will attack anything with anything. And they are very careless with their rifles in that damp and salty environment. Rusty .30–30 carbines and old .303 militaries were the commonest weapons. Of course these natives survived for generations before there were any guns, and they are the best hunters I have ever seen in action.

There are probably two species of *Alaskan brown bears*, though they are similar, and both are near-cousins of the grizzlies. They, and also the grizzlies of Alaska, are ethical as well as legitimate game. With sensible care, they should endure indefinitely, admitting that such care is somewhat uncertain.

Brownies suggest the same type of ammunition as the other big bears. Long shots may be necessary on occasion. Among long-range rifles that deliver when they really get out there, I put the .300 Weatherby loaded with 200-grain Nosler bullets at the top. The other *big* .300 magnums are not notably weaker. A friend from Pocatello some years ago took two with a .348 at very close ranges. He did all right, but felt that a little more gun would have been desirable. I have never heard that brownies attack people, but cripples might charge and a ton of great brown bear could be a rough customer in hand-to-paw combat.

It is doubtful if you will ever hunt a brown bear without a guide, and that guide will not only try to find a good bear, but see that you survive and hopefully come back for another hunt. He will also advise you in advance about guns, and you need not be surprised if his own rifle is an ancient but very honorable .30–06. Still, he will not look down his nose (which even the most polite guides are good at doing) if you have a .375, a .338, or both. If you lug only one rifle (weight could be important), it should wear that quick-detachable scope plus good iron sights.

Cougars may be second only to bears as American carnivorous game, and they are real carnivores whether you call them cougars, mountain lions, panthers, or whatever. Cougar is the best name as suggested by his scientific title. Panther is a name applied to other big cats and "mountain" lion is not so good if he happens to like swamps, as he does (or did) in Florida.

Cougars are on the scarce list and will be in danger of extermination unless there is prompt action, as will be discussed in Part II. Several Western states now rate cougars as game animals. Where their potentialities are greatest in Idaho, Wyoming, and Montana, as I write, they still rate as "varmints." There is a good chance that Idaho will improve their status at the next legislative session, but that may be partially wishful thinking. Many ranchers would cheerfully see them exterminated and some barbershop biologists feel that certain deer scarcities are the result of cougar predation. The fact that the "B.S." biologists are wrong does not make them less dangerous.

Cougars are sleuthy. Though they hunt some in daylight, a hunter in their territory might operate all season for years on end and never see one. He will see plenty of tracks. Cougars have been taken when hunters were after other game, but this is rare. If you find a cougar kill that still has plenty of meat on it, watching it at dusk or dawn will give an even chance for a shot.

The best way, from both the sporting and success angles, is to run cougars with hounds. They tree or come to bay in rocks. If the animal is a pregnant female, a kitten, or a tabby with kittens, the dogs are called off and another start is made. That is standard practice here in Idaho where it is still legal to kill any sort of a cougar at any time in any number.

Treed cougars may be killed by anything, and the hunters I know usually knock them out with some sort of a pistol. The hunting is usually on foot because of the exceedingly rough terrain these big cats inhabit; the hunter wants both hands for climbing and doesn't need the weight of a carbine. If a cougar is grounded and still has any life, he will injure and may kill a dog or two. Cougar hounds are expensive as well as treasured pals, and protecting them is the apex of importance. There are arguments as to how a treed cougar should be knocked out. Some favor a head shot so that the animal will be dead before he gets down to the dogs. That permits some reflex action, however, and nominally dead cougars have slashed hounds badly with their terrible claws. Thus, many favor a heart shot. The animal will then instinctively hang on to his tree hold for a few seconds, but will be incapable of any slashing by the time he tumbles to the ground. The method is definitely up to the owner of the dogs, but if he is an outfitter, his client, who will get the trophy, should do the shooting if he is competent to do it. That is also up to the guide. The dogs are in a sufficiently precarious situation without any carelessness or bungling.

Any admirer of dogs will see pretty much the last word in dog ability and total courage if he chases cougars. Embarrassingly often, a green but too-brave pup will get badly mangled if he actually attacks a cat that still has a spark of life. If the dog survives, he has learned something. A cougar cornered in rocks is a rough fighter.

The handguns used to finish cougars may well be powerful. I know some who use the newish .44 magnum that chambers the most powerful pistol charge known to modern shooting. Whatever is used, it should be most accurate, and should be fired with a careful two-hand hold. I would suggest that the .38 Special should be the mildest ammunition permissible, admitting the precision of the hit is far more important than the projectile that is fired.

If anyone gets a random shot at a cougar (and chooses to take it) when he is properly armed for deer, he will do all right with a big cat.

There are only a couple of the smaller carnivores that may rate hunting comment. *Foxes* and *raccoons* demand certain attention.

Both of these animals can get into the varmint category. Coons are not protected in Idaho, where they are relatively newcomers, are sometimes a nuisance, and are holding their own without any management. They usually are and should be classed as game animals.

'Coons, you are well aware, are normally hunted with dogs and at night. Night dogs will hunt only 'coons, 'possums, and skunks. They may or may not pursue other game in daylight. This is admitting night hounds sometimes run and *tree* gray foxes. These grays are the only dog-family creatures I know of that can climb trees fairly well, and cheerfully do so. Not that they can climb like a cat or a raccoon, but they do better at it than is predictable from their equipment.

After a 'coon is treed, the hunt may be far from over. There are various rules or conventions. I have been on hunts when no one had a gun. There were axes and saws and the tree was cut, or a good climber shinnied up and dislodged the 'coon in any way that he could. The dogs did the killing. That climber, incidentally, needed courage as well as skill. A cornered 'coon will fight. He fights anything, and fights until he is dead.

This was long ago, when cutting a tree, anywhere, seemed to be of little importance. Now, if a climber goes after a 'coon, he will have a flashlight and a good .22 handgun. For this climbing (I choose not to do it) any sort of high-speed .22 Long Rifle ammunition is good enough, but hollow-point bullets are an advantage. Shooting at the 'coon's gleaming green eyes from the ground suggests a little more power, such as the rimfire .22 magnum. Nor is a 12-gauge duck gun, loaded with No. 4 shot or bigger, any mistake on 'coons. Even with those iridescent green eyes and a well-held flashlight, rifle shooting at night is not my dish of tea. I prefer the smoothbore.

Occasionally one will happen on a raccoon when hunting squirrels or grouse. I have done so a couple of times, and once got one when I was not hunting at all, though it was open season. My dog chased it up a small tree in the Mississippi bottoms in Minnesota. I had a revolver in my canoe as a matter of routine, and shot it through the head. The November day was dark and drizzly, and the 'coon was on the ground where there were only small trees. My dog was an Irish setter, and I doubt if he had ever before seen a raccoon; but it looked like game, despite great pains not to get too close! Except for the dog, I would not have known the 'coon was around. 'Coons are sneaky, and night or day, seeing one is unusual unless a dog with his superior senses manages to seek it out.

There is little game meat that is as tasty as a fat 'coon in the fall, though the fat demands hot roasting and draining. Also there are a couple of lymphatic glands ("kernels") in the 'coon's armpits that should be removed, or the meat will have a musky flavor a bit like musk-polluted venison. An omnivorous feeder that takes considerable animal food should not be that good eating, but never pass up a 'coon roast. It is "out of sight," as is 'possum.

Foxes are also sort of equivocal animals. Where they are run with horses and hounds, shooting is regarded as anathema. But I recall when my native New York paid a bounty of $1 for a red fox scalp, even though the animal was a young whelp. (Further, I have collected on that bounty! Foxes *did* take chickens, and dollars were few. But that was long ago. Of course a fox will still take chickens, and I continue to respect a dollar, but bounties are a disgrace that we have rather well cleaned up.)

Running foxes with hounds, and the pink coats, "yoicks," "tally-ho," and all that is *the* way to hunt foxes. That is, if you have the proper fences, the good equipment, and the savvy to use it. Lacking that charming folderol, the occasional "John Peel," hunting on the simpler, lone-wolf basis has its points. In both instances, the hounds had to catch the fox, and that takes some doing. It's just possible that the American red fox is the smartest wild animal that lives, and his European counterpart isn't much different. Still, running foxes with hounds, the hunters afoot, expecting the quarry to be brought back from about where he was started, is sport enough. Then the hunter shoots. Usually he fires a scattergun loaded as for geese. Probably No. 2 shot is the best. However, I have done all right with No. 4, and the first fully grown fox I ever shot came by when I was watching for squirrels. I was loaded with No. 6 shot, but he ran within 25 yards and I got off a round out of the full-choked barrel. I was about thirteen. He did not go down immediately but did not run far either. It used to be standard practice to use BB shot for foxes, but that was in the days of less effective ammunition. I have blasted No. 2 pellets two-thirds of the way through a coyote that was upward of four times the size of a fox. Even a big fox is not very big or very hard to stop if he is in the middle of the pattern.

Occasionally a fox will be taken with a rifle, if you choose to shoot and are properly gunned. Hot .22 varmint rifles will tear a fox to pieces, and I will not shoot unless there is some chance for a decent skin. A powerful deer rifle may not hurt a skin as the animal is so light the bullet might not expand.

In any event, if you hunt in fox country—especially red fox territory—you should enjoy some association with these beautiful and really foxy creatures.

—11—

Rabbits and Squirrels

THIS SHORT CHAPTER on taking game is restricted to rabbits and squirrels, and since *cottontail rabbits* are hunted so extensively, I will consider them first. Definitely, more rabbits are shot in the U.S.A. than any other species of game. I am not quoting statistics, as they are too variable to be of any special use in this type of volume, but they are published perhaps every year by the Department of the Interior, and you will often find them illuminating.

Cottontails are usually taken on the run and thus demand scattergun shooting, unless you are as good a rifleman as Dan'l Boone and his ilk were alleged to be. A little gun will do well. Rabbits are anything but tough, in the brush or on the table. But I am a 12-gauge man, and reiterate my preference for double guns. The ruffed-grouse charges of 7½ shot in one barrel and 6 in the other are my choices, and early in the season you may knock off the occasional bunny while hunting grouse or any scattergun game. There is no reason to despise a mixed bag! And most of your kills will be with 7½ shot in the less-choked tube.

So, rabbit hunting may be incidental, while the season is frequently long and the meat tops. And while I mention this high-grade meat, please note that people have contracted tularemia and more from dressing rabbits. So rubber gloves are no mistake, and after dressing rabbits, at least you should scrub your hands with a brush and plenty of soap in as hot water as you can comfortably stand. (Few "bugs" can endure much hot water and soap, while infection is most unlikely unless one has scratches on his hands. Still, scratches are common enough if one is an active shooter.) Happily you do not eat your rabbits raw (I hope!), and even if any sort of meat is a bit buggy, cooked bugs may simply rev up the protein content.

Come the late season, preferably with tracking snow, the way to pursue elusive bunnies is with a doggie, and that means a beagle hound or (better yet) two or three beagles. Possibly rabbits and hounds can produce more hunting in more places than any other combination. Beagles are affectionate pets and making them into pets does not reduce their hunting efficiency an iota. And, though primarily rabbit dogs, I have seen beagles that were very versatile, including one that did a beautiful job retrieving woodcock. Beagle noses are as good as any, and if they find no rabbits, they will spring and retrieve anything that they have been trained to hunt. Further, their dedication in taking after a rabbit causes as much amusement as admiration. A beagle never caught a healthy cottontail, and never will. That keeps the rabbit so far ahead of the dogs that he takes his time and makes an easy shot. Further, the dogs are so slow that you rarely have to hold fire for fear of hitting them instead of the rabbit. The combination could not be more ideal.

Even slower dogs that also chase rabbits are dachshunds and bassets, both of which, in this country, have degenerated into pets and little else. But neither they nor anything else are comparable to beagles.

So we are down to *squirrels*—gray and fox squirrels for the most part, admitting the grays in some places are largely black. (These are melanistic freaks, like albinos.) These most important species are largely hardwood timber animals of the East, South, and Midwest. There is also a fine big Western gray that does not seem to get much attention, whether or not he enjoys (?) an open season. Kaibab squirrels are rigidly protected, and some Western states, including Idaho, do not permit any tree squirrel shooting, for reasons to be explained later.

The sportiest squirrel shooting is to plink them through the head with a .22 rifle, or a Kentucky squirrel rifle, if you would go whole hog. The rifle does not have to be of especially small caliber if you stick to head shots. You can also "bark" a squirrel with a big rifle, firing a slow ball or bullet. This takes careful shooting. If the squirrel is flat-out on a limb, you shoot just under him. A chunk of bark blasts up, and not only knocks the squirrel out of the tree, but knocks him out. He may come to and run, unless you swiftly bash him in the head. There are methods for getting more squirrels, but barking them is certainly sporting. If you discuss this and encounter skeptics, I suggest a bit of practice before you demonstrate its efficiency. Your rifle should be slow for barking. If a breechloader, the .38–40 or .44–40 class is right. For a more powerful rifle, handloads with any sort of cast bullets will do. Muzzleloaders should be .40 or bigger, using a ball. And a ball is standard excepting rifles that primarily use minié bullets. A muzzleloading squirrel rifle, primarily for head shots, can scarcely have too small a bore. Many were .31, and I have not seen one smaller than .28. My .36 Kentucky flinter would probably not be too big, though I did not have it when in tree-squirrel country and am guessing.

Of course a shotgun with any bore that is 20 or bigger is the best squirrel killer, though a 28 or even a .410 is all right if you are careful. A 12, with No. 6 shot, however, will do the best if you must take running shots through treetops, and those shots are the most fun.

Sitting shots, or shots when the squirrel is moving slowly, are naturally the most deadly. And patience is what gets the squirrels. I probably took more with a full-choke Stevens single, when I was a half-grown youngster, than I ever did with anything else. Get in the woods at daylight, where there are nuts or acorns, and sit tight. You can usually get a squirrel—rarely more than two—and then you should move and again wait.

I have known perhaps two squirrel dogs, and have heard much about others. The ones I knew were small and foxlike. Their owners claimed that the squirrels thought they were foxes. Since all mammals except man (and perhaps some apes and baboons) are color blind, I take this theory with a pinch of salt. I am inclined to believe that the half-beagle already mentioned would hunt squirrels if he got into squirrel country.

In any event, these "feists" (that is all the name I ever heard) would range the woods and spot a squirrel. If it was not in a tree when jumped it soon climbed one, and the feist would circle it, barking and screaming. To avoid a hunter, a smart squirrel will get on the tree side away from his pursuer, and stay there. But the circling dog made the squirrel circle, and the squirrel paid more attention to the dog than he did to the man who was sleuthing into range. That bad judgment on the part of the squirrel is what made the doggie valuable.

Squirrel shooting may seem a bit tame to one who has hunted many species of game, both great and small, but young folks can take them, and they are great eating. I have lost no zest for more important shooting, and still manage to take it. Still, my dotage is approaching—everyone becomes senile if he lives long enough—and occasionally I get a nostalgic yen to hunt squirrels. I well remember my first ones, not later than 1904, and probably there are still some in that same patch of woods. I will probably never go back, but it would be fun.

This ends my hunting advice, and I can only hope that you may hunt with as much pleasure, as successfully, and as long as I have. Or longer! I am still not doing badly after some seventy seasons. Hunting may not keep one young, but it adds to general flexibility, and it is definitely a sport that can be followed for a long, long time—if it lasts. But that is a problem I will deal with after one more specialized chapter.

—12—
Camping and Incidental Equipment

IT HAS BEEN suggested that Part I of this book, on game harvesting, can scarcely be complete without touching on incidental equipment for staying out for from one night to weeks. However, since there are libraries written on various phases of camping, there is no reason for elaborate instructions here.

The existing books vary, in my opinion, of course, from excellent to worthless. The most basic is Kephart's *Camping and Woodcraft*. It is old-fashioned, but will not be out of date until Gibbon's *Decline and Fall of the Roman Empire* is also outdated. Kephart could *write*, and he was there. It is a good combination.

Clothes and Footgear

It has long been reported that man can wear anything, *except* on his feet.

Man is a tropical animal. While he was slowly becoming human (more or less) he did not wear clothes. Sensitive and dangerously exposed sex organs—especially in males—resulted in breechcloths, and maybe some sort of moccasins came next. The only reason humans ever managed to make it in cold climates was because of their brains and hand-skills. Most North American Indians never learned to make sleeves or pants, though the Eskimos were fine tailors, and some northern Indians learned from them.

Human feet have horribly inefficient circulation; scalps are the reverse.

Our white ancestors wore wool socks ever since there have been historical records of ancestors in cool to cold climates, and nothing better has been devised. A few people have their feet seriously irritated by wool, and this suggests the thinnest cotton socks under the wool. So, for socks, wool, and as many and as thick as you need, should be in your boots or moccasins. At least one pair of those socks should be right up to the knee. Orlon may be the best wool substitute thus far developed. Some claim it is better. With this I disagree, but it certainly is worth careful investigation.

Outer footwear may vary vastly according to season and climate. In the tropics, shoes may be as light and porous as you can get. During an arctic winter, insulated boots are logical. Still, you are aware that if it is cold enough, dry chrome-tanned or deerskin moccasins are good for snowshoeing, or even for sitting in a zero-weather waterfowl blind.

Another sort of axiom is that if one is active, it is difficult or impossible to keep those badly-blood-supplied feet really dry. Feet sweat, warm or cold. If you have waterproof footgear, there is definite dampness. If the boots are porous, letting some sweat escape, water can come in from the outside unless the situation is plumb dry or plumb cold. You are on the horns of a dilemma, and must do your best.

An old guide friend, the late Lloyd Melville, whom I frequently quote, allowed that the only trouble with Indian-tanned deerskin was that it got wet three days before a rain! I have snowshoed some thousands of miles during subzero weather in those same deerskin moccasins. The sweat froze them in the course of a day, but the inside pair of three or four pairs of wool socks kept reasonably dry. I never froze my feet, though they seemed frozen often enough. If at night you can get into a cabin or a tent with a good stove, and get things dry, the discomfort is only nominal. Dampness is the outdoors problem in really cold weather and miserable feet top everything else.

Hands have a lot better circulation than feet, but they are of especial concern to me because mine are depigmented and I must wear gloves in the sun, winter or summer.

Returning to Indian-tan jobs, gloves of this material are the coolest when hot and the warmest when cold. Any sort of deerskin gloves come next to the Indian-tans, but the latter are my choice and not subject to argument. I have worn out a couple of pairs of long-wristed summer flying gloves that are thinner than the Indian-tans, and really better if you are handling a double gun with two triggers. They are a bit hotter, however, and I usually use a single-trigger double for early fall shooting, so the deerskin is more logical.

For real cold-weather shooting I prefer heavy mittens, sometimes with a separate trigger finger. This trigger finger is not especially important for cold-weather big-game hunting, however, if you have learned to snatch the trigger-hand mitten off with your teeth. If the shooting is fast and furious, like some jackrabbit hunting or using two guns in the canoe bow or waterfowl blind, the mitten with a finger has its points.

Though scalps have good circulation, hunting headgear is important. As I write, bare heads are stylish indeed on the campus within a dove-shot of my desk. If bare heads do not feel actually cold or hot, the fast circulation tends to influence one elsewhere. Further, a hat may be camouflage, and shades the eyes. For cold weather, a parka hood over a light cap is my favorite. The less hair, the more important the hat, and since I have not had much hair since about age twenty-three, my opportunity to study headgear has been extensive. The outdoorsman's headgear goes beyond the horseman's sombrero, or a ceremonial 'coon-tailed cap that is a must if you would be authentic with a long rifle. I have known good hunters who operated bareheaded, but I do not recommend it until you have given it considerable thought.

Possibly next-the-skin garments can engender more arguments than any other clothes. This because the majority of us now live with central heating and our buildings are usually overheated. This is not a serious fault at 4,500 feet elevation and halfway to the Boreal Pole, but if you are inside at all in this overheating, the professional outdoorsman's wool underwear is not comfortable. If you get out and stay out, living in a tent, itchy wool will not itch. Now rarely away from central heating for more than a couple of days, and still more rarely for over ten days, I make it with a cotton T-shirt under a wool jersey or light wool sweater. A wool flannel shirt covers both, and outer clothes are "to taste." Though I have heavy stuff, light cotton balbriggan drawers usually answer. I get them "too big" and let them shrink.

Wool, blanket-thickness pants are sometimes logical over these balbriggans. If I wear a knee-length parka, as I often do, and knee-high socks, mackinaw pants are too thick. You walk with your legs and lift your feet. The lighter the footgear and the less leg encumbrance the better, if other things are equal, which they often ain't. Heavy wool does not rattle, and this is an item if you are sneaking up to a wily whitetail. Then too, sometimes you are sitting. *My* experience is less important than *your* intelligence. Some people can stand more heat or more cold than others. Women can stand more heat, more cold, more starvation, and you-name-it, than men. Just tougher, as well as more "deadly," according to Kipling.

Sleeping Gear

No one can be happy if he cannot sleep. You will get used to a hard bed but it takes too long. That is, unless you prefer to sleep on a hardwood floor at home. Few do, and I recall the story about the chap whose bed was so *damned* hard he had to get up and rest occasionally or he could not sleep at all.

With all due respect to balsam boughs, dry leaves, and hay, the air bed was the greatest invention to facilitate outdoors on-the-ground sleeping. My first was purchased about 1925 and I have never been without one since. If you must lug your bed on your back, in a canoe, or even on a pack animal, you need the best air bed you can get or can afford. This is axiomatic, admitting I have seen some old-timer bed rolls on pack animals that might have enclosed an inner-spring mattress. Further, they were so heavy that just one made a stout pack mule walk sort of knee-sprung.

In mild weather, nothing is especially important except that air bed. Come the high-up November elk hunt, or whitetail shooting in snow, keeping warm at night is of the essence.

"Way north," and not so many years ago, either, I heard arguments *against* feather ("down") robes. Some believed that woven rabbitskin robes were the last word—but try and get one! Also try to get a double caribou-skin sleeping bag. Caribou skin, like wolverine fur, sheds frost. Don't ask me why—I am not enough of a biochemist to know, nor did I believe it at one time. Anyway, it is academic, and you will settle for a "down" robe, or possibly an orlon robe.

These feather robes, and coats, are indeed versatile. The lightest will manage on the coolest summer nights but not be so burdensome when it is rather warm. The best of the heavy ones will keep you warm in just about any known natural temperature from 50° to below 0° F or lower. To get warm you may have to duck your head under and blow hot air for a while, or sleep with a dog, but you will manage. You will manage so well that it is indeed a trial when you have to get out of it. But down picks up moisture, and a fire in the tent for an hour or so is very important if you would avoid that winter camping curse, dampness.

Good down robes cost fantastic prices, but they last. I have a so-called Arctic Three Star that I bought in January 1934, give or take a month. It has been back to the factory once for repairs, and again shows signs of wadding. It is 90 inches square spread flat, and weighs around 16 pounds. Though relatively big and heavy, it is as small and as light as can be managed if one craves the last word in cold-weather comfort. Naturally, it has not been used all winters since I bought it, but it has been used a powerful lot. I have worn out a lighter robe since 1925, and a couple of other light ones show some use.

To make them last and to reduce complicated cleaning, down robes should have blanket-sheet linings, or possibly ordinary bed-sheet linings in mild weather. And I am lost without a pillow, and feathers were invented for pillows. Sure, I have used a saddle for a pillow, also a small, too-lightly-padded spruce log. And so on. You do what you want, but for me, that feather pillow is worth lugging.

In addition to the lining, a down robe, if you sleep on the ground, rates a covering. So-called Stockman's Bed Sheets are the best, if you can get them, as you can from any Western tentmaker or saddler. Of course you can improvise something lighter, but scarcely better. These sheets were devised to cover the colossal bed rolls I have mentioned. Besides his saddle, that roll was the most important equipment and pretty much the home of the now extinct cowpuncher. Living where they once flourished, I do not recall seeing such a roll since 1940, so perhaps they are extinct too. But I do have a cover, and they are still made.

Tents

There are so many tents and they are so good, that suggestions about them require little space.

When lugging the whole outfit in a car or truck, it is solely a matter of choice. I despise the so-called "umbrella" tents, largely because they are commonest among the softest motoring tourists. That is a poor reason for dislike, but I have never owned one and never will, barring a gift.

For big-time camping, the universally known wall tents are unbeatable. If you travel by canoe or pack animal, the square, wigwam-type "miners tent" is my choice. They need only two poles, or none if there is a convenient tree limb. Backpacking or above timberline, you use the lightest shelter available. And above treeline, aluminum alloy poles and pins must also be lugged. If you lack experience, you rely on intelligence or advice. When I was teaching at Syracuse back in the twenties, I loaned some camp gear to students who, during Christmas recess, climbed Mt. Marcy. Certainly they tried to, and I dimly recall that they made it. When discussing the trip at a Forestry Club meeting, the leader allowed that the lightest equipment cost the most. What they used did not cost anything, and was thus not so light! They dragged it on toboggans, however, and dragging in the snow is easier than lugging.

Hunter's Cutlery

Next to the gun, or possibly fishing rod, the sportsman's most important actual tool is his ax. The knife or knives are parallel.

My experience shows that most town-raised axmen are poor ones. Rarely does one of them have a good sharp ax. If he has one, he does not know how to use it, and with this lack of knowledge, it may not stay sharp for five minutes. Further, he may have nothing to sharpen it with, and knows no more about using a whetstone than he knows about the ax. Bleak, but true. There are exceptions, but not enough.

The logical camping ax is called a "boy's ax" by dealers. Its weight should be some 2½ pounds and the overall handle length not less than 27 inches, nor more than 29 inches. There are instances where a 1½-pound hatchet with a 16-inch handle will get by, and the woodsman's 3½-pound ax also has its advantages, but single-bit small axes are favored by most of the best campers.

Patterns vary somewhat. My favorite is Plumb's National pattern. My next choice is the Michigan pattern. The National has something of a hammer poll, and a down-slash similar to the Hudson's Bay patterns. The latter types enjoy considerable popularity as I write, and are unbeatable for chopping. Their eyes are so shallow, however, that the handles loosen easily, and, further, they have such scant handle support that breakage is likely. Those eyes should not be less than 2⅜ inches deep.

Hickory with a straight, coarse grain is the best handle timber, but there is nothing wrong with good white ash or sugar maple. Good axes are fitted at the factory with good handles. The Plumb people glue their handles in with some sort of plastic glass that really sticks. My two complaints with this system are that a broken handle is hard to remove, and a handle that I fit suits *me* better than any job the factory ever does. I like my axes "hung in." That is, the bit slashes down, increasing the built-in cutting advantage of the Hudson's Bay or the National. Further, the handle should be straight and the ax "hung" absolutely square. The factories cannot be that fussy and make any profit. So I prefer to get my ax components separate, and compound them myself. The only good steel wedges I know of are made by the Sawyer Belt Hook and Wedge Co., 174 Cedar Street, Branford, Conn. 06405. This wedge is (or used to be) numbered 2000. These are easily driven out of a broken handle, and usually, unless something of a shop is available, removing the broken handle is a harder job than fitting a new one.

After fitting a handle, I like to soak the head in linseed oil to water-proof the wood. And wrapping the handle just below the eye with rawhide also has its points. When dry, the rawhide should be dosed with spar varnish. Of course, one should never "strike over"—that is, try to chop with the handle! But if you do, the rawhide helps—a little.

No ax is sharp when it comes from the shop. It needs grinding to suit the way it will be used, but there are some generalizations. If the bit is too thin, it can nick on frosty knots. If too thick, it will simply not sink in. The best grinder is the old-fashioned water grindstone that used to sit under an apple tree on New England farms. Try and find one today! So you must use what you can find and not burn the blade. A carpenter or a machinist can help if you do not feel competent. And once the bit is properly ground, an occasional touch with a file, using a whetstone to finish, will keep the ax going indefinitely. That is, if you do not cut anything harder than wood. Just a light blow into the ground, without touching a stone, dulls a sharp bit. Hitting shin bones is also tough on an ax, but even tougher on the bones. Most experienced axmen have scars, but they are not exactly honorable.

I have lightly referred to the hatchet as an ax substitute. It is light and portable but less than an ax. A double-bitted Cruiser ax, however, is a dog of different breed, and a valuable one. Mine is the same weight as the National single-bit, with a 29-inch Adirondack handle. This handle starts out like an ordinary double-bitter, but there is a slight curve and "fawnfoot" on the end like a single-bitter. You "hang in" the keen edge bit. No Solomonian wisdom is needed to be aware that you can take some liberties with the thicker, slightly "out-hung" bit and still have a keen blade for serious chopping. The double-bit, naturally, is poor for pounding. If you do pound with the flat of the ax, the eye may be flattened, inflicting permanent damage unless you get a blacksmith to rework that eye. Many old-fashioned, crossroads blacksmiths could make axes. I have watched them. If any still do, they are far from common.

I know of no reasonably complete instructions for ax use as I write. The Plumb people sold one at one time but it is out of print. Kephart includes some good hints. Anyone can learn to use an ax reasonably well if he practices slowly and carefully. It is essential to cut at an angle of some 45 degrees to the grain of the wood. Hair-splitting control is the secret. Well, perhaps it's unnecessary to split a hair, but you should be able to split a match rather frequently. And once past the preliminary training stage, ax work is fun as well as producing campfire wood and exercise.

Knives may be disposed of swiftly. I rarely *carry* any knife except a pocket tool with 3-inch blades. With it, I do ordinary whittling, as well as gut big-game animals and do all the dressing of small game and fish. Then I keep a big knife in camp. An ordinary butcher knife is good enough. There are many beautiful and super-efficient belt knives on the market, and I have my share of them, but they largely hang by the gun cabinet. This is another matter of choice. In any event, the knife must be sharp. A round whetstone, coarse on one side, fine on the other, is essential for the ax and will do well enough for camp knives. Again, practice makes perfect. Most kitchen knives I see are dull enough for plenty of opportunity to practice.

If a trip is big, demanding much cooking fuel, or the weather is cold, a saw may well give the ax an assist. Like the knife, it is not so exacting a tool as the ax, unless you go for professional cross-cutting or noisy power saws. Any advertised camper's saw is useful, but I get by with an ax unless the firewood situation suggests a buck saw with a 36-inch blade. The one I have now was bought from Sears, Roebuck and I have used it a dozen seasons. The blades are of excellent Swedish steel. I put in a new one each season. With minimum care, a blade will last a year. A new blade is cheaper than getting one sharpened.

Cooking Equipment

Since I despise cooking, and elaborate instructions are available, I will only mention the gear that is needed. That too is more efficient than ever before in recorded history, but experience suggests that many may profit from a few hints.

First, please note that there is really no such thing as specialized *camp* cooking. Cooking is cooking. There are limitations according to the conditions and environment. Here I assume that the cook is limited to the use of wood and an open fire. If you have a permanent camp, there will be a stove. A wood stove, usually, and an old one. We will forget oil and propane stoves that are pretty much associated with camping on roads. I have found that anyone who can cook in a kitchen can cook outdoors if he (often *she*) will try it. I have occasionally cooked enough to keep from starvation, and can prove it since I am still here! Once, on a woods assignment in the fall of 1915, I cooked for another chap as well as myself for nearly two months. You may guess what sort of a cook *that* guy was! We had a cabin with a good wood stove. Many men *think* they can cook and cheerfully try. Most women *can* cook, and are proud of it. My wife is as good as any and better than most. I manufacture the firewood, lug the water, and manage any essential chores for her or anyone who will work at cooking. I help as much as I have to but take few responsibilities. I can make good tea and coffee, but am not much of a coffee drinker. I can fry fish—or maybe anything— very well. I can big-scale cook meat. Never tried a whole critter, but can manage 125-pound quarters. I am fair enough at handling the fire for a reflector oven and even a Dutch oven. And that just about covers it.

Most reflector ovens are too small, but any tinsmith can make you a good one if you give him a model and suggest dimensions. Dutch ovens are too heavy for much lugging except to a somewhat permanent camp. For a long time they were almost off the market, but are easily available now. It takes practice, but you can cook or bake just about anything in a Dutch oven.

Aluminum and aluminum alloys make the lightest cooking equipment and are fine with certain exceptions. Those Dutch ovens are cast iron, and frying pans as well as the baking pans in reflector ovens should be iron or steel. Aluminum is too sticky. Cups must *not* be aluminum if you want to drink hot liquids out of them. For all kettles and buckets, aluminum is just fine. Stainless steel is fine for forks and spoons. Knives must be steel—*not* stainless steel, unless you are better at sharpening it than I am. Stainless steel is amazing stuff for certain purposes, and especially rifle barrels. It is newish and being steadily improved. I can hone a razor as well as a master barber, and put a razor edge on a knife or even an ax. But I have not managed edged stainless steel very well. So long as carbon-steel blades are available, I will stay with them, barring the emergency.

Trench shovel, waterproof matchbox, a good compass, and a map that includes the local magnetic declination are the principal other essentials, depending on conditions.

Since this is by no means a camping manual, I will not trespass further on a subject that rates a book. Instead, I propose that we turn over the coin and see what game harvesting or hunting looks like from the other side. Let us now consider the science, art, and practice of game management.

Part II
MANAGEMENT

Introduction

PERHAPS THE GAME-MANAGEMENT section of this book should have its own brief introduction, too, if you care to read it. As I have already indicated, I usually find prefaces and introductions dull indeed, but wade through them faithfully even so, and perhaps you do, too.

This section of the book is in some ways more technical than the section on game harvest, and perhaps some explanation of my treatment of technical nomenclature is in order. In accordance with my general refusal to follow a formal textbook style, I have avoided any extensive use of scientific names, even though I know a lot of them; instead, I have used what I think will be understood. If the reader likes technical names he can no doubt do his own translating. But if he is a one-gallus hunter who had trouble getting past the sixth grade, he should still get the drift. And perhaps he will be impressed by my hundred-odd shooting irons and seventy years of hunting, whether or not my academic degrees have any appeal.

Readers who like to keep up to date will be pleased to note that I have paid much attention to ecology in this section of the book, partially because I do not want to get behind the bandwagon myself. Let me add that I was somewhat familiar with ecology by 1906, and actively studying its applications by 1912. Until very recently, however, these ecological applications in game management were assumed but not elaborately explained; the subject was regarded as in the province of natural scientists, and general explanations were somewhat ignored. Now, "ecology" and "ecosystem" have suddenly become household words. There is a suspicion that some of those who write and talk glibly in this area may lack the classroom, laboratory, and field training an ecologist should have, but if they write and talk enough, they may still learn. I have been studying and applying ecology for many years, and am still learning, I hope. If I write about it a little, the masters thereof are invited to skip beyond if they wish, but those with less background may learn some basic principles. I have not gone beyond them.

Perhaps it is well enough understood that game management is some-what controversial, a relatively infant science (and art) in which opinions often differ, and can be difficult to substantiate. My exposure to both theory and practice has been great, and it is not surprising that I have occasionally disagreed with accepted authorities. They and others may well differ in turn with some of the ideas expressed on the following pages. This does not disturb me. We all have much to learn, while we all must hustle to do what we know must be done.

Though this part of the book deals almost entirely with game man-agement, I have occasionally touched upon one field not covered by the title—fish! I am no ichthyologist, but aquatic ecology is closely asso-ciated with game management. Moreover, I once worked a year with the old U.S. Bureau of Fisheries (1915–1916) as an apprentice fish cul-turist, and I planted a lot of fish for the Forest Service. Though not a fancy fisherman I am an enthusiastic wet flycaster, something of a canoe troller, and have been a licensed guide for fly-casting canoeists. Hence, no abject apologies!

—13—
Ecology

MOST OF GAME management's scientific details are based on ecology. By no means new, it has only recently become something of a household term, and questions suggest that a definition is desirable.

Ecology is a study of the interrelations that exist between living organisms and their environment. Possibly "among" would be better grammar than "between," but either will be clear enough.

So far as this book is concerned, I decline to recognize plant ecology or animal ecology as separate specialties. Botanists have taught courses in plant ecology. Possibly—just *possibly*—you may find a plant environment unaffected by animals. The botanists concerned, however, may not have known of or even hunted for such an environment. They simply assumed it. And I dimly recall a little green text, about 1914, with *Animal Ecology* in gold letters on the cover. If I believed it then, I have long since learned that no such thing exists. If a 100-percent zoological environment exists, it would be somewhere in the deeper seas, and I am ignoring oceanography. For our purposes, animals live in a botanical environment, or more exactly, on plants growing—largely—on soils.

Unrooted plants are common enough in water. Thus, freshwater biology as well as the geology of soils enters the broad ecological picture.

It may be trite to mention that the small amount of ecology we have room for here either just will, or just will not, take you out of the bridge-club ecology class. Ecology is a big subject, and you may earn a doctor's degree in it. Such a degree might not be a bad start in the study of game management!

Complicated and extensive in some respects, ecology includes many principles that are simple indeed, and I will draw some comparisons with the well-known human study of sociology. Really, much of sociology could be called ecology as applied to people.

One of the first items to note is that no living organism *necessarily* lives in the environment that it chooses or prefers. It is where it is because it can compete. It can *stand* its existence, whether or not it enjoys it. It can adapt. If it cannot or will not adapt, a more adaptable competitor will chase it out or root it out.

Please think about the environment of yourself or some of your friends. Are you or they exactly or largely where choice dominates? You are competing, or you would not be there. Only the individual himself may positively know how well he likes his slot. In class I have often called students' attention to their status. Do they like college? Did they definitely prefer *this* college? Are they helpless in their environment or did they choose it? Definitely they are competing! Come examinations, some may be tossed out. For the time being, they are making it.

If the reader is interested in *my* ecological status, so far as this choice of environment goes, I hasten to note that I am in Idaho through choice. Born in New York, I voted in that state, New Hampshire, Michigan, Wisconsin, Minnesota, Montana, and Nevada before coming to Pocatello almost twenty-five years ago. I have been in most of the other states excepting some of the Deep South and a little of the Southwest. I worked in Canada five years and have had considerable travel in three provinces. My European travel has been limited to France and Great Britain. Though I competed after a fashion everywhere, I finally made a decision. It must be admitted that Montana and Wyoming were even choices. And other parts of vast Idaho would have done as well. There was a job, however, in Pocatello, at Idaho State University. A reformer, naturally, or I would not have been in a natural-resources profession, I can thus see some things in the Rocky Mountain West that I do not like. Still, there are not (yet) too many people, and people are the world's number-one curse. Further, animosities in this West are rarely personal. One may violently disagree with another, but they can drink beer or hunt ducks together and keep the differences in abeyance. Poet Badger Clark in his "Old Cowman" rather summed it up when he wrote:

> With skyline bounds from east to west
> And room to go and come,
> I loved my fellow man the best
> When he was scattered some.

Thus, different people like different things, and possibly the psychologists know why. Sometimes they may even know what to do about it. Sometimes not. There are people who cannot endure a certain town, and others who can endure nothing else.

Animals are like people—or vice versa! Some twenty years ago, my section of Idaho was at the peak of a blacktail jackrabbit cycle. There will be more on cycles a little later, but we may emphasize here that when such a cycle gets going up, nothing stops it. Predators will increase, while you drive-and-club, shoot, poison, and do this and that. You may reduce the hordes of rabbits and cut down some crop damage, but only Nature really drops the population. She does this suddenly, and nothing can be done about that either. The animals survive to a limited extent, but upwards of 99 percent go out fast.

These jacks were most numerous on or near marginal farmlands. Farms that bordered sagebrush and greasewood cover made the best shooting. If the land was fertile, the jacks did not get so numerous. Farms that had been cleared from lands originally covered largely with greasewood and rabbit brush made a rabbit paradise. If the original growth was big sagebrush and bitter brush, or, better yet, native grassland, the rabbits were scarce. In one place they would eat down alfalfa hay stacks. Some twenty miles away, on good land, there were very few rabbits. One can look over prospective, uncleared, tillable-type land, and tell about what the local rabbit population will be when the next peak hits. I am not sure whether there has been enough research to prove just what careful fertilization and all-round land care will do for protection from rabbits, but there is reason to believe that it would help. Blacktail jacks just do not drift heavily into fertile, well-tilled land, if there is poverty land available. Ghetto-type farmers live in rural ghettoes, just as their parallel city cousins live in city ghettoes.

I have little knowledge and not too much interest in city ghetto problems, but I have seen proof of experience, early in this century, in trying to move New York slum families up into the Hudson highlands where farm labor was scarce. These people could not or would not stand the country. They went back to the slums. Whether or not I *can* stand a big city, I definitely *will* not. I have seen some of them and they are pretty much alike. The residential part of North London is the best of a bad lot, as I see it. It borders Hampstead Heath, and you can walk in an hour to the West End gun shops, and the museums. The Tower of London is further, but reachable for perhaps a shilling.

Like man, other organisms have their choices as well as their adaptabilities. Few if any big wild animals are as adaptable as whitetail deer. Their muley cousins are not so different. When we lived in Michigan, much whitetail research was in operation. There had been extensive efforts to move deer from disaster areas, such as the first winter after a fall fire. The deer would be wandering around, hungry and sad. Trap a truckload of them, haul them twenty miles to a location with excellent feed, and often they would be back in two days, hungrier, sadder-looking, but possibly happier since they were at home sweet home.

Though they have dumb streaks for smart animals, these Michigan deer assumed cute methods for eking out a precarious living. During a marking experiment, one old doe developed a trap habit. She had been trapped and ear-marked as soon as the first traps had been set. The traps were baited with clover hay, rolled oats, or something equally palatable. This doe spent the rest of the winter looking for traps. She would eat the bait, wait patiently to be released, and hie to another trap. A hopeless bum and a terrific nuisance, she was amusing enough to escape assassination.

An equally amusing muley doe resided in Pocatello's Mountain View Cemetery during a very snowy winter a number of years ago. Many deer had been driven down from the hills and were making only scanty livings. This doe browsed some on the planted shrubbery, but bore down heavily on the flowers left after funerals! To the credit of both the florists and the bereaved families, flowers that this vagrant especially liked were often selected! Though she attacked them (but daintily, as is the deer custom) immediately after the mourners departed, we heard of no complaints. There were human regrets when the snow dwindled and this lady bum departed for the mountains. No one can doubt her adaptability!

Though some animals, great and small, may readily enough adapt to a changed environment, others adapt badly, or at best slowly. Moose are in this group. When I was teaching at Syracuse, a colleague, the late Dr. Charles E. Johnson, had made extensive moose studies in Minnesota. He was raised in the Red River of the North area, and was a farmboy and a hunter before he was a scientist. Moose, around settlements, did not thrive. Though some hung around for a time, they did not breed and eventually disappeared. The Shiras moose of Yellowstone (assuming that there *are* three or more moose species) has adapted to human associates to some extent. In the first place, they have not been hunted, and I do not believe that they have ever had to be reduced (like the elk) because they crowded their environment. Some of them see many people, and they do not appear to be worried. The calf crop is all right, and everything seems satisfactory except that they are somewhat crowded by the elk. If whitetails are the most adaptable hoofed game animals, moose are probably the least adaptable American members of the deer family. This is admitting that native caribou have been exterminated in the U.S., of course excepting Alaska, and again excepting a handful in Idaho's Panhandle, that may be spilling over into the corners of Washington and Montana. Though caribou (reindeer) can be domesticated, American species have not been very adaptable to a man-influenced environment.

So adaptability is one of the ecological characteristics that is of top importance in game management. Another, which I have already touched lightly in connection with jackrabbits favoring poor land, is that weeds and pests take over as land deteriorates. I have also sketchily noted a few items about human pests, if that is a suitable term.

Good crops grow on good land. If the land deteriorates, the weeds thrive but the crops do not. This is as true for timber crops as it is for agricultural products. The virgin hardwood forests of the Northeast may be (or have been) the most fertile land in North America. However, like other virgin forests anywhere, they were not good game-producing lands. When they were cut and frequently burned, assuming they were not cleared for farmlands, the land deteriorated because fire burned out the humus. Nature, however, came in with soil-makers. First fireweed, then perhaps raspberries, followed by fire cherries, and other short-lived trees like gray and even paper birches, and the aspens. The way was paved for another climax type of forest, but as this progressed, the game-carrying capacity vastly increased. I re-emphasize that no old-growth forests anywhere ever maintained big stands of game. Squirrels, of course, when there were nut trees. Turkeys, where mast food was suitable. A scattering of everything that could *stand* that habitat, but only a scattering. Game increased after much of the land was cleared, even when it was heavily occupied for farms. Land that had been logged but not farmed was the game bonanza.

Though I am not sure that anyone can prove it, there is reason to believe that the grasslands of Ohio, Indiana, and Illinois may have produced the biggest poundage of game per the square mile of any part of aboriginal North America. The soil and rainfall favored grass and some shrubbery, except along the numerous water courses. These supported a rich fringe forest. There was variation in the environment. There was fertility, and fertile soil increases game capacity just as it produces bumper crops. The climate was less savage than it is farther north, so winter kill was less severe. Naturally, the game did not last as the farms came in. Most of the land was tillable. Of course the game was shot, but the species that were exterminated would probably have disappeared almost as fast if there had been no shooting. If a habitat disappears, the natural inhabitants who do not adapt go with it.

Perhaps I should note here what many readers are well aware of: the Biological Trinity. To survive, all animals must eat, must breed, and must have some home. If one of these items is lacking, the animal goes out. From the amoebae to the fleas and humans, that trinity is law. It is simple indeed and ecologically inescapable.

A further simple but equally definite set of principles involves the peculiar dependence of certain species on other species. (The biologist's term for this situation is symbiosis.) The weed and pest angle is also concerned in this complex. Consider water, for example, such as a good trout stream. The water must be fairly cold. We will assume that the fish are brook trout, which demand a good oxygen content and cannot stand continuous water temperatures much over 70° F. They thrive best if there are trees, ensuring that half of the water is in the shade much of the time.

Food is largely a build-up from minute plankton through infusorians to small insects, crustaceans, and molluscs. Young fish feed on these last three categories, the bigger ones eating just about anything, including each other. I am primarily concerned here with a piece of water inhabited by brook trout and no other fish. Frogs, crayfish, all sorts of insects, and even mice are included in the trout menu. This build-up, I reemphasize, starts with the minute green or blue-green algae. If something seriously interferes with this genesis, goodbye trout. This is the reason conservationists are so opposed to dredge mining. I have debated a couple of times with mining advocates. They insisted that the roiled water caused by a dredge did not kill fish. They were right, if the fish were fingerlings and bigger. But sadly, trout eggs are unlikely to hatch in muddy water. If they do, the mud blocks out light, and the algae disappear. That mud operates against all points in the Biological Trinity. It definitely wipes out the genesis of aquatic food.

There are examples of these sequences always in sight, and I will explain a few more that are most glaring.

Continuing with water examples, if my trout stream got polluted by municipal sewage, industrial wastes, or what-have-you, when the trout disappeared, squawfish, suckers, carp, or a combination would replace them. Weed fish, or pest fish. They appear from nowhere. I live almost within rabbit-shooting distance of the little Portneuf River. It was once a famous rainbow trout stream, and is still a bit better than a sewer, since Pocatello has a primary-treatment sewage-disposal plant. Industrial wastes still pour in, however, and there is still upstream sewage. Politics may demand secondary sewage treatment and laws concerning the industrial effluent may be enforced. Though the principal fish are now suckers, it *can* be brought back to trout production. The organic wastes promote rooted plant growths, including that great duck food the sago pond weed. I do not think it will become too foul for mallards, but a reasonably complete cleanup, if it ever comes, will be a long, rough job. The way to maintain a suitable environment is to not let it deteriorate. This is as axiomatic as preventing a disease instead of curing it.

A shocking example of ecological interdependencies is marshy Florida and its precarious alligator population. We must not only save them from extinction but build them up, or the miraculous Everglades environment will be violently changed and in many respects ruined.

If you have not studied this alligator situation, perhaps I should note that during the dry season (and the Everglades sometimes gets *very* dry) most of the available water is in alligator wallows. Alligators dig down to water. Of course, an unsuspecting little Floridian deer may end up as alligator bait when he sneaks in for a drink. Still, this charmingly ugly reptilian is not actually in his well all the time, and calculated risks permeate all of Nature's laws. It is better to risk being eaten than to die of thirst or migrate into dangerous, unknown territory.

So, no alligators, no game, yet alligator poaching pays so well that these great saurians face extermination. Their original range is now vastly restricted. If alligator leather goes out of style, or its use is prohibited by law, they still have a chance. Law can influence style. I well remember when the American egret and the snowy heron—bearers of aigrette plumes during the nesting season—were on the brink of extinction. Killing the birds had been illegal for many years, but plume values skyrocketed and the poachers accepted the calculated risk. However, when Congress passed a law making *possession* of the plumes illegal, excepting those that were legally registered, the styles changed, and fast.

This was achieved by embarrassment. Some fine lady would be wearing her gorgeous aigrette plumes when a polite young man, probably also formally dressed, would introduce himself. He would flip a lapel,

revealing a badge as gorgeous as those plumes, and state that doubtless
the lady had her plumes properly registered, but it was his unpleasant
duty to check. Could he make a date to examine the certificates? If the
plumes were registered, their owner did not like being thus accosted
and forced to prove it. If they were not registered, a federal court case
followed. Those aigrettes were soon relegated to the attic, and any that
exist are still there.

About gone at the turn of the century, I saw nesting American egrets
in the Mississippi bottoms of Wisconsin in 1937. They had been absent
for some fifty years. I saw nesting snowy herons in Idaho first in 1948,
but they were not new. A style change boosted by law saved them. Just
a style change would have done it, but just the law would not. With
very few exceptions, women are kind creatures. Those who could afford
expensive aigrette plumes are every bit as kind as their less opulent
sisters, but they did not understand all the details. They followed styles
thoughtlessly. It seems a far cry for the couturiers to be influencing
ecology, but the fact remains. The same precise route may save the
alligators—and the leopards. Communication is somewhat better than
when the egrets were threatened, and the stylists may not have to be
clubbed by laws. As I write, we are working for laws making the possession of alligator leather illegal. We may win. But again, we may not.

I am thus trying to emphasize that everything may lean on everything.
There are well-meaning people who would prohibit all hunting, con-
tending that it is cruel and inhuman. Few will claim that killing is less
than cruel, but enthusiastic hunters (I am one of them) believe that
hunting (man's oldest sport if not his oldest profession) is less cruel than
most other forms of death. Further, the game has a sporting chance.
If you are a meat eater (as most of us are, so far as we can *afford* meat),
you are aware that the abattoirs do not give their victims any sporting
chances. Given my druthers, I would sooner be shot in the woods than
be knocked on the head and then have my throat cut. Further, the
hunters have furnished most of the push toward protecting all forms
of wildlife. If they wish to perpetuate it so they can shoot it, the results
are better than extermination because of a destroyed environment.

One could cite examples of ecological interdependence indefinitely.
Few people would bother to kill blackfooted ferrets, but they are on
the endangered list nonetheless. They live on prairie dogs. If the dogs
go, they go too. An effort is being made to save a few "dog" colonies.
Possibly some ferrets are being saved with them. Prairie dogs, like many
of the small- to medium-sized ground squirrels, are destructive. They
demand some control. Rather parallel, sage grouse live during the winter

on sagebrush. To exterminate these grouse, all you need do is plow up the sage, or kill it with a weed exterminator. The birds simply do not adapt.

When an animal is dead, it is dead. If one side of the Biological Trinity triangle is erased, that is that. Animals have been exterminated by shooting, perhaps, but rarely unless so planned, as in the case of the buffalo. Trapping and poisoning finished the wolves. Grizzly bears have been shot out, but much of their environment disappeared along with the shooting. There are many wheels within wheels. We still do not understand them all, but are far enough along to do much more than the public will thus far permit.

Truly enough, ecological problems must be solved according to human values. I have occasionally been accused of not caring much about people. (This is partially true. My studies of people have been incidental and superficial; my animal studies have been extensive indeed.) However, the worst worldwide ecological problem is too many people; there have rarely been too many desirable game animals. Moreover, man can more or less control the animals, but apparently cannot control himself. At least he *has* not, thus far.

Presumably if one has studied humans as I have considered animals, he might understand them. Animals are governed by natural laws. Some are intelligent and adaptable, but they lack human brains and human hands. Humans are so adaptable and so mobile that the vast majority can manage some place in that Biological Trinity. That is, they have thus far. It is not my place to more than casually touch on human problems as such. Still, right now, man has progressed so far in destroying his own environment that thinking people realize desperate efforts will be just as necessary to save himself as they are to save game animals. There will be little excuse for managing game if man exterminates himself. A managed environment includes managing humans.

I will not elaborate heavily on this human management. Repeating that there are too many people, I will simply disagree with the demographers who predict standing-room-only in the foreseeable future. Of course, the Rev. Mr. Malthus was somewhat right, and we may be past the reasonable population peak in North America. The same is probably true for Western Europe, and we are *far* past the peak in much of Asia. For there have always been some controls on all populations. Though man has increased steadily since the Plague despite war, famine, and pestilence, he may—in the long run—be cyclic like lemmings and snowshoe rabbits. If so, his cyclic peak is just around the corner.

Cycles build slowly but go down fast. In any case, something is going to break. I believe man may intentionally control his overpopulation in what are popularly called the enlightened nations, but if progress is too slow among all nations, a shocking debacle will result long before that standing-room-only stage is reached. I will not suggest the form of this debacle, but it is certain.

While still on this somewhat lugubrious ecological chapter, I must repeat that essential research is by no means complete. But I would add that enough is known to make most of the needed improvements if these improvements are permitted. The conservation of all natural resources is scientifically dependent on only two principles. The first is observation; the second, sound interpretation of the observations. There the science ends. What follows is the *art* of doing what observation and interpretation indicated must be done. Religion, politics, mores, economics, and what-have-you all tend to prohibit the application of that art. Theologians allow that man has dominion over every living thing, and insist that he "multiply." Politicians crave voters and taxpayers and realize that deer and ducks never vote. Chambers of commerce are interested in payrolls; so factories are permitted to pollute, ruining the wildlife environment, in the name of progress. And progress, scarcely excepting the flag and sacred motherhood, is the most worshipped American term.

Existing technology can eradicate all forms of pollution. We can eliminate much that is ugly. The management of game and fish can be immeasurably improved. Those of us long trained in ecology must be given something of a free hand until the less learned can progress. Salesmanship is the crucial lack. And if the population upswing continues, game has had it. Eventually that same upswung population has had it too, so that is the ecological *sine qua non*. Of course, I believe the population problem *can* be solved, or I would not be writing. That it will be is a logical guess for the U.S.A. and much of Europe. The outlook for Asia, Africa, and much of Latin America is not so promising. An enlightened island in a sea of ignorance may or may not be able to hold its own. Protecting a planned environment by armed force is an unpleasant prospect, but a possibility before the twentieth century is over.

—14—

Poisons

CHEMICAL POISONS ARE the most recent types of dangers to wildlife. I do not recall any extensive and specific example until about 1954, when cattle suffered serious damage and some game and some farm fish were killed the same way. Interestingly enough, the public knew little and cared less. The press knew something but said nothing.

The situation I learned about occurred just out of Pocatello, Idaho, and involved a big phosphorus plant. In fact, there were and are two plants, with something of a common working agreement. They take ores from the same general types of mines, on the Fort Hall Indian Reservation. One refines phosphorus while the other produces phosphate-type fertilizers.

Fluorine escaped from the stacks. It drifted to a ranch and killed calves in a big way. The son of a neighboring rancher, who was in one of my classes, told me the factories settled out of court for $62,500 damages. I believe that a reporter investigated, but no story ever ran. The paper's front office probably thought it would be bad for business. Somewhat later, a neighboring trout farm sued these companies, and that did get into the press. The court award was something over $90,000 but did not remotely cover the destruction. Rainbow trout were the crop. The fluorine washed into the rearing ponds, and eggs of the infected fish hatched badly. Many of the fry died and many of those that lived had twisted backbones. It was typical fluorine damage.

Much of that fluorine is now being recovered, and public feeling has so changed that I doubt if such a story could now be suppressed. I repeat, I doubt it, but I'd hate to have my life depend on it. The payroll is still king.

On my desk is a report that just came, listing the serious chemical wildlife and fish poisons. I hesitate to list them as this is a relatively long-range text and conditions will change. I do not want too much of what I write to be out of date before it sees print. However, I have already referred to the dangers of DDT and will amplify briefly, since DDT and its near chemical relatives are the worst of the lot—so far, in any case.

The main problem with DDT is that it does not break down, but continues to accumulate in water and perhaps everywhere else. It affects fish especially, and at one time we were so naive that we thought that if DDT dusting was kept away from watercourses, we were safe. Not so, or else it was *not* kept away from the waters. Dead fish were eaten by scavengers, especially eagles. It is stored in the bird's fat. Their egg shells are weakened and break before the young birds can hatch. It is likely that bald eagles and ospreys are doomed, and golden eagles are seriously affected. Possibly there will be survivors in less-poisoned Alaska or Canada, but that is questionable. DDT has been found in Antarctic penguins, and that is a far piece. If DDT use were to be absolutely prohibited as I write, some of the damage from it could still be around for a half-century or longer, according to careful estimates. The stuff is going to go off the market, I am reasonably sure, in a relatively short time. It may be too late to save certain species, but immunities are possible, and I am somewhat optimistic, just as I am optimistic about controlling the eruption of humans—in this country, at any rate.

I mentioned immunity, and I am not well informed as to what immunities may be worked up in connection with these newer chemicals. Of course some insects do become immune to the poisons that are supposed to kill them. Perhaps 99.99 percent of the bugs are killed. The .01 percent survives and breeds and you may have a new and immune race of pests. Then you must find a new insecticide. This problem will never end.

You are aware that immunology is something of a medical specialty, and people may become immune to very serious diseases. Game and fish may develop the same condition. Our African slaves probably had an immunity to malaria. They have pretty well lost it, for an American Negro in malarial zones will get it as easily as his white associate. In France during World War I, I saw something of an American nurse who had helped in Serbia during a serious typhus epidemic. She was medically famous because of apparent immunity to *all* contagious diseases; nonetheless, she came close to losing a hand through infection of a minor injury.

I went through an amoebic-dysentery epidemic myself in France in the summer of 1918. Yankee soldiers got it but apparently the French did not—they had worked up an immunity. I could go on with examples, but I am not suggesting that animals may get immune to DDT, mercury poisoning, lead poisoning, and what-have-you. Any of us may be immune to diseases that might cause neighbors to shuffle off swiftly. I reiterate that I know little about it but can see that it must be reckoned with for its possibilities.

It must be emphasized that insecticides are absolutely necessary in modern agriculture. I have not felt that there was any necessity to elaborately consider insecticide history, but insect damage has been recorded for thousands of years. I was farm-raised. Our most important income came from milk and fruit, but we raised a considerable variety of crops. The Colorado potato beetles would have taken the entire crop if we had not poisoned them with Paris green. San Jose scale would have likewise taken the peaches. Practically everything had its enemy. The fight was continuous. Still, at that time, I did not hear of any accumulative effects from these poisons. There are ways of killing insects without killing everything else. It is just a matter of more research and more attention.

Besides DDT and its relatives, mercury poisoning rates special mention. Though long known, emphasis on mercury damage is recent so far as I can find out. Further, the danger may largely be to humans but transmitted by game and fish. In 1969, some Canadian seasons on gallinaceous birds were closed because the flesh of these creatures contained so much mercury that they were unfit for human consumption. There was no evidence that the birds themselves were unhealthy. As I write, the Idaho Fish and Game Department has reported a somewhat similar situation. Pheasants particularly manage to get mercury-treated grain, and this especially toxic metal seems to be accumulative. A recent report on Great Lakes fish showed such mercury content that they were taken off the market. Again, there was no report of the fishes themselves being affected, but there is always a danger to spawn or young fish, as was pointed out on a preceding page.

I emphasize that the mercury damage reported thus far indicated potential danger to people only. Still, hunters and fishermen are frequently the principal donors of the funds that finance wildlife management. If you poison some of them and their families, with these products of field sports, it would really be killing the goose that laid the golden eggs.

Mercury is of importance in both paper-making and agriculture. Something can be done about it. In fact, something can be done about all the industrial poisons and every other kind. With tertiary treatment, water that goes through municipal sewage-disposal plants may be safe to drink without any risk. I confess to not especially liking that prospect! Boiling and a pinch of tea would add to its palatability, as I view it, or a spoonful of 100-proof bourbon might answer if boiling was not convenient. (I have at least the soul of a teetotaler, but am aware that far more people have been killed from drinking bad water than from drinking good whiskey!)

Much thought has been given to natural controls. Many of our pests are imported. In their home environment there were controls, but the controls were not imported with the pests. In Europe, I never saw hordes of "English" sparrows and starlings comparable to those infesting this country. They were deliberately imported. So were carp. So was the mongoose in Jamaica and Hawaii, the European hare in Australia, and the nutria in Louisiana. The walking catfish may be loose in Idaho as I write, but it is doubtful if he can take our winter climate.

Later, some of these bigger-creature problems will be considered, but basically, the principle is the same as with the insects. Insectivorous birds are the best controls for many insects, and there we have really been off the beam. The insecticides have killed the birds that prey on the insects so we have to use more insecticides, and so on *ad infinitum*. If you can envision a more vicious circle, please describe it.

Insects and spiders eat insects, and there may be the real controls. I was casually associated with natural control methods for spruce budworms as far back as 1920. Entomologists have done wonders in that field more recently, but it was not fast enough. A dangerous insect outbreak (cycle?) is normally followed by some sort of a reaction. That is, if there is anything to react. There was nothing to react against the sparrows and starling and Down Under rabbits. Something must be done while you are dredging up the natural controls, but you must not ruin potential controls with that dredging. The U.S. way has always been to do things in a hurry. Too frequently, a policy turns into a boomerang that is hard to catch.

I must reiterate that the population boom is back of all these dangers to game management and back of all the menace to the general environment. Agriculture has always been a sacred cow. It should be, since, with certain exceptions, it permits us to eat. Still, it is peculiarly regulated economically—or possibly *un*regulated economically. Because of mechanization, fewer people raise bigger crops on bigger farms. Insecticides are spread on a bigger scale. Haste is essential or the bank will have the farm. And on into the night.

For all this apparent pessimism, DDT is on the way out. Still, we cannot predict the conclusion of its violent damage.

The less toxic poisons, organic wastes, and silting should be easier to manage than this violent stuff that could be dangerous for a century. It is solely a matter of routine knowledge and continuous attention. There has been some progress.

As a small boy, I was fond of eating shad from the Hudson River. Pollution wiped them out by about 1910. I was back in Poughkeepsie in 1960 for the fiftieth anniversary of my graduation at the high school there. In a small way, the shad had come back! The Hudson is still polluted, but it is gaining.

The earliest pollution that I studied was from milk-processing plants. The still-nitrogenous whey went into the waters untreated, and oxidation, among other contaminants, dangerously reduced the oxygen content so that game fish were destroyed.

There was a battle that lasted a generation over this milk-processing pollution. Big names were involved. They knew how to clean up, but it cost something, and no one would do anything until the law demanded it. I believe this milk situation is pretty much under control as I write, but nothing was done until the creameries were threatened with legal padlocks.

Each region has its own pollution problems. These regional types of pollution—aerial, aquatic, and terrestrial—often intermingle. Each is a separate but related problem and must be attacked at its source. Among the most venemous organic pollution situations, and Western regional, is duck botulism. It is confined to the West, since the water is somewhat alkaline, and cannot proliferate without organic pollution. Botulistic ducks can be picked up and put in a "hospital" situation where the water is clean, and they will recover unless almost totally paralyzed. Maintaining fresh water is the simplest preventive, and that varies from difficult to impossible.

Fortunately, there is little botulism in the Canadian nesting grounds, though it gets worse if the water is low. There is continuous research going on, and the U.S. Sport Fisheries and Wildlife Service in Washington provides the latest information. During five years on the Upper Mississippi Refuge, I never saw a botulistic duck, not even on the western side. As indicated, water showing a distinct alkaline reaction is essential for the botulism "bugs" to reproduce, and waterfowl biologists are thus happier in the East.

The East, however, with bigger human population and more intensive hunting, has a waterfowl problem not serious in much of the West, thus far. I refer to lead poisoning. Dumb ducks, including smart mallards, cheerfully swallow shot thinking it is gizzard gravel. A duck has been killed experimentally with a single No. 6 pellet, pulverized and fed so that the duck would get the full lead poison dose swiftly. While I was biologist on the Upper Mississippi Refuge, 1935 to 1940, I estimated that on about 300 miles of Mississippi bottoms, some 65 tons of shot fell on the shooting grounds annually, enough to poison all the ducks in the world if they got it all, as fortunately they do not. Vegetative rubbish or silt covers the shot rather swiftly. I believe that few ducks are poisoned if they miss the shot fired in a specific hunting season. The next spring covers it fairly well.

If one is accustomed to spotting lead-poisoned ducks, diagnosis is fairly easy. In addition to just "the way they act," there are stains from a green diarrhea that is characteristic. In twenty-five years of Idaho duck hunting, largely on the Fort Hall Reservation, I have seen only one lead-poisoned duck. This was a goldeneye on Spring Creek, in the fall of 1950, give or take a year. It was sufficiently paralyzed so we caught it without shooting. Dissection showed one badly worn shot (probably a No. 2) in its gizzard. Whether or not that had done all the damage, we had no way of telling. I was with Dr. Rufus A. Lyman, M.D., Ph.D. (Zoology), who is also a hunter, and he helped with my examination. We had no way of knowing whether or not the duck would have recovered if we had let it live. It was not especially emaciated, but it was so helpless that even the weakest predators or scavengers could have taken it.

When on the Upper Mississippi Refuge, as the shooting seasons closed and the marshes froze, we gathered hundreds of crippled or lead-poisoned ducks and gave them another chance. We had some big chicken-wire enclosures with lean-to sheds. We fed these birds carefully and about half of them recovered. However, since the ducks were picked up on shore with the help of our dogs, we were rarely absolutely sure whether a duck was crippled or poisoned. We *were* certain if a wing was broken or that green diarrhea was conspicuous. Lacking this damage certainty, I will not risk more than an estimate, but it looked as if about half the poisoned birds, as well as half the cripples, recovered. Recovery of the poisoned ducks depended on how many shot were picked up. The birds we retrieved would all have died, of course, whether or not they were taken by predators, since the water was frozen.

In that Mississippi country, crippling and lead poisoning probably took as many ducks as the hunters actually bagged, and possibly more. There is evidence here in this springy Idaho area that sometimes a wing-tipped bird may live indefinitely. If the water froze, he would not last very long. Predators usually get them if humane hunters do not bother to finish them. A couple of magpies can swiftly tear up a duck if he is on the shore edge, and weak.

Lead poisoning has had considerable study for at least a half century. Though not as critical as wintering and breeding grounds, it is still of vast importance. Soft iron shot currently exists that kills ducks satisfactorily at short ranges, but there is evidence that crippling increases rapidly beyond 40 yards, not to mention the potential damage to the choke in thinner and softer shotgun barrels. Maryland has already made the use of this shot mandatory as I write, and it seems likely that other states and possibly even the federal government will soon adopt similar requirements. However, if these steps lead to a simple trade-off between losses due to lead poisoning and losses due to increased crippling, of what benefit is that to the ducks? On balance, the most encouraging factor in the whole picture is the very much aroused concern this controversy has engendered. Given the technological resourcefulness of the ammunition manufacturers, it is a better-than-even bet that they will soon solve this problem, *somehow*. It is as important to them as it is to the game managers and hunters.

—15—

Conflicts and Confrontations

For well into the centuries, game management has been in conflict with other land uses. You may have heard diplomatic efforts at sportsmen's clubs, trying to prove that there was land-room for agriculture, industry, and what-have-you, without seriously handicapping the management of game. I admire diplomacy, but have little respect for an out-and-out liar, no matter how conscientious he may be about making concessions. Compromises are often unavoidable—this is as true economically as it is essential in science. Political expediency must often take precedence over logical scientific action, for in general, the promoters of game fight for what they get. However, the iron hand should wear a velvet glove; it is axiomatic that you catch more flies with honey than with vinegar. The opposition is usually solidly entrenched within the slogan of Progress. Progress will cheerfully donate to game whatever it does not want or cannot use, but leavings are not enough; we must demand our due. It will be considerable if Progress also applies to the modern management of wildlife.

I have had considerable contact with agriculture. In previous pages

I have referred to being raised on a farm in Dutchess County, New York. I was past twenty-one and had struggled through two years of forestry school before getting away from it for good. (I did not mind the work, but milking 365 days a year was most confining, and in those days of handpower and horsepower, the financial rewards for the farmer were slim.) However, I have always stayed close to the soil, while employed as a federal biologist and a college teacher, and I continue to have many friends among neighboring farmers and ranchers.

Mechanization, electricity, good roads, and so on have completely changed the agricultural picture. Utterly essential farming is alleged to not pay very well even now, though the farmers I know seem prosperous. They work very hard and there are many gambles. Still, there are agricultural surpluses, the U.S. Department of Agriculture is paying many millions for *not* growing crops, and farmers generally are getting concessions undreamed of at the turn of the century.

A number of situations seem unethical to one who has long since left the farm and entered a profession that is directly competitive. Millions are spent paying farmers for *not* growing crops, yet more millions are spent to put land under irrigation so that ultimately more money can be spent for not raising crops on it. My studies of land economics have been reasonably extensive, but nothing explains *that*. Ask any agricultural specialist—preferably a federal employee—to explain it, and he will swiftly get beyond his depth. The simple fact is that the U.S. Department of Agriculture is an overgrown bureaucracy that has *partially* outgrown its usefulness. The employees are honest, dedicated, and skilled, and usually do the nothings they are supposed to do with speed and ability. But having worked for the U.S. Forest Service both full-time and on summer jobs, I learned something about the other bureaus. Much of the work is important, but some results in self-perpetuating contradictions fostering most unsound land economics.

Another shocking contradiction that may (or may not) have been abated involves the wetlands-purchase problems of the Sport Fisheries and Wildlife Bureau (Interior). They got some money, but the purchases could not be final without the consent of the governor of the state involved. Further, agriculture was subsidizing the *drainage* of these same lands that Interior was trying to buy and protect! All of which proves that there are ways of getting rid of ducks that are much more efficient than shooting them with big charges of No. 4s. Of course the governors of these intensely agricultural states were not approving the purchase of these wetlands very liberally. They naturally wanted to stay in office.

The only cure for these shocking situations is a complete overhaul of the too-numerous land-use bureaucracies. This is not possible unless public sentiment changes. It may. Ecology is now a household term, though few even know what it means. As I have said before, agriculture, like progress, has been scarcely less revered than the flag and sacred motherhood. I trust that the flag has not lost any luster, but the pregnant damsel is now Public Enemy Number One. Collectively, of course. Personally, our affection for her does not waver, even as we wish that she had been a bit more cautious!

A change in viewpoint may also be essential for the conscientious do-gooders. Americans are a kindhearted race. From the time I was a small child, someone was always collecting for the starving Armenians, alleviating a famine in India or China, or something. We were told that two bits might buy enough rice to save a child's life. If I saved any, their descendants are now aggravating the existing Asia crisis for all I know. Yet today there are touching advertisements concerning donations for saving starving Asiatic children. Why? To continue the crisis? True, the children did not ask to be born—which of us ever did? And it is cruel if they should starve. Still, the more of them that are saved now, the more that are likely to starve later. Or be wiped out by atomic bombs if the population explosion goes far enough. Shiploads of wheat to Asia may be humane. And they may immeasurably add to starvation and other deaths within a period that can be closely calculated.

Though all this is easy for me to predict with little fear of contradiction, I am glad that the decisions are beyond my reach. Definitely I oppose agricultural surpluses, Department of Agriculture shenanigans, and the farm worship that still exists. I am as aware as anyone that agriculture feeds us. I cannot condone its overemphasis and the artificial efforts to stimulate it.

Commercial efforts outside of agriculture and its products are as serious a danger to game and even more complicated. Mining may be the most spectacular, admitting that water corruption and fish damage are especially conspicuous among the mine problems.

Sadly, mining and oil production are almost as essential as agriculture. These are nonrenewable resources, and their study is on the periphery of my professional field. I would first emphasize that these nonrenewable riches are just that. When they are gone they are gone. We enjoy (?) a gasoline economy as I write. At least 99 percent of this situation has developed during my long life. I saw my first motor car in the summer of 1897 shortly before starting school at the age of six. The importance of automobile transportation at that time was zero. But the growth was swift. Without gasoline and internal combustion engines, we would be paralyzed. Steam transportation seems to be just around the corner, and more electrical and atomic energy transport are probabilities.

The handling of all these nonrenewable resources causes pollution. Much or all of it is preventable, but industry is another sacred cow. Cleaning up costs, and few industrialists *will* clean up until so forced by law. There are exceptions, of course. I chance to know that certain big oil operators have taken strict precautions to prevent oil escape during water transportation. Others may be doing as well, but some are doing badly indeed. Oil is tragic for water birds and more or less damages everything. It is my belief that all petroleum damage can be eradicated and that the oil companies know how to do it.

The whole conflict with industry may still ultimately be won, but intense dedication must be maintained. Mining most minerals is more destructive than most of the "mining" of oil. Miners are necessarily a ruthless group, irrespective of their normally fine personal characteristics. We must have their products, but I prefer that they shall come from Africa or Siberia. My adopted Idaho is a mining state, and there is a bitter battle about mining molybdenum in the beautiful White Clouds Mountains as I write. There is no shortage of molybdenum, but the producers believe it would sell profitably. The proposed strip mining would be devastating indeed. It is touch-and-go, but, as I write, the conservationists have a slight lead. The industrialists and the chamber-of-commerce-minded politicians object to "locking up" resources in wilderness areas. I would lock them up cheerfully. You can always un-lock them, and in the meantime the unrenewable resources stay there. They are stored cheaply indeed in the ground. Even timber may be stored better on the stump, very frequently, than in the lumberyard. You cannot stockpile game. And the dangers inherent in progress and the logical use of resources is that the resources disappear. If locked up, at least they are still there! Good game management demands that mining be kept to an irreducible minimum. Dredge mining, during the foreseeable future, may well be absolutely eliminated.

Highway construction is another form of progress violently conflict-ing with game management and all other renewable-resources conser-vation. Our country is afflicted with a road mania. The reasons for it are simple and understandable. Too many people exist and these too many are living in a culture dominated by motor transportation that depends on roads, streets, and parking space. Mobility is also stylish. Many families move frequently. Many business and professional people are routinely transferred. Vacations usually demand travel. Just racking up mileage is one form of vacation pleasure that has been the vogue

for many years. I have known vacationers to "do" Yellowstone Park in
a day, tear to Glacier Park and "do" it in another. Hopefully they
remembered Old Faithful and the Going-to-the-Sun Highway, but the
facts are that it would take a busy fortnight to cover *either* park reasonably well, and a month on each would be worthwhile. Such activity,
however, would mean largely abandoning the car that owns them, which
would be intolerable.

Not only do the vast highways destroy equally vast acreages, but the
by-products are even more destructive. Roads through steep grades result in terrific erosion. They are easiest built along streams. Altering
streams, as they have been altered, reduces their fish-carrying capacity
by 87½ percent, according to some Idaho figures I recently saw. The
water birds and water vertebrates other than fish may be even more
seriously damaged. Nature reduces the erosion in time, but much of the
injury is permanent because the road is there and will stay there. Watercourses are used for roads because the easiest grades result in the
cheapest construction. The essential roads often *could* have been built
away from the streams. Discussing it now is rather academic, because
the stream-following roads are pretty much built.

Some relatively small-time roads are getting attention. The U.S.
Forest Service is a magnificent organization, possibly the biggest and
best that is devoted to the conservation of natural resources. They are
inclined, however, to be road-happy. Existing laws scarcely give them
the authority to deny roads to destructive miners or only slightly less
destructive loggers. Under our existing educational system (or its lack),
simple accessibility often ruins important areas. Naturally, this ruin results from our gasoline economy. If accessibility demands pushing one's
feet, leaning on a paddle, or forking a horse, a vastly different tourist
is the result.

For four summers I was ranger on Yellowstone's rather remote Shoshone Lake. A car could not get closer than four miles. Motorboats could
get to within another four miles, by a different route. A canoe had to
be dragged about a mile and a half up the Outlet. Motors were prohibited on both the Outlet and the T-shaped lake that was four miles by
six and almost 8,000 feet above sea level. And the lake was inclined
to be rough and wild. Perhaps 2,000 people got in there every season,
for periods of from an hour to upwards of a week, but they were a far
cry from the "madding crowd's ignoble strife" as seen around Old
Faithful. Actually, my quotation lacks some descriptive accuracy. The
Yellowstone mobs are most orderly and peaceful. Middle-class America
at its *average* best. But 99.99 percent held to within 200 yards of its

cars, and that may be twice too far! They were frequently overweight, normally tense, and usually doing exactly what everyone else was doing. In that specific environment, they were as original as earthworms. Of course, the few that made it to Shoshone Lake were different. More than one party told us that it was the only part of Yellowstone that was worth seeing. It recreated their faith in the great park. But other people, naturally, would like a road into Shoshone Lake. So people could "use" it!

The road-craving public, that pushes the Forest Service into this road-happy trance I have mentioned, could be educated. But public attitudes are to appease rather than to train. The "multiple use" slogan is congressionally passed law applying to this great Forest Service. Commercially minded folks have not been taught to understand wilderness use. An official Wilderness or Wild River prohibits motorroads, motorboats, and all permanent installations. What use is it if the great majority *cannot* use it? Really, its greatest value is because the great majority *will not* use it. Possibly another quotation from what may be the greatest medium-length poem written in English could explain the basic philosophy back of wild rivers and wilderness areas:

> Full many a gem of purest ray serene
> The dark unfathom'd caves of ocean bear:
> Full many a flower is born to blush unseen,
> And waste its sweetness on the desert air.

It may be overly presumptive for a forester with a game-management specialty to attempt the interpretation of any verse written by such a genius as Thomas Gray. It is my belief that the fact the wilderness is there is reason enough for its existence. The flower cannot waste its sweetness. Sweetness, like beauty, may be greatest when there is something to appreciate it. I have smelled sweetness and seen beauty, but there is much of both that I have missed. Because something desirable is beyond my reach is a poor reason for its eventual destruction. Making everything easily available to everyone is very likely to end with a condition unsuitable for anyone.

Before dismissing roads and their progress-promoted path to oblivion, I must explain that people can be trained to ignore the ugly chaos that they, and many other manifestations of progress, will produce. Human senses are easily numbed. Our sense of smell is almost gone, and what little is left can be educated swiftly. This is fortunate if you live in a paper-mill town, have occasion to police a dairy barn, or must clean skulls and skeletons. Having survived all of these examples, I am well enough qualified to prove that one can learn to endure odors less enticing than new-mowed hay. Further, the eyes can be taught to discriminate but still learn to ignore. And if the eyes still see, the mind can learn to not interpret observations rather than the all-important reverse.

One of the courses I was assigned to teach at Idaho State was dubbed "The Conservation of Plants, Soils, and Waters." It was a tall order, and one semester involving three hours' credit was confined to water study. The students came from more or less all over, but many were Idahoans and some came from Pocatello, which did not then have any sewage-disposal plant. As I recall it, none of the Pocatellans had thought what happened to sewage when a toilet was flushed or dishwater sluiced down the kitchen sink. On the first field assignment, I took them to the main sewer outlet. The stuff went, totally raw, into the potentially beautiful little Portneuf River. It made the students think. There is primary treatment now. I believe it will be improved to secondary and even tertiary treatment in the foreseeable future.

You may multiply examples of little observation and less interpretation to the nth degree. It may be comforting to not see and interpret, but it is very very dangerous. Few people notice highway advertising signs, which, to everyone except the promoters and the advertisers themselves, are just about the ugliest things in Christendom. I have often been asked to explain my hatred of these signs. They would seem to have no connection with natural-resources conservation in general and game management in particular. Sadly, this failure to see the ugliness of highway signs is a manifestation that people cannot see ugly erosion, the ugliness of dying rivers, or the tragedy of an overgrazed range. If you carry the analysis far enough, advertising has taught the public to ignore noise (including vile music), accept atrocious art, and so on *ad nauseam*. Those highway signs are especially mentioned as a manifestation because we are discussing the direct highway menace. If a substantial majority would hate those signs and eventually get rid of them, further hatred of the ugly would result in an intellectual climate that would reduce the difficulties in the way of sound game management. This is simple, if you give it thought and remember the wheels-within-wheels angles of ecology.

Even timber and paper-pulp production has certain conflicts with game management. Since they are part of the natural-resources picture, their coordination with other facets of it should not be too difficult.

Though tourists do not like the smell of a paper-mill town, I do not know that the fumes are especially injurious and one gets used to them, like a cow stable or a tannery. The liquid effluent from a pulp or paper mill, however, is venomous indeed, but subject to treatment. This has sometimes been neglected. When I was an employee of the Chequamegon National Forest, with headquarters at Park Falls, Wisconsin, I lived within a few blocks of the Flambeau Paper Company. You could catch bass or muskellunge right under the main drain from the mill. I first checked it in 1933, and the situation was not new. I am under the impression that none of the Wisconsin paper mills are any pollution menace, but I know of others that are apparently poisonous. This situation will soon change. The laws are ample, but have not been enforced. They will be.

The logging and milling of timber is not vastly different from the paper business. The actual mills are criticized for their smoky refuse burners, but I deplore them more for their waste than for their fumes. You are doubtless aware that scrap wood is ground up into "hog feed" before going to the burner. Heat is energy and power. Much hog feed can go into useful products. The burner smoke is a minor pollutant. I have been very unhappy if not actually sick from smoke when fighting forest fires, but burner smoke never bothered me, nor have I heard that moderate amounts of wood smoke would hurt the average person.

Mill sawdust or any sort of wood refuse that goes into streams is another matter. It is better to burn it, if no economic use is practicable for it.

Though the U.S. Forest Service is inclined to put roads where roads should not be, as previously mentioned, the timber sales as handled by them are managed rather well as I recently observed them. Watershed protection is most important where the biggest forests are located, and so is grazing. Where there still is road damage and general erosion damage on National Forest lands, I expect to see it reduced to reasonable harmlessness within the existing decade as I write.

I am less happy about National Forest grazing. Both the Forest Service and the Bureau of Land Management know overgrazing when they see it, better perhaps than any of their critics. Ranchers contiguous to federal land have no more *rights* on them than citizens 3,000 miles away, but they manage to exercise their privileges too heavily at times. Overgrazing on private lands is even more of a problem. Why grazers should destroy their own property seems hard to understand. It comes from miscalculation of precipitation, or more exactly, of hoping for the maximum when the average or less may fall. As overloading increases, production lessens. On steep grades, severe erosion may be the next catastrophe. I can point out places where good potential grazing has been reduced to nothing. Nature repairs, but in the meantime there is no stock production or game production either. Good stock land is always good game land, and the best game land is often good agricultural land. The conflict is thus hard to resolve. Game has usually lost.

The greatest potential advancement in logging and milling is developing slowly because of professional views in the forest schools. Earlier, I noted that the State College of Forestry at Syracuse offered a minuscule game-management course by 1914. I am rather sure it was the first such course. The University of Michigan followed, but it was some years before graduate work in actual game management was developed anywhere. This slowness in general natural-resources training was noted by farsighted observers. One humorous comment referred to not being able to see the forest for the trees. Further, while I was still an undergraduate, one of the great German foresters—probably B. E. Fernow— remarked that "forestry in the Empire State is doing very well except in the woods." So far as I know, the fine Forest Products Laboratory at Madison is still called exactly that. Further, I would state that it has never been concerned with forest products, only tree products.

Many forest schools now have professional wildlife-management courses. They were just slow; it was not totally ignored, but just swept under the rug. Still, the loggers have slowly learned from the forest schools, and, the Forest Service, too, gradually came under forest-school domination. The Yale Forest School is the oldest in continuous operation, and may have had the strongest Forest Service influence for many years. Yale gave perhaps two lectures on game management as late as 1920, or later. Perhaps it was the result of assuming that hunters, on the average, were something of a bad lot. It has been said that all hunters are not bums, but lots of bums hunt. Unfortunately, this was true, and still is, though it is further admitted that the percentage of bums has been reduced if not the numbers. Hunting popularity has so increased that even a small percentage of bums results in them being numerous enough.

In terms of forest game, correct and cooperative logging management comes incidentally close to good game management. Virgin forest is unproductive of game in general. In fact, it is unproductive of everything except very important tourism and concomitant recreation. Logging is essential, but it must be coordinated with all other natural-resources management, and in many places the greatest of these is game. If, at times, the tail wags the dog, this fact should be analyzed and acted upon as well as observed.

—16—

Game-Management Errors

SOMETIMES GAME-MANAGEMENT STYLES develop that are open to question, and practical hunters may have the temerity to criticize "scientific" methods. Occasionally they are right enough to be embarrassing, which is my excuse for this important chapter. In discussing specific management problems for individual species a little later, further occasional references to what I consider questionable practice may be made.

It is first necessary to emphasize, with respect to game-management practice, that only research dealing with a specific problem is usually worth undertaking. I am the last to decry pure research, but it belongs in a liberal-arts area. Scientific knowledge starts as an abstraction in a scholar's mind. A hypothesis develops into a theory, and finally a law, or something that approaches a law, may result. Game management needs much research, but I have noted that we already know enough to do much more than we are doing, if it were not for the interference of politics, religion, general education, mores, and what-have-you. Sadly, research time is still being spent in proving certain things that the gamekeepers of Henry VIII knew well. Possibly the guides for Philip of

Macedon or even Rameses II had this knowledge. If modern research "proves" it, so what? It was known anyway, and was more or less axiomatic. Presumably no one still bothers to "prove" Euclid's geometric axioms. They seem obvious to me, but no more obvious than some problems that have had careful but useless investigation.

One example stares me in the face as I write.

An excellently trained zoologist has spent several summers investigating pronghorn antelope. He is not a professional game specialist, thus I should not, perhaps, be critical of his methods. Still, he has been working on a professional game problem. His final report is not out, but after several summers' work, I heard him give a progress report. After forty minutes, and some very beautiful colored slides, he came to one apparently profound conclusion: pronghorns did better during a wetter-than-average season! Since they live in what the old geography books call the Great American Desert, what could he expect? Of course a pure researcher should not expect anything, but there may be limits as to how far one should blank his mind. It is like the supposedly intelligent prospective juror who has not read or thought about a crime that has been headlined for weeks. The "one-gallus" hunter certainly cannot comprehend that reasoning, and far too few hunters have much basic scientific learning. They are getting it, I hope, but in the meantime, there is research they can understand that is far more worth doing.

Any sort of research knowledge *may* be useful, and I will not decry it. Federal and state game-management departments, however, and the graduate schools, might well be more practical until "practice" has gone somewhat further. Basic education need never be practical, but vocational education and specialized graduate studies should have some visibly useful angles.

Banding, marking, loading with electronic tracing equipment, and similar techniques demanding the capture of game have been popular game-management methods for many years. Of course the electronic devices are rather recent.

If the creatures marked are caught when rather young, there is reason to believe that they suffer no harm whether or not useful scientific results are finally obtained. Much has thus been learned about bird and fish migrations, and I will not question that *some* important values have resulted. But when enthusiastic banders try to prove how the duck and goose bands I turn in will produce more birds, they may get confused. I have done my share of this tagging, getting instructions from administrative superiors. They may or may not have known the values of what they directed. Sometimes I was suspicious as to their knowledge.

The worst marking results I ever saw was on the Desert Game Range in Nevada. We were to trap and mark bighorns. The idea was to see where they went, admitting that it might not do any special good. We could not stop them from going, nor did we care. Anyway, we trapped them, and painted their horns a brilliant orange with a type of enamel supposed to last for years. The only trouble with the experiment was that neither I nor anyone else I heard of ever saw one of those sheep after their horns were colored. They evaporated. The marking was not my plan, but the seeming result was that it made the sheep disappear, orange horns and all. We quit marking them. With that I implicitly agreed.

This dire result does not suggest that marking game is a failure. Some cougar marking in a specific research area in Idaho did not scare the animals away. Some were caught several times. I have noted that some deer apparently like to be trapped and certainly do not object to being marked. Those high-desert bighorns are peculiar creatures, however, and our marking proved only that we were making a mistake in marking at all.

When on that same Desert Game Range, a couple of perhaps too-pure research problems came to my mind, and I would have liked to have seen them developed. They involved water, and some proof *might* have helped management.

The Federal Fish and Wildlife Service managed this range, and it did not know much about these dry-country animals. Bighorns were the most important species, and they were supposed to be a *sub*species, scientifically called *Ovis canadensis nelsoni*. I am not a taxonomist, so my criticism of nomenclature may not be worth much. On the basis of what I have seen, however, many definitions of "species" are rather specious, and when *sub*species are described, I doubt their existence. The desert bighorn is a useful creature to complete "grand slam" collections of American wild sheep, but otherwise they are wraiths of the imagination. One authoritative text has said that they were "smaller and lighter" than typical *Ovis canadensis canadensis*. I watched them for six years and if some had been any darker they would have been black. Furthermore, some were bigger than any of the "typical" sheep I have seen in Idaho. There were differences between the high-country and low-country sheep, their breeding season centered on September instead of December, and they were very moderate drinkers! That about covered it. Comparatively, perhaps, it could be noted that a tall blond Swede is the same *species* as a little black Hottentot, and the taxonomists do not divide *Homo sapiens* into subspecies. Which leads to the conclusion that there may be too many taxonomists working too faithfully. However, I am not a taxonomist, and I am presenting a belief rather than an argument.

As to the research, I wanted comparative urine studies between this desert sheep and the "typical" northern animals. Empirical observation suggested that the desert sheep's urine was thicker and presumably "richer" in urea than that of any other hoofed animal I had worked with. I wanted to have a couple of animals collected each month during the driest part of the year, doing the same with some Northern "subspecies." I am reasonably certain that my guess could be and should be proved by research through the simple process of urinalysis. I could not persuade my Portland, Oregon, and Washington, D.C., superiors to direct this research. The Washington office's decision was that we could not "spare" the sheep for this urinalysis. This though we had ancient rams dying from old age.

Closely parallel would be research concerning the apparent ability of some mammals to manufacture water from the basic elements.

During my early biology studies, we were given examples of animals that maintained body moisture with no water available and while eating food with far less moisture content than the animal itself possessed. The finest example was the little silverfish "moth" that all of us have seen scurrying around bookcases and chest corners. (In fact, he is something of an enemy to book bindings.) This is a juicy creature, though his diet could scarcely be more desiccated. He has to manufacture water from the oxygen and hydrogen that he eats or breathes or something. No more physiologist than I am taxonomist (perhaps less!), I have not understood the processes by which this water is manufactured.

Getting up to mammals, however, I have some knowledge of their anatomy. Many species of rodents and rabbits in a desert environment maintain their considerable body moisture for months with no water to drink, with little if any dew, and with a diet of vegetation that is far drier than they are. This has been proved in the laboratory. Half-grown pocket gophers have doubled their weight over winter in a dry laboratory with no water and dry rolled oats for food. I had known this through desert observation before I had known of the gopher research. No one that I have questioned had heard of research directed toward knowledge as to *how* they manufactured the water, but there is nothing in anatomy to indicate how they do it.

Again, I am not sure how my research project might have assisted game management, but it might have. I first worked on a desert in 1942, and my curiosity was aroused. I had been told nothing about it (though some students of deserts knew it well) and was assisted by only one report. The Andrews expedition to the Desert of Gobi proved that the Mongolian wild ass drank no water and excreted no liquid urine, only a paste. Whether or not he managed enough green feed to maintain his body moisture was not explained in the report I read.

Another stylish game-management policy that I sometimes question is counting. I am especially critical if this counting is termed a "census." A census is an actual enumeration that is exact or approximately exact. You can rarely count game that closely.

Estimates of numbers are essential enough if you know what to do about them, but sometimes a "census" is called for when there is no apparent use for it in view. And the objectives may be trivial even if an accurate count were possible.

In 1934, when I was biologist for the Chequamegon National Forest in Wisconsin, we were asked to estimate the numbers of deer. An open season, limited to a single buck for each licensee, was coming up. I had plenty of untrained labor, as the CCC program was in full swing. Further, I knew that there were plenty of deer. There was shooting only every other year, and I had had a winter to see tracks and observe deer yards.

I decided upon a counting method that was approved by the regional office. We selected what I hoped were typical sample areas in each Ranger District. These sample few acres were estimated for size rather carefully. We would surround an area quietly, with the boys some 50 yards apart, wave brush and yell at a given signal, and drift toward an open-end funnel where the counters were located. I was usually there myself, with two assistants. We had tally registers, and one would check bucks, one does, and one fawns. There is little doubt that we counted rather accurately the deer on the sample areas that were selected. Occasionally an animal would break back through the beaters, but this was always observed. Interestingly enough, old deer did not like to be driven.

After we had sampled as many areas as we conveniently could, we assumed that the whole forest would have the same deer density as our samples, and the rest was simple arithmetic.

We could scarcely have been less accurate. Come the open season, we had checking stations on all the roads that left the forest. You *can* count dead deer accurately enough. The bucks taken were about as numerous as our total estimate for both sexes, and we still had plenty of bucks left. Antlerless deer constituted upward of 75 percent of our count. We soon knew that we had not counted more than 25 percent of the deer that were on the forest during the open season. Perhaps we were off worse than that.

There was little chance that deer drifted onto the forest from the time of our count to the shooting season. No one knew what was wrong except that everything was wrong. Further, the count was pretty much useless even if it had been accurate. Later, I will discuss buck laws that are now rather well outdated, but at one time were among the popular errors under discussion.

Counting is now less of a sacred cow than it was at one time, but too much scientific labor is still used for it. About 1942, *The Journal of Wildlife Management* published an article of mine, "The Animal Census." It was critical, and my federal superiors would not have permitted its publication had not Editor W. L. McAtee insisted on it. However, I believe that its main points are still valid.

The basic faults with counts are at least twofold. First, counting does not increase the countees by a single head. Second, there is small occasion to count unless you know what favorable results will accrue from the count. However, there are also virtues in connection with counting, or "close estimating," as I would prefer to call it.

As to numbers, all game species must fall into one of three categories:

1. You have too few, and management suggests increasing them by the most logical methods.
2. You have plenty, and a judicious harvest is indicated.
3. You have a balanced population, just about right for the existing environment. A very limited harvest is permissible, to see what the results may be.

Numbers mean little. I have worked with whitetail deer where the winter "yarded" estimate suggested as many as thirty-five head to the square mile. The food supply, though used heavily, was still sufficient to get them through. Contrarily, I have been on mule-deer range where there were not more than four animals to the section, and yet there was evidence of deterioration from over-browsing. The game manager must be able to read the condition of the habitat. Relatively brief observation will show him whether he has too big or too small a population. The easy animals to count are the dead ones.

Incidentally, range estimates as to populations and condition are most valuable when made year after year by the same observer. He carries the picture in his mind and he knows whether the range is deteriorating, holding its own, or improving. Skilled observation will stand up against the gibes of poorly enlightened critics, and I have assumed the responsibility of defending myself under these circumstances and managed very well. When I got into a tight spot was when superiors gave orders that I had to obey or resign. When bureaucrats are ill-advised or ill-informed, the situation gets sticky. Ideally, of course, everyone involved should know what he is doing, but mistakes are inevitable. Eminent physicians, learned judges, and brilliant theologians often disagree about professional matters in their own fields. Certainly game managers are cut from no better cloth. Still, the worst game-management blunders I have seen, those that engendered the worst criticism, concerned situations that should have been obvious to anyone with minimum professional training, routine experience, and horse sense.

Sometimes a good salesman acquires prestige even though lacking in all these essential advantages just mentioned. As an example, I was transferred to the Desert Game Range in Nevada in June of 1942. Somewhat earlier an employee presented a paper to a learned society concerning the management of the desert bighorns that were the principal crop there. Though everything in the report was pretty much wrong, it was cited for years in game-management schools. Eventually, however, it was discredited because of one strategic blunder. The writer claimed to have *seen* seventeen bighorn-lamb eagle kills. The Audubon Society became vitally interested. The man had probably not seen seventeen eagles, to say nothing of even one taking a lamb. I saw perhaps three eagles a year, and no remote evidence that they were a factor in bighorn management. This is not saying that eagles have *never* killed lambs, but it *is* insisting that if eagles were the worst bighorn enemies, these sheep would be as numerous as chipmunks. The observer I criticize did his field work behind a desk; he was a salesman, and his superiors were incompetent, careless, or both.

This somewhat dismal chapter can scarcely be complete without noting some wasteful and nonsensical shenanigans that could have been lessened by better knowledge and experience. I have seen many such antics, and relate one series because it could happen again.

When the Upper Mississippi Refuge was developed, the Nine-Foot Channel Dams flooded thousands of acres of bottomlands that had largely been covered with hardwood timber. Of course the trees had all been removed. It was logical to get waterfowl food established on all this flooded land. I was given careful planting instructions, the most important planting areas were spotted on the map, and I was furnished with the essential seed. We planted it from a canoe, the seeds properly embedded in balls of clay. Though I was far from a beginner, it was my first experience with fairly big-scale *aquatic* planting. I was very careful and naturally hoped for success.

Interestingly enough, the seed we planted grew luxuriantly—or perhaps it did. The stuff we planted certainly appeared, but it likewise appeared on all somewhat similar habitat that we did *not* plant! Nature lays down exacting laws but grants many reprieves to innocents. She brought down seed all the way from where the Mississippi rises in Itasca Lake, to those great fertile flats. The habitat was suitable, so it grew. We wasted a lot of work. Someone should have figured it out. I had not, nor would it have mattered if I had. Orders are orders. My experience is now such that I could diagnose a similar situation, if there were such a situation. By now I hope that same front office has similarly gained, but I would risk no big wagers.

An indefinite number of real or apparent blunders is in mind, and I do not know that any more examples are desirable with a single exception that is very conspicuous. It concerns the U.S. Army Corps of Engineers.

The Engineers are admittedly dam-happy, and unquestionably have done some work that seriously damaged anadromous fish and injured game only slightly less. They have, however, been too seriously damned by too many for too long.

I was intimately associated with Corps of Engineers work on both the Upper Mississippi Refuge in Minnesota, Wisconsin, Illinois, and Iowa, and the Fort Peck Game Range in Montana.

Dire predictions were made for the Upper Mississippi. Actually, waterfowl increased by *at least* 1,000 percent—ten times over, and perhaps much more. (The increase was well started before I got on the job in 1935.) Muskrat production was parallel, and fish also gained, though I paid little attention to them. A few species lost, including raccoons and squirrels. The increase in ducks, of course, vastly overshadowed everything else. The Engineers could not have been more cooperative. They did not know anything about game management as such, nor did they care especially, though some of them liked to shoot. Their cooperation consisted of doing anything we asked within their legal rights.

At Fort Peck, we literally lived with the Engineers, and while I was working on the organization of the game range, we leaned on them very heavily. Both the military officers and their civilian engineers were men of high professional caliber. They had enough brainpower to immediately grasp what we were trying to do, and helped us materially even when much extra work and extra expense was involved. Their view, like mine, was that when two federal organizations were accidentally associated, we should do what we could to help each other. They were in a position to help us very substantially.

For the last couple of generations I have heard the Engineers cursed by many prominent conservationists. Their damage to natural resources is unquestionable in certain areas, but I have always given the Devil his due. They cooperated with me without asking me to lower my professional ideals. I believe they would have cooperated with anyone, if they had been approached reasonably before any specific job started. They have been with us a long time and their demise is unlikely. They are hard to fight, and when faced with violent criticism, they go their own independent way. I reiterate that some of their work has been conservationally desirable. I insist that in most instances where damage was inevitable, it could have been materially reduced if they had been shown logical methods for getting our desired results. Vituperation and ignorance cannot do much against Corps of Engineers brains, but they are easy to educate if properly approached. If it comes to a fight, the fact remains that they are in the Army! I suggest common sense and sensible strategy—in politics, if you can't lick 'em, you can always jine 'em. If you can't beat an inevitably damaging situation, you can hope to mitigate the damage through cooperation and compromise. In the previous chapter I tried to illustrate the impossibility of compromise where the issues were clearly cut. However, the Corps of Engineers situation is an exception—we *must* cooperate or take a beating under the existing conditions.

—17—

Waterfowl

WATERFOWL-MANAGEMENT THEORIES are not especially complicated or difficult, but their applications are complicated indeed. They hinge on our polluted water and lack of water.

In addition to the Biological Trinity in our own country, we are involved with both northern and southern neighbors, and Canada is the key element in the problem. So let's consider Canada first.

Some years ago, a couple of well-informed Canadians told me that though Canada raised 85 percent of North American waterfowl, 85 percent of the harvest was garnered in the U.S.A. Therefore they saw little reason to increase waterfowl production. They had all they would use during the foreseeable future, so why worry about conditions south of the border?

I am by no means sure that those percentages are accurate now or if they ever were. But the fact is that Canada *does* raise many or most of our water birds, and it is our role not only to shoot some of them, but also to winter them and send the nesters back.

There are millions upon millions of acres of northern marshlands that are good for waterfowl production. As I view them, they are good for little else, or at least are better for ducks than anything else. Difficulties, however, are conspicuous.

Among these difficulties, drainage for agriculture looms the largest. Canada still has a relatively small population in proportion to her size, but it is growing rapidly. Some crops, and especially wheat, will grow during a short northern season. Hardier strains of grain are being developed, and in those long June and July days, wheat really jumps. Every acre that is drained takes an acre away from the birds.

The U.S. does finance some waterfowl production, largely through Ducks Unlimited. You are of course aware of their competent program. The only drawback is its minuscule size. Proportionally, the Ducks Unlimited area is only a small dot on the map. It is one thing to applaud their efforts and acknowledge their local success. Further, their research has been most valuable. However, it is questionable if the Ducks Unlimited effort has made any measurable contribution to the numbers of birds we have available in this country. It would take a hundred Ducks Unlimited, or maybe a thousand, to do what should be done. Naturally, we are thankful for anything of the sort. One brood of ducks is a brood of ducks!

Canada has plenty of skilled game managers. It would be logical simply to hand them as much as half of the U.S. "duck stamp" income, and ask them to please raise waterfowl. Of course we would have to get in agreement with them, and maintain a token staff to inspect their work. It is my impression that they would undertake this job.

This plan is, of course, just improbable utopia. Or totally impossible, international politics being what they are, even with so friendly a neighbor.

Another Canadian problem is their aborigines. This is admitting the U.S. natives are equally problematical, even if their numbers are proportionally fewer. During my extensive Canadian travels, I found that Canada's Indians and Eskimos hunted, trapped, netted, snared, and so on anywhere, at any time, on Crown land. It was their heritage, and theoretically, this policy is above criticism. Practically, it can wreck fish and game management. Moreover, the U.S. is parallel wherever any old treaties are recognized. As an example, the Fort Bridger Treaty was recognized in Idaho some years ago. Under it, the Shoshone-Bannock tribe can hunt on public lands "wherever game can be found." The courts have ruled that fishing rights are neither less nor more. Most of the big-game hunting for everyone, and most of the fishing, is on public lands or waters.

Thus these Indians can (and do) shoot pregnant does in April, seine spawning salmon during the closed season, and so forth. It is their heritage too, and understandable indeed, even though it is also wrecking our game and fish management.

As natives become more responsible and better educated, it is my opinion that they will stop "playing Indian" and assume routine citizen responsibility. Neither the U.S. nor Canada has managed its Indians very well. Further, I am enough anthropologist to know that the tribes varied unbelievably in intelligence, leadership, and responsibility. The best are the equals of any people, anywhere, but most are unquestionably culturally deprived.

This opinion, I am aware, will not add to my popularity, but I am simply stating facts as I see them, and maintaining that they are facts.

I do have some faith that the Indians themselves will see the light. The *very* intelligent Eskimos likewise. But there are many who now seem to believe that anyone *not* white is automatically right, and that could hamper progress. I fully agree that we have treated our Indians badly. They owned the country and would have liked to keep it. We have treated our Negroes little better. They came here in the holds of slave ships, and did not want to come. We owe these races something. How we will pay seems obscure. I am here concerned with enough obscurities to not hunt for others out of my field, but I assure you that Indians are important in general game management, as well as concerning the ducks, from which I have slightly digressed.

It can scarcely be overemphasized that Canada must raise most of our waterfowl, and we know what they should do: let those vast wetlands just sit there and keep the natives from stealing eggs, catching "flapper" young, ignoring limits, and spring shooting.

As to U.S. waterfowl production, we have made a fair start, but politics are dangerous, the public has been indifferent at best, and organized agriculture has been ruthless. Ecological interests have recently been escalating rapidly, however, and this may change the picture.

Ducks like to nest in swampy lands. There are many natural hazards. The worst is to have the marshes dry up before the ducklings can fly, for then *they* dry up and die. This is a calculated risk each year. In general we cannot do much about it.

There have been a few nesting ducks almost everywhere. They have been more important in the North, and the Dakotas were (are) the best of that North. Unfortunately the agricultural mania has resulted in drainage and cultivation of much of this land. Even where there still is some water, the presence of people with their livestock, including dogs and cats, interferes with much potential small-scale nesting.

Naturally, we must encourage *large*-scale nesting where we can, but settle for small-scale production where we must. If you get them started, a pair of ducks will nest around any permanent puddle. They must be undisturbed. Few birds like people around during nesting, and ducks are typical. They do not like to have their eggs smashed by wandering cows either. Feral cats and wide-ranging dogs are all part of the problem, admitting that a mallard momma might give a cat a bad time if her ducklings were threatened.

In Montana, I once made plans for some simple duck production wherever there are rangeland springs or waterholes. I was transferred, and do not know what, if anything, was ultimately done. My suggestions were for the state to do the work, but in or around the Fort Peck Game Range and the Indian Reservation with headquarters at Poplar.

Rural Montanans are the most intelligent as well as the friendliest (to strangers!) of any folks I have known during long and wide traveling. But they were primitive and careless in the handling of their very meager supply of water. If there was a spring, they would dig it out so there was room for a little accumulation of water, or put up a small earth dam in a strategic place to make a reservoir. All in the name of watering stock. But the stock are far from neat—they wallow and paw and stomp. The water swiftly becomes a mudhole, and the reservoirs especially may lose 75 percent of their watering values because the cattle have broken the silt seal and there is seepage out of the bottom.

You are aware that when any sort of a puddle is formed, if there is fine clay in the soil, it seals the bottom. The water sits there until it evaporates, unless something drinks it, as is the reservoir plan. Western soils are extremely variable, but northeastern Montana is blessed (or possibly cursed) with as fine-textured clay as I have seen anywhere. It really seals the bottom of a reservoir—until a cow walks through it. Then the water runs out. These reservoirs, or the cleaned-out (and hopefully permanent) springs, should be fenced. A pipe should run to a watering trough that is automatically filled by the action of a ball-valve. A master plumber, who was also a Fish and Game Commissioner, figured out the system. The fence enclosure should be large enough to manage space for a brood or two of ducks. Blue-wing teal especially like that country. A thousand such spots (few indeed in that vast expanse) would result in a lot of blue-wings.

A little ingenuity used everywhere you can find some reasonably permanent water can result in a few ducks. I have not been everywhere, but some method will work everywhere. An observer need not have studied any game management. He only needs to see, to interpret, and then do something. At times this is obvious, as when there are a few wood ducks and not enough hollow trees. Nesting boxes are the solution. The box should have a nest space 15 × 15 × 15 inches, or a bit deeper than that. The hole should be 4 inches in diameter, with a bit of "front porch." Some sawdust or a mixture of shavings and sawdust in the bottom will make it look natural. Weathered lumber is logical if you want nesters at once. Slabs or hollowed logs are more authentic-looking, and I would be the last to discount authenticity, but weathered boards look all right to the birds. Wood ducks are charming creatures, and possibly the world's most beautiful ducks, but I have already noted that they are not very bright. If they were just a wee bit smarter, they might not insist on nesting in trees!

In planning nesting, certain care is essential. If squirrels are numerous, the wood-duck boxes might need some protection, or more boxes so there would not be undue competition. And bull snakes (pine snakes) cheerfully climb trees and swallow eggs—any sort of eggs! So thinning out bull-snake concentration is part of the program. Likewise, inspection of those ball-valve-operated watering tanks is essential. But a boy or a girl with a jeep or trail cycle (or even a pony, if you would be authentic) could do it—or an oldster. Definitely this patrol does not demand a top hand unless something is amiss, and then all it needs is a good range plumber.

If you are concerned with big-time nesting, as on a refuge, there are extreme variations. Nesting islands have been subjected to considerable experimenting. Making them entails a lot of work, and I have been where the ducks were slow about renting them. Muskrats are our best allies. They work hard and cheerfully, ask no wages, and grow valuable pelts. In fact, if a waterfowl manager manages his rats, the fowl may well manage themselves so far as production goes. Muskrat houses make perfect nesting sites for both Canada geese and many species of ducks, and the rats can manage the emergent vegetation if *they* are properly managed. Ducks need some emergent vegetation for protection. If there is too much, there is no open water for them to light on; if there is too little, they lack the protection. So the logical number of rats is trapped and skinned. This takes a little doing, and the results are not necessarily perfect. Muskrats are rodents and the rodents and rabbits are the most cyclic creatures. If you skin too many, vegetation may overrun the marsh. If you do not take enough, they could open up too much water. There is no rule of thumb. As a general thing, there are often more rats than most of us usually estimate to be present. In any event, they cannot be overestimated as the duck manager's allies.

Later, I will give brief attention to fur management. Trapping was ignored in the harvest section, Part I of this volume, and I have taken pains to avoid a definition of "game." But some of the fur animals that must usually be legally trapped and not shot rate notice here, because of the wheels within wheels. Muskrats help with ducks, but mink may be the rat's worst enemies, and the ecological plot thickens.

When you have raised some ducks, and harvested what you could— maybe too many, maybe what you have been able to get—then the problem is to keep the breeders over winter and send them north. That is, if they have really gone south, as they should.

This, too, is simple in theory. The federal refuges in the South may be the best examples of government game management that we have. All you need is a fairly decent aquatic environment, and then leave the birds to themselves. They naturally have to eat, and cheerfully take what they can get. This is normally their water-plant choices, with a seasoning of animal food that may be handy. Lacking sufficient aquatic food, they go to the fields. That is, the dipping ducks and geese do. The divers usually stick to the water. A couple of times, I have seen scaup (bluebills) eat corn when it was available, but that is the exception. Not that any game duck dislikes corn, but the divers normally decline to accept the environment in which corn usually grows.

In fields, waterfowl may do damage. This is true whether or not they are wintering or get into crops in the fall. If 100,000 ducks invade an unharvested barley field and are not promptly chased out, there may not be any reason for harvesting it. Field feeding is not normal. In the West, which is the principal part of the country where fall and winter field feeding is common, there was no grain to speak of until the last hundred years. But ducks, and especially mallards, learn many things fast. They eat grain the first time they see it. They resemble a range horse that has never seen an oat. He learns all he needs to know about oats in ten seconds or less.

While mentioning waterfowl interest in eating grain, some discussion of artificial feeding is essential. This is admitting that I am against do-mestic-animal-type feeding of any wild creature if there is any way of avoiding it. Basically, making a bum out of anything is a mistake. How-ever, unusual weather or some other calamity suggests feeding until normal conditions return. It is doubtful if artificial feeding is *ever* of long-range value. It is tough to make the decision, but possibly whatever cannot make it naturally, may as well die. I have managed quite a bit of this feeding, and saved some needed breeding stock, but there is uncertainty, that will be mentioned when discussing some other game a little later.

When I was organizing the Fort Peck Game Range in Montana, 1940 to 1942, warm water was seeping under the gigantic dam and ducks—largely mallards—started hanging around all winter. There was always some open water in fast spots in the Missouri, and of course there were wheat fields that would feed ducks if they were not snowed under. Northeastern Montana has a very peculiar climate. It can get beastly cold, with several feet of snow, yet chinook winds can melt it all in a matter of hours. Which suggests floods. Cloudbursts do not attract too much attention either. Montanans expect anything in the realm of weather, and usually get it.

By January, when snow got bad, some of that passel of ducks got so weak they could not fly. I could get some government-surplus grain, largely wheat. So I fed them maybe 200 pounds every two days. It just kept them alive. They took off very early in the spring and appeared to head north! The next winter there were more, and they had to be fed twice as much. But in the late spring of 1942, I was transferred, and did not have to worry.

The ducks had no business trying to winter in that spot. They liked the warmish, quiet few acres of water below the dam. And that raft of ducks was interesting to watch. None ate out of my hands, but they would shovel up wheat not six feet away. I threw most of it in shallow water and made them tip for it. Some would stay under for three minutes before they tipped back. I did not want them to starve, but I did not know that feeding them was the right policy and still do not know. I had the approval of my Portland, Oregon, and Washington, D.C., superiors. They got the grain for me. But their judgment was no better than mine.

A situation developed in January and February of 1949 when I would have cheerfully fed ducks if there had been anything to feed them. This was the first winter we were in Pocatello, and the *worst* winter in recorded history.

Hundreds of thousands of ducks, largely mallards, winter in this vicinity. There are warmish spring creeks, and usually the birds make a fair enough living off the wheat stubble. This particular winter the fields got snow-covered and stayed that way. Ducks starved by the thousands, possibly by hundreds of thousands. They were sports to the end. They scrounged around little gardens around town and even tried for kitchen garbage. I saw a couple that fell dead on the university campus. They were flying seconds before they died. Skeletons, they tried everything but what was logical—they did not go south. They thought they *were* south! Late in the game some feeding was done and some birds were saved, but the losses were sickening. Fortunately, there have been no such winters since 1949, though several times it was touch-and-go. Of course there is some excellent natural feed in the creeks, the Portneuf River, and the Snake, and ducks clean it when the fields are covered. Since 1949 there has always been a break before the ducks starved. I hope this will continue.

The weather is milder on the Bear River Refuge some 150 miles south, and I believe they can manage emergency feeding. However, there is no way to persuade the ducks to go there. Mallards are smart, but they have their blind spots.

Thus, it is of great importance to raise grain especially for waterfowl where there is need. The Tule Lake Refuge, in extreme northern California, raises grain, and tries to shoo the ducks onto it and away from the farmers, using special efforts to scare ducks away from where they are not wanted. About 1942 I met a Tule Lake old-timer who was a professional waterfowl scarer. He drove from field to field in a pick-up truck, armed with an old Model 1886 repeater, caliber .45-70. He hand-loaded with black powder and cast lead bullets. He mutilated the bullets so that they would howl like banshees. Approaching a fowl-infested field, he fired a howling shot over it. The birds would rise, and he would howl a couple of other shots through them to speed them on their way. Of course he had a federal and state permit for this shooting. Occasionally he would kill a bird. It had to remain where it fell, for the magpies or gulls to clean up. Such a permit did not include the authority to eat a bird that was killed. The reasons for this policy are obvious.

Perhaps I should amplify my statement that waterfowl rarely do any field damage except in the West, and also a knowledge that I have done little checking in the South where many birds winter. I am reasonably certain only on the migration routes. Presumably in the wet East there is proportionally more water and the birds can feed sufficiently in or immediately around it. For five years I was biologist on the Upper Mississippi Refuge, which at that time straddled the "Big Muddy" for 300 miles in Minnesota, Wisconsin, Iowa, and Illinois. During those five years we had a special record that included a single complaint of ducks attacking unharvested grain in Wisconsin. Usually the wheat was harvested before ducks in any numbers showed up. Corn, harvested later, was more vulnerable.

There was one other slightly parallel situation that was grimly amusing, and scarcely normal field feeding. It again was on the Wisconsin side of the river, a few miles below LaCrosse.

A big field—perhaps 100 acres—was protected by a dike, and planted to corn. These bottomland crops are usually excellent. The alluvial soil is rich and there is plenty of moisture. In fact, it would be flooded much of the time, if it were not for the dike and the pumps. In this instance, after the corn was cut and shocked, but before it was husked, the dike broke and the land was flooded. The farmers decided to wait until spring, then repair the dike, get the pumps going, and salvage the grain. Some hundreds of thousands of ducks, largely mallards, arrived very early in the spring. There was still some water all over this field. The ducks literally tore the corn shocks to pieces, and ate the grain. It seemed incredible that birds of that size could scatter a corn shock all over the landscape. I watched them, usually from the dike, for a couple of days. They were hungry after their migration flight, and found a bonanza. Every duck on that vast flyway stopped for a go at the corn as long as it lasted, which was not long. They did not miss a grain, so far as I or the men who owned the corn could tell.

These farmers, with or without any real hope, wanted the Division of Wildlife Refuges to reimburse them for the loss of their corn. It was worth many thousands of dollars and represented a season's work for two or more men. As biologist, I was asked to make a recommendation as to whether or not the government was at fault for this damage. You are presumably aware that the government stubbornly resists illogical claims and can refuse to accept a suit for damages if there seems to be no governmental fault. They cheerfully pay if there *is* an obvious governmental error. My report was brief and to the point. I admitted that the ducks were federal ducks, since they were within the general boundary of a federal refuge, admitting further the damage was on privately owned land. But the owners, when they diked the land and pumped the water out, were taking a calculated risk. It was no governmental fault that the dike broke and the land was flooded in the fall. I did not feel that the Refuge Division had any responsibility, or that any damages should be paid. Farm-raised and fully aware of the seriousness of a crop failure, I found this a hard choice. Still, one calls them as one sees them, and duty sometimes leaves little room for sympathy.

Duck diseases must be recognized by game managers, and treated by them to some extent, though specialized pathologists are essential for diagnosis. Of course, as in the cases of other wild-animal diseases, often the disorder must run its course, leaving you to salvage what is left as best you can.

Possibly crippling should also be considered briefly, though this is really an educational item, on the fringe of management as such. Crippling has been charged with destroying as many birds as go into the hunter's bags. I will not question this figure, even if I think that I and my duck-hunting associates do a lot better than that. We occasionally get our six-bird limits with no known cripples, though losing one cripple while getting six may be better than our average.

It is axiomatic that a good gun and good shooting are the elements that lead to clean kills. Shells with plastic wads enclosing the shot are a decided advantage, since they prevent some shot distortion and help make a clean kill or a clean miss. While waiting for commercial iron shot most of my reloading for ducks is with the too-expensive copper-plated shot. Soft shot kill better than anything, if they get to the game. But they jam each other, jam in the forcing cone, and jam in the choke. Too many get flattened or almost square, and come close to turning around and starting back before they get halfway to the hoped-for ducks.

Next to good shooting with good loads and a good gun, a good dog does the most to limit crippling. While I was stationed at Winona, Minnesota, I knew one duck hunter who frequently brought in his ten-duck limit without firing a shot. I am not sure he owned a gun. He had a boat and a good Labrador retriever. He hunted shallow marshes, with heavy emergent vegetation, where his flat-bottomed boat would just float. A big canoe, pushed with a duck-bill-tipped pole, would have been far easier to navigate. Early in the season, on weekends, his doggie would bring in a limit of just-killed birds, or cripples, before noon. Later, when long-since-crippled birds would be skinny and unfit to eat, he might have had to bring in twenty ducks in order to get ten fit for the pot. Or maybe more than twenty. Which, as a general thing, he cheerfully managed.

If you shoot over open water and watch for birds to drop, you will not lose many ducks. Similarly, when canoe-jumping ducks on a creek or small river, it is important to land them in the water. I often hunt on two brushy creeks where a bird that lands on shore is often lost without a dog or even with one. A season or two back, I had been paddling a faculty friend who was a good jumpshot, on our little Portneuf River. He took his limit, and we had to walk back maybe three miles through the meadows to get the truck and drive down for the canoe. I had not fired a shot, but lugged my Beretta 10-gauge magnum, loaded with No. 2 shot, in case we were attacked by geese. Well back toward the truck, we saw ducks milling around a springhole that was

easily approached. I was to take the shot, Dr. Holte staying back with
his dog, a smart German shorthair–black Lab cross. When the ducks
boiled up, I fired one shot, raking one edge of the flock that may have
totaled 200 over an eighth of an acre of water. I saw ducks showering
down. My partner shouted, "Fire the other barrel!" which I did not.
The doggie picked up six ducks. Half of them were cripples. Maybe
I hit all of them. Maybe not. Other hunters had been in the vicinity.
Without the dog, we would have found two birds easily. Possibly three.
I had to more or less flock shoot, or not fire at all. It is management's
duty to try to confine crippling to an irreducible minimum.

As to actual diseases, duck botulism in the West, year after year,
probably kills more ducks than all others combined. If the season is wet,
with a lot of snow-water early and heavy rains later (a too-rare situation)
few ducks are affected. If there is some source for fresh water in a nesting
area, it may be reduced. This was done on the Lake Bowdoin Refuge
in Montana when now-retired Ben Hazeltine was manager. He was
entitled to draw a considerable number of acre-feet of water from a
relatively deep reservoir handled by a different agency, the Bureau of
Land Management, if my memory holds. He let Lake Bowdoin get very
low, and when there were signs of botulism, he took perhaps half of
the available water in one swoop. A few weeks later, he took the rest
of it. This action vastly reduced the cases of botulism. They had a "duck
hospital" with spring water, where affected birds were kept, and they
recovered unless they were in very bad shape. The shore was patrolled
daily and dead birds were gathered and burned. The total losses were
thus kept low.

Botulism develops only in warm alkaline water, and is not known in
the East, where the water is not alkaline. I do not know that it can
be totally eliminated, nor can it be treated satisfactorily in many instances. Fortunately it is not in the Upper Canadian muskeg country
either, and will certainly not wipe out ducks in the foreseeable future.

The other waterfowl diseases, like diseases everywhere, ebb and flow.
Some involve alternating hosts, including black flies, that are Canadian
insects, and big-time as all know who have had to endure them. But
the cycle goes down after it goes up and there are survivors to keep
the race going. Usually, you cannot do much about it. Cut down the
season, probably, to save what you can, because there is not much else
to do.

Another terrible duck killer, though not a disease, is oil. This has been
written up for at least a half-century, so far as our East Coast is concerned. Oil tankers filled up with water ballast for return trips. They

"blew" this ballast with considerable oil in it, and the slicks coated the ducks so they could not fly and they died miserably.

The big oil transporters have been unmercifully criticized for this practice, and I believe there is now little of it. Offshore drilling, however, has made some very serious mistakes. They killed not only ducks, but a tremendous amount of other aquatic life. If this oceanic drilling must leak oil, it should be stopped entirely unless there is a national emergency. In fact, as I have said before, if we keep *most* of our *unrenewable* mineral resources in the ground, it would be advantageous for perhaps everything that *is* renewable. With very few exceptions, miners are our archenemies. Many industrialists are enemies enough, but the miners are among the worst if not the worst. This especially applies to ducks, as they are water creatures and water pollution could be the worst phase of an all-round pollution mess. Also the easiest to clean up if a real effort is made.

Local conditions, especially on refuges, or where sportsmen's clubs can do some work, may often work toward small-scale duck protection, just as it is possible to get small-scale production. "Many a mickle makes a muckle," if I have correctly spelled an old Scottish proverb, or, quoting *Poor Richard's Almanac*, "If you take care of the pennies, the pounds will take care of themselves." If everyone can produce a few extra ducks, or save a few, we will continue to have some ducks. Perhaps!

As an example, when I was on the Upper Mississippi Refuge, we saved some ducks by taking care of our skunks. We issued permits for trapping muskrats and mink. Skunks were not especially important fur animals, but they were valuable for digging out and eating turtle eggs. Big turtles will pull under and kill big ducks. Ducks are especially dumb about being attacked from under water. A smallish snapping turtle will catch young ducks. There were a lot of turtles, and we recognized their rights to exist, but we sort of let the skunks and turtles have it out. The skunks were doing a fair enough job of snapper control. Snappers are excellent on the table, but few bothered to catch and eat them.

Waterfowl hazards are great. Many are natural, and man has created many more. Some will shortly be reduced if they are not eliminated, but others could crop up on either a small scale or a big one. About 1930, waterfowl were at such a low ebb that there was question as to whether or not there was any use to try to save them. Let them go, and much later, try to build up the survivors—if any—and get them back on the shooting-game list. The decision was to try to save them, and this was done. The weather improved. It could again go bad, and the waterfowl season would have to be drastically curtailed or eliminated.

It is drastically curtailed now. In some places there is only a three- or four-duck limit. In Idaho only six a day or in possession, and two Canada geese. I recall the market-hunting days when twenty-five ducks, eight geese, and eight brant was the daily limit. And, as I mentioned in the duck-shooting chapter, there may not have been any limits during my early life. And there was spring shooting too.

Most do-gooders and gun-haters blame shooting for our present relatively small waterfowl population and reduced bag limits. Shooting was an influence, especially when shooting was not reduced and production was. We have too many people (the greatest hazard of all), and with limited production, the remaining ducks must be distributed the best we can manage, among the too many hunters that stem from the too many people.

In our heavily populated East Coast areas, and the somewhat parallel West Coast, waterfowl shooting for the "one-gallus" hunter is pretty much gone. It has become a sport for the well-heeled club member. And it is now so common to be well-heeled that you may not buy your way into a club. The Midwest and Far West have many public shooting grounds, where the small chap still has a chance. Even then, waterfowl do not come really cheap. Since nothing else comes cheap either, that may be a statement that is so obvious it is not worth the making.

It is re-emphasized that waterfowl management is dependent on basic water management. If we keep some spare water, we can manage some water birds. However, if so many people demand so much water that we have to drink it two or three times over during its return to the sea or air, then duck shooting has had it. Possibly by then, people will have had it too, or will be about to get it.

—18—

Upland Game

RUFFED GROUSE ARE an easy place to start, for their management is almost totally an environmental problem. The theory is simple: If you have a suitable habitat, you will have some birds; if hunting pressure is heavy, you limit the season.

As to habitat, water is a key essential, though I have seen ruffs in the West a couple of miles from any water I knew about. Usually, if the weather is dry, 100 yards from water is far enough. There is no distance limit when there is snow, or during damp weather. Perhaps, when eating Dutch clover or green strawberry leaves ruffed grouse do not drink water very often, but usually you assume that water is an essential part of the ruffed-grouse habitat.

Next to water, winter food is of primary importance. Ruffs always do all right during spring, summer, and fall.

I could scarcely pick ruffed-grouse food choices nationwide, for they eat many different things. In the spring, as soon as the snow melts (and these grouse are northern or high-country denizens), the clover and

strawberries are much in demand—where they exist. Young grouse are
of course insect feeders, and momma does not disdain animal food.

Later, berries almost monopolize the menu. Currants and gooseberries
are so important that their eradication, so essential in combatting white
pine blister rust, may sharply reduce grouse as well. I would scarcely
say there is definite proof of this, but there is evidence.

Later, the wild cherries are followed by viburnum, hawthorn, blue-
berries, rose, and dogwood berries. Even seemingly impalatable bitter-
sweet attracts grouse when other berries are scarce. Favoring these
shrubs also favors grouse.

The important winter foods are buds and winter catkins. When I was
on the Chequamegon National Forest in Wisconsin, birch winter catkins
were definitely preferred. Both paper and yellow birches were abundant.
The buds of all the birches are also important winter food. Possibly the
buds of most of the Rosaceae family are equally important. I have observed grouse feeding on wild black cherry *(Prunus serotina)* buds very
extensively. They are as popular as the cherries themselves. The other
cherries (including the cultivated varieties) also produce palatable buds.
So do common apples. During my farmboy days, grouse used to fly to
our apple orchard, only an eighth of a mile from a patch of woods. There
was no evidence to show that this budding reduced the fruit crop.

I have also seen grouse eat aspen buds, and the closely related willows
must be equally important. When big-game hunting in Idaho, I have
seen ruffs wintering in willow thickets. They had to be feeding on willow
buds, as there was nothing else—and "willow grouse" is one of their
common Western names.

During a beechnut year, these nuts are the main fall food.

It is interesting to note that ruffs may have either gray or "red" tails.
The "red" is really a chestnut brown. I have seen what I was reasonably
sure was a brood of ruffs with both tail colors. It is a variation commoner
in the East and Midwest. The Idaho and Montana grouse I have shot
ran heavily to gray tails, but I have not studied these differences, nor
are they of any practical importance.

Two characteristics tend to protect ruffed grouse. The first may be
that they are hard to hunt. With very few exceptions, they prefer dense
woods and brush. If the woods are big, hunters rarely if ever cover them
completely. In the East where I was raised, a 200-acre stand of timber
was big indeed; most patches of woods were 10 acres or less. But the
brush was thick, and some grouse survived. Again considering the Chequamegon Forest, there was considerable grouse hunting, and I was one
of the hunters. But I doubt if 10 percent of the probable grouse coverts

were hunted, and I doubt if many hunters got 300 yards from their cars.

Those situations are common enough everywhere. Even when the ruff cycle is down, our Idaho Fish and Game Department is quite correct in not worrying much about them. I have heard that not over 10 percent of their vast area is hunted. When found, they often sit and chirp, or fly to a low limb. To get a sporting wing shot you may have to pelt one with stones or clubs, and you may thus kill it!

As soon as hunting becomes heavy, however, the ruffs' safety education soars. When I was a boy, there were spots where I could almost always put up a grouse or two, in season or out. In season, I burned powder without additionally worrying the birds. They were always worried. But only once do I recall seeing a grouse sitting except fighting females with young, and winter budders. The latter rarely let one get within gunshot range. The one exception was a bird that sat on a rail fence along a field where we were husking corn. This grouse was at least a half-mile from any normal grouse habitat. The date was probably early November. This creature was a dumb one that should not have lived to grow up! But we happened to have my single-barreled Stevens 12, and the bird's career ended swiftly. This was typical behavior where the birds are not hunted.

Twice I have known ruffed grouse to fly through windows. Once on the University of New Brunswick campus in Fredericton, and I myself saw one fly through a school window in Park Falls, Wisconsin. They smashed fairly heavy glass, and of course were dead or dying when picked up. This type of behavior is not very well understood. It is psychosomatic for all I know.

I emphasize that with the maintenance of some brush, some water, and intelligent open seasons, ruffed grouse will not be on the endangered list.

A few other species (or groups) of grouse deserve a paragraph or two.

The *Eastern spruce grouse* is unsavable wherever humans assume control. By the time you attempt any establishment of management, there are none to manage. The *Western Franklin's grouse*, which may be the identical bird that has assumed different feeding habits, is in the same category. I would not forget them, but they are on my songbird list. Some will hang on wherever there is magnificent isolation. They are wilderness birds, who can exist among humans if these humans, as well as their dogs and cats, are extremely tolerant.

The *ptarmigan* are parallel—what few there are in the U.S.A., barring Alaska. They will exist in the mountains if left alone. And the mountain climbers usually do just that. The willow ptarmigan, way north, do not get hunted very much. They are no songbirds, but they are getting along well enough so far. Being dumb, they could not stand much hunting.

The magnificent *dusky (blue) grouse* are not in an especially different slot. Though tough and fast, they are not smart. Denizens of the high, back country, they are not hunted much. When land is settled, they go. Maintain some Western wilderness, and you will maintain some blues, and get some shooting, if you work at it.

I would write off the *pinnated grouse* (prairie chicken) about like the spruce and Franklin's grouse, but something might reverse the present trends.

At one time they were very numerous in the Middle West. Grain lands interspersed with prairie seemingly boosted them. As the grain fields gained and the prairie all but vanished, the birds went with the prairies. I never saw any except in Wisconsin and Minnesota, from about 1929 through 1939. A couple of times I saw flocks of forty or thereabouts, in the winter, on little Trempeleau Refuge, some 20 miles up-river from LaCrosse, Wisconsin. They may hang on. The few suggestions I can make about sharptails may apply equally to pinnated grouse. The Eastern variety, heath hens, are gone.

Sharptail grouse are pretty much identical to prairie chicks in size, in color, and on the table. Sometimes they are in the same flock, and a hunter would need a fast eye to tell which bird he was taking, but they are vastly different birds. The sharptails also consort with ruffed grouse in the thickets of the northern Lake states. Out of the thicket, they more nearly follow prairie chicken habitat, but are more adaptable.

The best sharptail shooting I have had was in Montana when I was stationed on the Fort Peck Game Range. All they ask is not too heavily grazed range, and interspersed farms. Decent general land management results in good enough sharptail management. At times they drift into woods, but they are basically plains and prairie birds, that should make it.

Pheasants, where they can live, are more important than any of the other gallinae, including the ruffed grouse. They are farm birds and this is an agricultural country. (Partly!) Of course I refer to ring-necked, or Chinese, pheasants. Most of the other pheasant species have been imported and have failed to take hold, though a black-necked species has had limited success. (Apparently it could and did interbreed with the ring-necks, and disappeared.) At present Idaho is experimenting with the smaller green pheasant. I am not ready to write them off, but I am not optimistic.

As to range, pheasants cannot (or will not) stand much continuous heat. They are rare below the Mason-Dixon Line, and down there you had better not give them much thought. They may slowly spread, on their own. Plants have not amounted to much thus far.

I do not know that cold as such curtails their spread. They do all right in northeastern Montana and go on into Canada, and it gets powerful cold in those parts. Cold and soil conditions do curtail their food, however, so let us say they are farm birds. They do not go into the woods very much. I have seen them sitting in trees rather frequently, and in England they sometimes roost in trees, but trees are not essential for their U.S. happiness.

As to food, they can be rather omnivorous. While taking a master's degree in game management at the University of Michigan, I worked on a big pheasant problem. Basically a forester, I have more concern for wild-land game, but the pheasants were there, and students follow instructions—or at least, they did! Further, I had a chance to work on a very fine private game preserve, where there was a special long season. Many birds were artificially reared. Pheasants, luckily, are not "tamed" when raised behind wire. I had a chance to examine many hundreds of crops.

Pheasants will eat any field grain, as far as I know, despite a consensus that they prefer corn when given a choice. However, they seem to like what is handy, including beans, peas, and alfalfa and sweet clover seed.

As to wild vegetable foods, the big green seeds of the arrow arum (*Peltandra virginica*) seemed the favorite. It was handy, in some marshy ground, and that may have been the reason.

Again, when they are available, pheasants will apparently live on grasshoppers. Some crops were crammed with them, and nothing else. But they will grab about any insect, and the occasional spider. Also the occasional mouse. The mice I recovered from crops were juveniles, apparently half-grown (or less) specimens of the genera *Microtus* and *Peromyscus*. In other words, anything is fish that comes to their net, though I have not heard that they catch and eat fish. (However, I would risk a substantial wager that they would, given the opportunity and the shallow water. If they swam and dove for fish, that would be more surprising, though they swim well, like their not too distant relatives, the turkeys.)

Pheasants' favorite roosting and hiding places are in low-ground sedge grasses. After the freeze-up, bullrush or reed (*Phragmites*) make equally desirable cover.

To raise pheasants you must literally raise them, and they hatch best on wild land, such as sandy sagebrush pastures, contiguous to cultivated fields. The young feed on insects, and water seems important during warmish weather. Western irrigated farms near big patches of wild land produce the most pheasants.

Clean cultivation is deadly to any farm game. The worst situations are nests in cultivated fields where hens are killed by the cutterbars of mowers or harvesters. Flushing bars have been developed that saved the hen, but rarely saved the nest. Nor will a hen pheasant, or any bird, usually go back to a wide-open nest that has been mowed over. Pheasants are often smart enough to nest in uncultivated land, if any exists. Having such land available is one of the biggest problems for the pheasant manager.

There are some conflicts of opinion as to laws protecting hen pheasants. "Save the hen" was once the loudest cry. It is still important enough. Pheasants can be very polygamous birds. A cock will gather a sizable harem and mainline his crowing ground against intruders. Few hen pheasants become dedicated spinsters. However, hens can be too numerous for the available habitat. Idaho allows one hen in the bag at certain times late in the season. Total hen protection may not be necessary. Careful local attention is essential.

Naturally, excited hunters shoot hens and leave them where they fall. I recall doing this myself once or twice, and I believe I am more careful than the average. And once I missed a cock and hit a hen that I thought was a safe distance from where I aimed. Since game wardens cannot be everywhere, there are bold hunters who fire at anything that gets up. I have been with them.

But pheasants will stand tremendous hunting pressure if the Biological Trinity is in good working order. Pheasants are farm game par excellence if the farming is organized to give them a chance. They are strong, tough, and adaptable over a tremendous area.

A last pheasant item may be consideration of winter feeding. In general, my principle about making bums of wild animals (or anything else) holds. Feeding stations attract predators as well as pheasants. There must be handy cover as well as some sort of cover over the actual feeder. It is possible to feed with good results, even though pheasants are great rustlers and can stand very meager rations without giving up.

Special field crops, left standing, are far better than actual feeder feeding. Short milo that keeps its grain heads above the snow is fine for winter. Late-planted and unharvested grain of any sort is all right if it is not totally bogged down in snow. Not very palatable food that is ignored until the pinch is most desirable. Russian olive is in this category among trees, though I do not know that pheasants will eat them. Sharptails will. Unharvested corn and some of the sorghum types taller than milo may keep the grain available even in fairly deep snow.

Hungarian partridge management so closely follows pheasant management that we can dismiss it swiftly. In places, the Huns have adapted slowly, and I have been West since their general spread. But they get along, once they are established, pretty much like pheasants, and sometimes in places where pheasants will not survive. I doubt if Huns can get on indefinitely with no water, but I have seen them in Nevada where it was very dry. Likewise in Idaho, far from pheasant habitat, such as above the Salmon's Middle Fork. But I generally feel that the imported Hun goes along with the imported pheasant, though somewhat more adaptable.

Chukar partridges are the only other imported game birds to have established themselves in this country. My personal experience with them has been confined to Nevada and Idaho. They are not dependent on farms, for they definitely prefer rocky territory, and apparently they can winter on a diet confined to the seeds of cheat grass (chess). Much of the West has plenty of rocks and plenty of cheat. These birds thus demand little attention. Further, they swiftly learn about hunters and take long flights. They also thrive where few (or no) native game birds exist. We have reason to fear the competition of exotics, but that situation cannot remotely apply to chukars.

Bobwhites, where they can thrive, are high among the game birds that have been subjected to some management practices.

Bobwhites cross the pheasant-tolerant range in the North, but are at their best where the pheasants peter out. Farms, with wild cover close by, are the essentials. Farther south, they rarely winter-kill, but bad weather may wipe them out on their northern periphery. Dutchess County, New York, where I was raised, was close to their boreal limit. You may raise some quail where you can raise peaches and watermelons. They spread from a southern habitat until a bad winter takes most or all of them. Many gallinaceous birds roost under snow, and any of them can be fatally caught under a crust, but bobwhites are especially vulnerable to snow crust. Occasionally I saved a few by digging them out. Farmboys, who are incidentally trappers, see a lot.

Not too peculiarly, bobwhites thrive under fairly heavy hunting pressure. Most gallinaceous birds are fast breeders, and created to be eaten. Since it is axiomatic that no game can be stockpiled, this especially applies to the Gallinae, with bobwhites the finest known example.

I have often referred to bobwhites being on the protected song bird list in many states, and have done considerable investigating of this practice for upward of a half-century. At the risk of wrath from my Audubon Society friends, I will clearly state that, with reasonably decent management, there are more quail under shooting than there are under total protection.

There have been many examples to prove this statement and none to disprove it, so far as I have heard. One striking situation came to my attention in 1938. I was in Ohio on a drainage-inspection trip for the U.S. Fish and Wildlife Service, but had an opportunity to make observations on other specialties.

I talked to a farmer who owned some 320 acres, and had a definite interest in game. He had purchased the farm some fourteen years earlier. Two coveys of ten or a dozen quail each had wintered on this farm. There had been open seasons on quail for many years before this purchase, but during the last legislative session, the season was closed and it stayed closed. He was reasonably certain that no shot had been fired at quail during these fourteen years. There were a good many in the fall, but they thinned out. That 1938 spring (I believe it was April) he said one covey of maybe a dozen birds had wintered. He found them for me by driving his pick-up for ten minutes. That one wintering covey had been average for years. It was his guess (and I agreed) that at least fifty quail each fall could have been harvested on his land, without reducing the breeders. Possibly the breeders would have increased in numbers under shooting.

It seems contradictory to believe that birds can be favored by killing half or more than half of the fall crop. I do not know that anyone knows the whole story, or ever will, but nature's plans suggest that all the Gallinae were expected to be eaten by something. Bobwhites lay a hatful of eggs and momma bobwhite is a very smart and devoted little momma. She loses some chicks, but I have often seen broods of ten or more when they could be classed as raised. If the breeding stock is very low, the birds may stockpile a bit for a season or two. This Ohio man felt that some twenty-five birds were as many as would survive over winter, on the average. If they increased to a hundred by October, reducing them by half would be conservative. It is essential to cut-and-try to some extent. Probably a landowner with absolute control of shooting could best devise a reasonably exact harvest number.

Possibly this is the place to briefly discuss the views of the hard-boiled bird protectionists. I recall that a few years ago, the Audubon Society authorities were not willing to admit that starlings should be reduced. This view is totally nonsensical. Ignoring simple scientific principles gets these conscientious extremists disliked, for some people doubt if they know anything when they show such utter damnfoolishness in one area. Most of us can condone certain failures among many successes, and these bird enthusiasts have done much that is important indeed. However, it is deplorable that they cannot always recognize reason. Game managers have a rough enough time dealing with their obvious enemies; when they also have to fight with their friends, it is sadly discouraging.

As a situation parallel to many other species, bobwhites, in their suitable weather environment, need little more than a suitable mixed habitat, and a carefully planned harvest.

Management of the *true quail*—Gambel's, valley, mountain, Mearn's, and scaled (all Western)—closely follows the simple suggestions for handling their bobwhite cousins. These quail have somewhat exacting habitat demands. When trapped and moved, they may succeed to some extent, but real shooting populations are rare except on areas that the birds really like. Their ranges coincide to some extent. Both scaled and Mearn's quail may be found on the same square mile. I have seen valley and mountain quail in the same covey. Gambel's quail were decidedly by themselves when I hunted them rather extensively in Nevada and somewhat in Arizona. The Gambel's quail imported to Idaho live fairly close to other game birds. Their success, as I view it, is not spectacular.

I re-emphasize that these birds only need room and a hunting season they can stand. They need not be coddled, just given a chance.

Turkeys are the last gallinaceous birds I will discuss. My personal experience with the Eastern birds is such that my suggestions are better than those of the barber-shop biologists, but less than the last word.

If there is a habitat suitable for them, turkeys can definitely be brought back to their original range. This would be from Florida to halfway up New York, and including lower New England. The bigger state parks and all the few national forests through the East and Midwest will produce turkeys. Mast food is the most desirable. Like the timber grouse, turkeys can live on buds in the winter.

Merriam's turkey, as I noted in Part I, seems to demand a habitat that is at least somewhat dominated by Ponderosa pine. It will be interesting to see if they will spread beyond this habitat. Though no game can be stockpiled, several consecutive good breeding seasons may cause birds to drift out of their normal range, and stay. Our existing Idaho turkeys were imported. There is no evidence that they drift extensively, but they can adapt if the environment is suitable. I repeat that many exotic gallinaceous birds have been imported to this country, but only three species have done well.

Before abandoning turkeys to their (we hope) happy fate, this may be the time to generalize a bit on importations. If you rob a wild turkey nest and hatch some poults under a hen, you will raise some turkeys, but they will just be turkeys—not *wild* turkeys. In contrast, our common pheasants can be raised in captivity for ten generations, and still be plumb wild. I knew one old cock pheasant in Michigan that was hatchery-raised and became domesticated. He hung around the kitchen door, fraternized with the dogs, and was almost a pet. He was one in a million. Certainly the only tame pheasant I have seen.

Under the right conditions, you can tame a full-grown mallard duck in ten minutes. Fed well, he may get too fat to fly, if he is interested in flying away, as often he is not. To produce game, and especially game birds, they do best when they stay wild, though captive, or near captive.

Conversely, many domestic creatures, and all of the common farm mammals but one, may go totally wild in one generation. Many of the wild horses in Montana were cleaned up during World War II. I saw quite a lot of them in 1940, and no wild animals are wilder. "Razorback" hogs in the South are simply hogs gone wild, and I believe the European "wild boars" are the identical *Sus scrofa* as are our domestic pigs. They can all revert to type except sheep. Our sheep have become so specialized that they cannot exist without man's care.

Of course we have some relatively wild humans still hanging on in South America, Borneo, a few spots in Africa, and so on. Socially, reversal to type is common in war. White human predators are normally—and fortunately—rare, but we can be trained into hard-boiled killers rather swiftly. Nor is such a killer easy to reinstate into his former "human" niche.

Some of these aspects of human management are of the greatest importance in game management. The latter is ancient enough abroad, but has developed entirely during my life in the United States. Human management was first thought of by Malthus, so far as records go, but it has had little enough notice as I write. I can only reiterate that game has had it unless human management develops. Without management, humans have had it too, which might give the game some satisfaction if they could think that much.

Non-Gallinaceous "Upland" Birds

The two species of "shorebirds" still on the game lists (and one is never on the "shore") only partially fit into my chapter heading. Still, they have to go somewhere.

Woodcock, rather Eastern and only technically a shorebird, have had very intensive biological studies. To the best of my knowledge, however, no one has been very lucid in showing what should be done about them—or, more accurately, what *can* be done, if anything. Jacksnipe (Wilson's snipe) are in the same boat.

These two "shorebirds" have remained numerous enough to stay on the game list. Their future is on the knees of the gods, if I may risk a B.C. quote. Apparently they are more adaptable, or better breeders, or smarter (my guess) or *something*, and thus have been able to partially hold their own.

I well remember when there were perhaps a dozen species of shorebirds that enjoyed an open season. Browsing through files of game laws before 1900 would be historically interesting, even if they showed nothing valuable for the present. At least two species of curlews, two species of yellowlegs, and possibly everything down to sandpipers were listed since I could read. I read a little by 1898. I have eaten yellowlegs and curlews as a child. And I distinctly recall my father mentioning the shorebird season opening in New York on August 15 or maybe 16. The birds petered out and were either off the game list by 1904 or thereabouts, or so scarce they were not worth hunting. Except, of course, the jacks and timberdoodles that are still struggling on.

None of them could be very adaptable, as their environment was too specialized, but those that still exist may continue to make it if we maintain some wilderness and show some population control. If I had a few millions to spend on woodcock and jacksnipe, I would make a frantic effort to use it well. Right now I would not know what to do. I could "study," but studies, though essential indeed, do not produce game in a hostile environment. I do not know how to lessen this hostility. These birds need luck beyond their rather good ability to avoid No. 9 shot.

The *doves and pigeons* are in another category. At least, the white-winged doves, in their Southern environment, and the mourning doves all over, are doing fairly well.

Mourning doves' worst danger may be their proclivity for getting on the songbird list. Their "coo, coo" is indeed musical, and they have been exalted as "a bird of peace." If we can trust King James' translators, a dove was the first creature to leave the Ark.

Doves, though rather dumb, are adaptable. They can nest close to man and get away with it. Controlling cats helps them, but they can get along without much wild land if they have to. Further, though I have never seen over two eggs in a dove nest (and it is a horribly poor nest), those few eggs are very likely to hatch and mature. And three broods a year are not phenomenal if the weather is good.

As long as doves are listed as federal and state game, at least they get some attention. The songbird dove boosters are never logical. One of their commonest plaints is that mourners are the closest relatives of the long-extinct passenger pigeons. The pigeons were not adaptable. They were killed mercilessly, but there is some reason to believe that if none had been taken by man, they would have gone out anyway. At least one leg of the Biological Trinity collapsed—breeding grounds, as a guess. Of course, netting them for the market in millions (repeat, *millions!*) was reprehensible indeed, and guns may have finished them. My father saw a little scud of pigeons light on the dry limb of an oak tree in the fall of 1888. He shot all of them, and never saw another. I saw the dry limb, and have the gun that he used! Which is more history that does not help any.

Whatever little is being done to boost mourning doves, they are getting by under the present limit of ten birds a day and twenty in possession after the first day. Possibly more attention is due on their wintering grounds, about which I know too little. Many drift to Old Mexico, and I understand they are not heavily hunted there.

In spite of expensive ammunition, dove hunting has vastly increased in popularity during the twenty-five seasons I have hunted in Idaho. There were ten dove hunters in 1968 and 1969 to one in 1948. This is all a part of opulence and too many people, admitting neither of these conditions are especially applicable in the Intermountain region. Meat hunters will not bother with them. (My doves cost *at least* $10 a pound, on the hoof.) These situations help the doves. And if some states keep them on the songbird list, so much the better for the rest of us!

In short, doves may do all right if we simply maintain the *status quo*.

—19—

Deer

EVERY OUTDOORS WRITER seems to find it profitable to write about deer, largely whitetails, and many of them deal with management as well as hunting. I have been reading much of this output, since 1900, or at least I did, for maybe fifty years. During my latter life much of it, though by no means all, has seemed a bit repetitious. Thus, I am treading heavily cultivated land. In my harvest section, Part I, I noted that the written instructions on deer hunting varied from excellent to worthless. I cannot be so harsh regarding the management information. Much of it is good enough.

With so much information existing for so long, I will try to be brief, while considering all members of the North American family Cervidae.

Whitetail deer have been given some attention earlier in this volume, and must come first. When Americans think "deer," over half of them think whitetails.

These whitetails are adaptable. They have not been really domesticated because, like our antelope, there was no reason for it. However, though does are gentle, "tame" bucks are dangerous. Not as dangerous as Jersey bulls, but rough enough. When not frightened, wild deer, when hungry, will learn to eat out of a human hand. And safely enough too.

Basically, deer ask comparatively little in order to reach harvestable numbers. I am ignoring situations like Westchester County, New York, where deer roam the bigger rural estates. They are tolerated and charming nuisances. They could scarcely stand shooting, and their numbers are naturally (or artificially) limited by that old Biological Trinity. They are something like the two or three species of deer in London's green belt. These are sort of unconfined zoo animals—of great interest, but not subject to game management.

In general, you have to have a little wild land for deer. With too little wild land and too many farms, deer can damage crops. They can get to be bums, even when there is plenty of wild food, though they never become as obnoxious as human bums.

If deer are getting along quite close to humans, dogs, in deep snow, are a terrible menace. In Wisconsin, in one day in one deer yard, I knew of sixteen deer being run to death. Not a tooth mark was on any animal, but all were dead. Here in thinly populated Idaho, we have also had dog trouble. It can happen almost anywhere.

Another civilization-deer problem is the automobile. I have never hit one, but several have come close. Both whitetails and muleys have missed my front bumpers by not more than inches. Signs may help, but most motorists of all ages are inclined to be immature. Even killing people does not worry some of them especially. However, the fact that a deer is likely to damage the car has some influence. I might note here that cars take a terrific toll of all sorts of wildlife. I do not know what to do about it. If human car deaths start declining, methods that save humans may also apply to game. This is simply a part of the "too many people with too many cars" problem.

I discussed crippling in Part I, and will only briefly mention it here. Good guns and careful shooting are a part of good deer management. If enough people keep forever at it, there are some results.

Another problem compares to the presence of doves and bobwhites on the songbird list: many well-meaning people do not want the beautiful deer shot.

There are places where deer, or anything else, live in such a limited terrain that hunting is illogical. I have already referred to New York's densely populated Westchester County. But a game-management beginner, or even a high-grade moron with some common sense, can size up the deer situation on the average national forest. Without any harvest, the deer can do devastating damage before nature takes over and controls them. Each forest is its own problem. Managers do not always hit proper management methods. You must cut and try. If a deer crop is poor, you can cut down the kill. It is parallel to handling sheep, beef cattle, and hogs, or chickens and bobwhites—but more complicated.

Somewhat like the "song mammal" problem is prohibiting the harvest of does and fawns. Buck laws have their places, but they can work out badly. Pennsylvania had a notoriously bad buck law that took years to repeal. The sex disparity became 30 to 1 or worse. The few bucks that were left covered the territory the best they could, but it was poor enough. Many does went unbred, and breeding habits were eventually so mixed that fawns were being dropped every month in the year. Of course many of these did not have a remote chance to survive.

I hunted in Wisconsin under a buck law, and did not approve of it. The same was true of Nevada, though it involved another species of deer and had some exceptions. However, there are instances where a buck law can have certain merit. The knowledge of conditions and judgment of the managers must determine the management. Usually, buck laws have not worked well and have had to be abandoned.

The holes in these restrictive laws are obvious, but I will mention some briefly.

Most deer hunters will take a buck if they can find one, and the bigger the better. Nonetheless, I have become a meat-deer hunter, and I know others. I look for a fat doe, or a very young buck. I have taken many big bucks, but now leave them for whoever wants them, unless time is getting short and a trophy buck is all that is available. If hunting parties are reasonably big (six or more), it is ethical and presumably legal to swap deer around so that everyone gets what he wants.

It should be noted here that there are managerial differences of opinion as to enforcing (or trying to enforce) a who-shoots-what policy in various states. Idaho, where most of my shooting has been done for twenty-five seasons, tries hard to apprehend anyone who shoots game on another person's license. This is hard to enforce unless an officer sees the violation, and I feel that such observation effort is a poor use of his time. It is parallel to big, strong, well-trained police officers spending time on parking violations.

When I hunted in Wisconsin, the buck law was silly, but the interpretation as to who shot what was liberal. If a party filled out the legal number of tags, that was good enough. As a grimly amusing example, one of my late friends in Park Falls was an old railroad man. He was a good deer hunter, and a good shot with his old .25–35 Model 94. He sometimes went to a cabin owned by the railroad magnates, late in the season, where hunting was good and access only by rail, and shot all the deer—as many as eight in three or four days. The tagholders stayed in the cabin, playing poker and drinking whiskey. Jack (that was not his name) *did* make them get out and help drag in the deer. They needed a little air and exercise! Everyone went home happy, with a nice buck. The local game warden knew what was going on and did not object. Further, a party in camp rated a deer (any kind of a deer) for "camp meat." This one animal could be shot and eaten, untagged.

I feel that this is satisfactory management. Everyone usually prefers to shoot his own deer, or whatever game he is hunting. If he does not, he has paid for his license and his tag, and deserves his deer if he has made a reasonable effort to get it. Of course, things can get a bit thick under these liberal interpretations. Nevada was apparently as liberal as Wisconsin when I hunted there, but I knew one man who was fined for shooting a deer and using his wife's tag. The day he dated the tag, his wife was in the hospital with a one-day-old infant! The investigating game warden thought this was too bold, and I fully agree. Nevada has the most liberal laws of any place we have lived, but those laws are strictly enforced.

I call attention to some of these examples and interpretations because it is good management to make hunters as happy and as successful as you can. A disgruntled hunter may become a lawbreaker. I have emphasized in an earlier chapter that apprehending 5 percent of small-game violators is topflight law enforcement. On big game, smart officers, covering logical territory, should do better than that. Market hunters are the worst menace, and many apprehensions come from tips, but an unhappy hunter does not give tips to his "enemy." A policeman on a routine beat may have to be a bit liberal with his underworld friends if he would net big fish.

Though I have mentioned possible liberal interpretations of deer laws, law enforcement is a *sine qua non* in deer management. If a violator kills twenty and you catch him with one, it is bad enough, and close to average. Deer are sleuthy when hunted, but they cannot hide as easily as cottontail rabbits and ruffed grouse. And a deer is a desirable hunk of meat. Identifying a small piece of meat is possible with long and expensive laboratory testing, but a hair is a simpler method. Grabbing the whole carcass is the desirable result, but an apprehension does not bring back a dead deer. The best law enforcement is preventing the violation. You cannot do anything about the confirmed poacher except keep him in jail as long as you can. However, most hunters are pretty good guys, and maintaining them as good guys is an important phase of deer management.

I discussed the artificial feeding of game in my chapter on wildfowl management, and the same basic principles apply to big game and especially deer. If there are too many deer for the winter food supply, there are too many deer. More should go into the freezing locker, or hang on the wall.

There are exceptions, of course. During an exceptionally hard winter, if deer are starving and you can feed, it is logical to do so. But skill is needed. I have heard a federal specialist in game management state positively that alfalfa hay would poison deer, in this instance, muleys. He was wrong, of course. Both muleys and whitetails can live on alfalfa hay. But it was true that deer were found dead with their stomachs crammed with alfalfa hay, just as a starving man might die from an overdose of T-bone steak. The dead deer got too much hay, and it was a new and different food. I have known a couple of horses to die from overeating ground feed. Whole oats are safer. Horses can also die from too much water when they are too hot. Mules and donkeys do not die from too much feed and water, so far as I know, but they are animal smarties.

I have kept a herd of whitetails going on whole oats, dishing it out carefully so that no deer would get over a pound a day. At the same time I cut trees that could not mature into anything valuable. Two species of birch, aspen, and three species of maple.

Logging can be regulated so there will be an abundance of browse. In New Hampshire, back in the winter of 1916–1917, I helped with a small logging operation in good deer country in Grafton County. Those deer especially liked hemlock browse. They would stand hopefully while we felled a tree, and chew on the top while we were trimming and logging up the trunk. We were also logging some yellow birch and sugar maple, which they liked equally well. They also ate sedge hay that we scattered on the hills to make them less slippery going down. (We were hauling with horses.) It was not very good hay, but we had lots of it and it was easy to haul some out on return trips with empty sleds. None died from eating *that* hay! The deer remained fat and sassy and there was no danger that they would overeat anything.

In winter logging, timber management can easily be coordinated with game management but it demands common interest in both crops. Naturally, a big deer population might build, and if a winter with no logging was planned, a long open season and two-deer limit should precede it.

Where there is little or no snow, nature herself manages to limit populations. Predation is her favorite reduction tool, almost everywhere. Hunters in general, and barber-shop biologists especially, do not like to have deer chewed up by wolves, cougars and coyotes. But unlike feral dogs, the normal predators *usually* just take what they can eat. They take the valuable fawns, but also the old and sick. Predators must not run ragged, but a few may improve the deer herd. We have all but exterminated gray wolves except in Alaska, and it was a mistake. Cougars are scarce enough, and will be discussed later. Coyotes have spread, though overly persecuted in some places. They kill deer, but where I largely hunt in Idaho, there are lots of deer, many coyotes, and fair cougar hunting. Nature has done most of the managing in that Middle Fork Wilderness and Wild River area, and she has done it right well.

Briefly reconsidering dogs, the wild "coydogs" that have become somewhat established in some of the East and Midwest are undesirable indeed. This smart coyote and renegade dog hybrid should be exterminated if it is possible to do so, as presumably it is not. Coyotes and wolves are real dogs, and domestic dogs may get to associating with them. Coyotes will feed their less skilled cousins. But hybrids resulting from this fraternization are dangerous. Mules are about the only truly satisfactory hybrids I know about, including the field of human management. (Some of my friends will resent this view; but while all races may be equal, nature is very careful about mixing them. People can very possibly learn something from wild animals.)

Mule-deer management is not very different than whitetail management. In general, they need more room. Further, though some are bushy enough, they like open country fine, as the whitetails do not. Nor are they as adaptable to human association, with certain exceptions. Possibly muleys have not lived so close to people for so long. In the early spring, I have fed sandwiches to Yellowstone Park muleys out of my hand. Back in 1947–48, we visited Carmel, California, a couple of times. The little Columbian blacktails—pretty much muley small brothers—were all over the landscape. The gardens were fenced to keep them out. I questioned one householder whose garden was enclosed with a 7-foot board fence. He explained that he did not like to see deer looking wistfully through a wire fence! When the gardens were growing there was plenty of deer food, so pillaging them was simply an adaptability habit. The deer made themselves into bums because the opportunity was handy.

Muley range includes most of the remaining coyote and cougar country. Coyotes eat deer when they can get them and are hungry, but rodents and rabbits are their natural prey. Cougars may live on deer, but oddly enough, if you can locate a range where cougars are reasonably common, you will find good deer shooting. This is another provision of nature—we do not understand all the details at present, but we are learning, and we *do* know the results.

The dog menace to muleys is not as common as with whitetails, though it exists. Muleys, when persecuted, will simply get out of there unless the snow is exceptionally deep. Their mobility is great, and their management is thus extensive rather than locally intensive.

This mobility has been a puzzle on my favorite hunting ground in Idaho. On the Salmon's Middle Fork, deer are numerous in the late fall—the later the better, so far as shooting goes. And they pretty well use up the winter food supply, though there has been no starvation I have heard of. In the spring, they get out. I spent much of three summers on the Middle Fork and did not see a deer. Only two were seen by our party in these three seasons. There has been some trapping and tagging to see where they go. This situation is biologically curious, and rates investigation, but may not be important. They leave, but they come back. If they did not come back, it would indeed be a problem. When gone, they may rate some care. No results have been reported so far as I know. The territory looks as good to me for deer in the summer as in the fall and winter, and the elk and bighorns stay. My only positive conclusion is that I cannot reason like a mule deer—certainly not like a Middle Fork deer.

Possibly this stubbornness on the part of game needs further exploration. You will recall the notes on Michigan whitetails who preferred meager living or starvation instead of good living conditions elsewhere.

I have been bragging about Nature's sound laws. No opinions are being reversed, but it is definite that this same Nature has not instructed all of her denizens as well as she might. Most migrations and drifts make sense, to say nothing of the amazing instincts that are displayed, but there is no sense in some types of behavior. Ducks, for example, may be wiped out in some good breeding area. It may go duckless for some seasons while other breeding grounds are crowded. The birds will eventually rediscover the place, and re-occupy it, or they probably will. However, there are other good breeding areas that have never been occupied in any numbers by good game ducks. I have paddled over a thousand miles of Quebec with very few breeding ducks except worthless mergansers. (That is, worthless except for their feathers.) A wild creature that does not like some particular territory does not like it and will not stand it. If moved, he tries to get back home and often dies in the attempt. Or, if he survives, he becomes a non-breeder. In many instances, humans know what constitutes good living conditions for a bird or animal; we have done some importing and exporting and got away with it. But often we could not get away with it. We cannot transmit our superior knowledge to a sometimes adaptable creature. By trying long enough, we may convince some leaders, who will do what we want, and slowly reproduce and populate.

This stubbornness is peculiarly human. Some people who are apparently normal will not accept normal teaching or live under what are assumed to be normal conditions. I will admit, however, that wild animals at least know what they want and try to achieve it, with or without reason and judgment. Off-beat people, however, are often negative; they know what they do not like without knowing what they do want.

I am rather sure that those Middle Fork muleys would be better off if they did not migrate in the spring. If we could argue with them, I am sure they could show no reason for what they do except that they have always done it. It is a situation we have to live with, and do the best that we can.

It may be advisable here to add a word on the possible planting of deer food. This applies especially to mule deer, and to other hoofed game, especially in the dry West. Hoofed game can eat after the snow leaves, and until it gets deep again, barring catastrophies of one sort or another, such as a big fall fire. So winter food, usually above the snow, is essential, and that means browse.

In the damp Midwest, damper East, and the Southeast where snow is rarely severe, winter browse is usually available. Burns, slashes, margins, abandoned farms, and what-have-you are inclined to produce the food. I have already discussed possible artificial feeding emergencies. Further, in these damper areas, game has comparatively little competition from domestic stock. Hogs in the South are an exception—"wild" razorbacks are of course the animals I refer to—and there is evidence that they are being handled better than in the recent past.

In the dry West, a fire can wipe out browse shrubs. Grass comes back swiftly. It may be inferior, like the imported cheat grasses. Still, it comes in. The shrubs and small trees are slow. Browse shrubs in New Hampshire make as much progress in three years as they do in the dry parts of Idaho in twenty. Further, the West has domestic stock competition, which I will discuss further in connection with the bighorn sheep that are most vulnerable to this competition. Thus, browse planting has advantages where it has been reduced because of either catastrophes or bad management. This situation is most important when the precipitation is scant.

Probably bitterbrush is the favorite winter food of mule deer. Deer will stay alive on poorer vegetation, including sagebrush, but I can scarcely imagine anyone cultivating it. Bitterbrush (family Rosaceae, which is a *very* important browse group) has been hard to raise because small rodents preyed on the seed. This has been overcome fairly well. Both our Fish and Game Department in Boise and the U.S. Forest Service are now raising it. I will not elaborate, as methods are changing and improving, but both planting and layering are successful. If deer have plenty of bitterbrush, they are happy. Mountain mahogany (another of the rose family) is also important, and especially for elk. It is equally hard to raise, and the animals may eat it up as soon as it is above snow. The Eastern "white cedar" *(Thuja)* has been exterminated in some places because whitetails love it not wisely but too well.

There are federal, state, and university reports existing and being developed on browse planting. Routine inquiry will permit anyone to get hold of them at little or no expense. (The Superintendent of Documents, Washington, D.C. is suggested for inquiry.)

Among the rest of the deer family, *elk* may be the most important. They are in the type genus *Cervus,* and close indeed to the European red deer. (Or "stags and hinds," in England, or "beasts" in the Scottish Highlands.) Our elk have been satisfactorily crossbred with red deer, though one English authority told me that the hybrids usually had poorer heads than either parent species. The English and Scottish deer I have seen—all under fence—were a little smaller and blockier than elk, with proportionally bigger racks. I saw a skull with something like a total of forty-seven points on the pair of antlers.

Presumably elk were so called by early East Coast settlers because of a seeming resemblance to the Old World elk that is in the genus *Alces,* blood brother to our moose. The best Indian name for our "elk" is wapiti. To be English, our animals should be red deer and elk; to be native American, wapiti and moose. Nothing will be done about it. Taxonomists can change scientific names, but colloquialisms stick. (I know Texans who call large-mouthed bass "trout," but anything can happen in Texas and Alaska, and frequently does.)

Elk ranged across the continent at one time, but they have long since been exterminated in the East. They are adaptable so far as moving around is concerned, and probably could be brought back wherever there is suitable habitat. This is unlikely, however, as farmers hate them.

They eat farm crops, tear down fences, attack hay stacks, and are nobly obnoxious when next door to civilization. I would call Idaho, Wyoming, and Montana the elk states. There is elk hunting in several more, but it seems to be restricted and spotty. You have to have big country for elk. Lacking it, it is logical to have the territory occupied by deer. Elk country is always deer country, but the reverse is not always true.

When uncontrolled by shooting, even in wild country, elk can become a nuisance because of their adaptability to any range. You have probably heard of the much-advertised "elk slaughter" in Yellowstone Park a few years ago when some five thousand were made into meat in one winter. This got too much publicity and was the result of typical federal bungling. Yellowstone is legally set up with no provision for public hunting. Even if some public shooting was in the realm of sound game management (which is open to question) it is impossible in the foreseeable future. If, for example, a Wyoming congressman wrote a bill to permit park hunting, he would be castigated by every organization from the Isaac Walton League to the WCTU.

The National Park Service (or more properly, its predecessor organization) started the trouble originally by exterminating the wolves and cougars. Ranch pressures were partially responsible for this. The buffalo were exterminated except for a few park animals. Cattle came in and wolves took them cheerfully. So they had to exterminate the wolves. The cougars were killed as routine protection from all "varmints." (It is remarkable that a few grizzly bears were spared. No one has told me why.)

With no shooting and no predators but the too-few grizzlies and too-small coyotes, elk proliferated. They spread from their normal elk range into bighorn range, antelope range, and moose range. Unrestricted, they were going to pretty much crowd out the other hoofed park animals, and then pretty much exterminate themselves. The situation was foreseen for years. The superintendent was a nice old bureaucrat who was doing a good routine job, with retirement a few years away. The "book" did not demand elk control. He was not going to risk trouble, so he let it drift.

By the time a new (and courageous) superintendent was appointed, the situation was desperate—a terrific winter kill of everything was only a year or two away. So he ordered the "slaughter." His only error was trying to explain it to the public and the press. Elbert Hubbard's philosophy was: "Never Explain. Your friends need no explanations; your enemies will not believe them."

Various people who should have known better, including some highly placed politicians, made asinine criticisms of this absolutely inevitable elk killing. Their contention was that honest American hunters should have been allowed to do it, but this was against the law; it had to be done by sworn Civil Service full-time Park Service employees. There was no time to attempt to change the law, which probably could not have been changed even if there had been time.

What was needed were some wolves and cougars, but there was no time for that either, and ranchers 500 miles from the Park boundaries would have howled to high heaven (as well as to their congressmen) if such importations had been suggested.

It is just possible that these larger predators *are* coming back in Yellowstone, or have been smuggled in. If smuggled, I am sure that the importers have chosen animals that habitually prey on elk. Otherwise the too-scarce deer and bighorns might suffer. Antelope are too fast and moose too pugnacious for the predators to bother with them if there is anything else to catch. It is my understanding that the proper numbers of Yellowstone elk are now being disposed of every winter. Some are trapped and sent to whoever wants them alive; others are shot with a minimum of publicity.

So you manage elk where there is room to manage them. They can be pastured like cattle or they will browse like deer. They are big, strong, hardy, often magnificent and sometimes obnoxious. They will survive and prosper to some extent where there is wilderness. If, like deer, they can adapt to civilization, civilization will not adapt to them, unless it be a few in a pasture like the English deer parks. They are not universal game.

Moose are more wilderness animals than elk, and are not going to change very much. They are even bigger, stronger, and more magnificent, which is saying something, but they are not as smart. Their management is further complicated by their being so good on the table that poachers will take risks. Further, moose ranges sometimes overlap on elk, and moose in Idaho are killed every year "by mistake." Our Idaho Wildlife Federation posts a handsome reward for anyone who reports an illegal moose killer and assists in his conviction.

There is going to be moose hunting in Canada and Alaska for an indefinite period, as conditions now exist. In the West, there is limited (*very* limited) moose shooting in Idaho, Wyoming, and Montana and possibly a few other states. In Idaho you have to draw lots for a moose hunt, and if you get one you are not again eligible during your lifetime. I drew one on my first try in 1949, but have known people who tried for twenty years without getting a permit.

I do not believe there is any moose hunting in the East or Midwest. I saw moose in the Mt. Katahdin country in Maine in the summer of 1925, and saw moose tracks in Minnesota the last time I hunted deer there in 1939. There are some on Isle Royale off Michigan and should be a few in the north part of all three lake states. And besides Maine, they could get along in the rest of upper New England and New York's Adirondacks. Moose imported from Canada have been known to head back for home, though I doubt that they ever got there.

Moose are the largest deer in the history of the world, including such paleontological records as exist. They also have the heaviest horns, though the long extinct "Irish elk" (a giant fallow deer) had a bigger antler spread. I believe the Irish elk spread record is 9 feet, 3 inches. This seems unbelievable, but I have seen similar mounted heads in the Oxford Museum and the British Museum. The animals themselves were far smaller than moose, however, and seemed out of balance. There is nothing wrong with the balance of a big bull moose. The biggest moose horns come from Alaska, though eastern Canadian records may show heavier bodies. It is not simple to get live weights of moose, or weights of fresh kills. Quarters are easily enough weighed, and the quarters of my 1949 Idaho moose totaled 556 pounds. This was a comparatively big Shiras moose. I would estimate it at just over 1,200 pounds live weight, but I saw far bigger bulls in New Brunswick.

To manage moose you have to have a big, suitable environment, and leave them alone. They are northern animals.

A word may be in order concerning the human fear of moose. You hear all sorts of tales about people being "treed" by them. About 1952 a faculty friend of mine was so treed, close enough for me to hear the moose roaring and him calling for assistance—or possibly enlightenment! An active young man, he shucked off his heavy coat and climbed a convenient tree, with his rifle, which was one of *my* .30–06 Springfields. Of course he could have illegally killed the moose. By the time I got there, the bull had made off, still roaring, and my friend was back on the ground and in his coat.

Bulls, during the breeding season, frequently "make passes" at people and scare them, but there is no record that one ever closed in. They roar and "charge," but sheer off. This has been carefully investigated. I have never heard of a moose really attacking and hurting anyone, but I advise no one to risk being the first statistic! Bull moose act gentle enough except during the breeding season. Then they chase cows (who make little effort to escape) and cheerfully fight other bulls. There have been instances when they "charged" locomotives and came out second best. It is my guess that the charge meant no more than when intimidating a human, but the engines caught them before they sheered off.

Just possibly a cow moose with a very young and very confiding calf could be really dangerous. Several times I have walked to within 50 feet or a bit less of a cow and a young calf. Then the cow's hump-hackles stood straight up, and her unwinking eyes showed a blaze I felt was ominous. At that time of year I never carried a rifle, and the last animal one wants to shoot is any sort of a momma with young. I was dead sure she would come for me if I got closer. Whether or not she would have kept coming when I ran, I do not know and never will. I have been chased by a Jersey cow with a woods-born calf, and a bull who really meant business once ran me out of his pasture. Moose have killer potential. If cattle that have been domesticated thousands of years will attack and kill men who feed them, it certainly shows bad judgment to bait a moose. Because one has never really attacked a person is no reason to be sure it never will.

I will only add a word on *caribou*. They are doing well enough in the wilds of Canada and Alaska, and will continue to do well if roads, airplanes, and pipelines are kept in abeyance. It is probable that there will eventually be a limited caribou hunt in Idaho's Panhandle if they continue to progress as they have in the last twenty years. Maine and Minnesota have also had some, and they could be brought back. They can (and do) live on lichens that nothing else is especially interested in, so food is available. Their impact on game management through the foreseeable future, however, is so slight that there is small reason to dwell on it more than lightly. Caribou (reindeer) can be domesticated, but the wild American species (probably three) are wild-country game that belong far from Main Street. Further, the Barren Ground (and most numerous) animals are migratory. The woodland caribou are more fixed as to range, and Idaho's mountain caribou are rather local. They are spreading slowly, but I have not heard that they really migrate.

—20—

Antelope, Sheep, and Goats

THE NON-DEER UNGULATES (cud chewers) are all Western and all problems.

I consider *antelope* (close to goats) as charming animals that are out on the periphery of game. Like the magnificent African and Asiatic cats, I prefer to watch them and let them live. A good buck antelope, however, has a very beautiful head and rates as a trophy even though the meat is often poor and the hide worse.

Throughout their normal ranges, it is possible to have as many antelope as are wanted, or as many as the countryside will stand. It takes a lot of them to do much crop damage, though they eat anything. In a wandering way, they are as adaptable as whitetails, but they can move so easily that a 25-mile radius for one small band is common enough—that was about the range of some hand-raised antelope we had in Nevada.

Antelope are plains creatures who crawl through fences rather than go over them. They can be high-jumpers, however, as well as long-jumpers. In fact they can do about anything possible to four-footed animals except climb trees!

Antelope are easily driven into rope nets, and can be moved around. When exported to a suitable environment, they "stay put," though if they saw fit to go places, 100 miles a day would be no task.

When alarmed after a shooting season opens they run like fury, and picking up a decent trophy is hard enough. When just hanging around, however, they are very easily poached with a long-range, scoped rifle. Laws must be respected rigidly if you want to maintain antelope. I consider them game, but do not plan to shoot any.

Rocky Mountain goats, which are much nearer to being antelope than goats, have very restricted ranges. At least, their *present* ranges are restricted. They can live on very high mountains with very limited vegetation. When any were lower, they got shot. The best climbers of any American hoofed game, their only defense is to get where hunters or big predators cannot get at them. I have never seen a cougar chase a mountain goat, but in such a contest I would put my money on the goat. Their agility among rocks is incredible.

All that is essential to maintain goats is to maintain wilderness conditions, as wilderness is legally defined, in high country. No roads, no motor vehicles of any kind. The hunter should push his feet to get his goat.

A skin with mounted head used as a "wall rug" is a trophy that is rarely excelled. Goats are easy to take if you can get where they are and locate a good one. The hunt, however, can be the most laborious of anything on this continent.

Bighorn sheep are the last of the ungulates that rate detailed notes. Because good sheep heads (or a series of them) are the most coveted trophies in America (or perhaps in the world) they rate careful attention, and since I have spent more time on them than any other individual species, I can provide it.

Further, and incomprehensibly, our wild sheep have been subject to more mistakes and handicapped by more ignorance than several other game groups combined. There have been several comedies of errors.

With all these comedies (or tragedies), plus innate difficulties in handling them, it is understandable that the sheep ranges have dwindled and that they are in bad enough shape.

Bighorns originally ranged East as far as the Nebraska Sandhills, if the reports I have heard on the so-called Audubon's sheep are correct. They certainly were common along the Missouri Breaks of Montana, and the Dakota Badlands. In the vicinity of Glasgow, Montana, I talked to three different men who enjoyed the dubious distinction of claiming that their fathers killed the last sheep in the Breaks. This occurred not later than 1916. They certainly were long gone when I was investigating that area in 1940 to 1942. It is my understanding that they have been re-imported and are slowly coming back. This is comparatively low country as sheep ranges go.

There were also bighorns in the lava beds of northern California, just off of Tule Lake. The last of them supposedly died in a blizzard back in the last century. I have seen horns that were picked up on a hill called Sheepy Peak.

You will recall my pointing out in Chapter 16 that these comparatively eastern and northern California animals are supposed to be *sub*species of typical bighorns, like the so-called desert bighorn; they are dubbed *Ovis canadensis nelsoni* while *O. canadensis canadensis* is the *typical* species. You will also recall my skepticism about this whole subspecies business. In my view, some Alaskan sheep, and certainly the beautiful white *Ovis dalli*, are different species (whatever a "species" is) but all the others that exist or have existed in the contiguous U.S.A. are the same animals so far as I can make them out. In any case, I cannot for the life of me see differences between the average Idaho sheep and the average Nevada sheep.

I would not have used this space on speciation except for the fact that the Boone and Crockett Club, which officially classifies trophies, lists the desert sheep as a separate trophy animal. On the basis of geography, I will not differ. I *will* differ to the extent that I can pick an animal in Nevada's sheep range, trap it and move it to a band of sheep in Idaho's Bighorn Crags, and once you have taken your eyes off it, you cannot distinguish it from its new associates. Further, if one would make a long-range wager, it would be a good enough bet that desert bighorns will not be recognized as different animals by A.D. 2000, if any are left!

Though I insist that there are little differences between these geographical races of bighorns, breeding seasons are not the same. For the last fifteen years I have been on over-Thanksgiving hunts on the Salmon's Middle Fork in Idaho. Though I have ridden the Middle Fork trails extensively, these consecutive hunts have been near the middle of the river's length, not far from the mouth of Camas Creek. I have been leaving the area from the last days of November to the first couple of December days. Some sheep-breeding activity has been noticed on all of these trips. The outfitters are in agreement that December is the sheep-breeding month. That is three months later than it was for the desert sheep I worked with.

There are apparently considerable differences in bighorn breeding habits in various areas. James Morgan, who is the sheep specialist for the Idaho Fish and Game Department, knows more about bighorns in our state than anyone else I have met. He reports that breeding ewes are inclined to spurn any but big-time rams, and may walk away from any males they feel are secondary. Mr. Morgan is authentic and does not copy his data or do his field work from behind a desk. Contrarily, the sheep he studied have been subjected to some harvest, and an appreciable number of their heads adorn den walls. A big-harem ram in Nevada often had two or three rivals almost his match. The ewes might allow that any of them were proper poppas. Mr. Morgan's sheep (and he has beautiful photographic evidence) showed a greater variation in ram power. Young rams hung around the harems, but they were usually pipsqueak types that did not go over very big with the ewes, and the reasons seemed apparent.

My own experiences with bighorns suggest that they are the most polygamous, or perhaps promiscuous, of any of the ungulates. And they are genuine sheep! An antelope may be a goat and a goat closer to an antelope, but a bighorn sheep *is* a sheep—a far cry from his plebeian domestic cousins, but definitely a sheep.

Bighorn management is a complex problem from the breeding season to the time when a noble head is turned in to the taxidermist. A good lamb crop in Nevada was a fifty-fifty bet, or worse. Wherever one had an opportunity to watch a band of ewes and lambs rather closely, the lambs slowly declined. I know of no record of twin lambs, though it seems logical enough. If a dozen mature ewes produce eight lambs, that would seem to be a fair average. If four of them survived to go into the winter, I would expect nothing better. Occasionally production is better. On the Salmon's Middle Fork, about July 1 in 1959, I saw ten ewes with ten lambs, on the same hillside. I watched them carefully for perhaps two hours. It was a record in Idaho or anywhere else, as far as I know. I diligently looked for the eleventh lamb, hoping for two records! If ten ewes ordinarily had six or seven lambs among them, all around two months old, they were doing well.

I could not find out what happened to the Nevada lambs, nor does anyone anyplace seem to do much better. Surely those imaginary eagles did not get them, and we did not think coyote depredation amounted to anything. A bighorn ewe is a different breed from her domestic sister.

She is strong, smart, courageous, and can fight with either her head or her feet. A canny coyote might sneak a lamb, but he would not survive to sneak very many. I never totally eliminated bobcats as lamb killers, for cats are better among rocks than coyotes, and paired, they might manage the essential strategy. Cougars could of course kill a ewe as easily as a lamb, but they were few in Nevada. The predator hunters (we had them in too great numbers) did not take a cougar in six years, but tracks were not unknown. I saw one track that I am sure was made by a very large cat.

So, without being definite, predators did not appear to be serious killers of bighorns, old or young. Moreover, deer are increasing as big-horns decrease. A ewe will protect a lamb far better than a doe can take care of a fawn, yet the doe generally has two fawns, and she often raises both of them.

Mr. Morgan, in the areas he has studied, blames overgrazing for the sheep deterioration that he feels is going on all over the Idaho ranges. I believe bighorns are increasing a little in the Middle Fork range, but there are no domestic sheep, hunters have to ride 16 miles to get to a base camp, and there is no starvation.

Dr. William T. Hornaday, in his *American Natural History* (1904) was a great admirer of mountain sheep, and felt that domestic sheep diseases were their greatest enemies, possibly excepting hunters and rifles. I am inclined to agree, while pointing out that the hunters are their protectors as well as their killers. In any case, it is certain that bighorns need room, with no grazing competition and especially no competition from do-mestic sheep. Bighorns also need some winter browse, often enough, and prefer mountain mahogany and bitterbrush, but they eat almost every-thing, like domestic sheep. Grasses and weeds are their *real* food. It does not reduce breeding if only full-curl rams are shot, but the seasons should be early. June may be the month in Nevada, early September in Idaho.

There is also the probability that sheep populations go peculiarly up and down like almost everything else, not in short cycles like lemmings and snowshoe rabbits, but still in cycles. Man, too, may be cyclic, and his population has been irregularly going up since the Plague Year. I feel sure that this population curve will turn down materially by A.D. 2000 at latest. There are several methods to force this turndown, of no importance except to presume all living organisms are subject to the same natural laws. These laws may demand the extermination of any organism that has been unable to compete. Bighorns are touchy in this category. They can be domesticated after a fashion, and are being hy-bridized with domestic sheep; hence we may get a woolly hybrid that is much more independent than our silly domestic varieties of sheep. Domesticated thousands of years ago, farm sheep rate some pepping up by their wild cousins, and may get it.

Even to an optimist, however, the wild-sheep situation is precarious. I hope they will make it, but risk no predictions.

A final thought suggested by this bighorn situation can apply to any sort of wildlife, big or little, in any environment, but is especially applicable to public lands.

As far back as 1925, when I was teaching in Syracuse at the State College of Forestry, we read many accusations that public lands were being overgrazed. It had to be true, as they still are. The worst I have seen are or were in Utah. Some Eastern extremists felt that no domestic stock whatever should be permitted to run on National Forest lands. That was an unsound view. Grazing diminishes the fire hazard, and dry lightening storms, igniting grass, start the most embarrassing blazes on the widest fronts. National Forest grazing can produce a lot of beef and mutton at low cost without reducing game. It takes a little doing, but the Forest Service knows how. However, while there is less politics than in the past, there is nevertheless considerable overgrazing. And it especially affects game that largely live on grass—sheep.

Domestic stock should be (and can be) so managed that game can be produced in *maximum* numbers on public lands. No one complains about too much game unless it attacks crops raised by man. A ton of game meat is just as nutritious as a ton of domestic meat, and far cheaper to raise. And the public owns the game as well as the land. One who borders on this public land has privileges he can easily use, but he also takes a calculated risk. Yet I suspect that a single individual, with capital for travel, publicity, television time, and clerical help, could get laws passed totally prohibiting domestic stock from grazing on Forest Service land. The laws would be foolish, but they would not be the first foolish ones!

—21—

Carnivorous Game, Fur-Bearers, and Small Game

MUCH OF THIS chapter involves simple solutions that are often hard to put in practice.

Bears may be the most important of the game animals under this heading. Certainly they are rather spectacular.

Black bears are valuable. Aside from sport, they provide excellent meat, and often pretty skins. They should be removed from the "varmint" lists, where some are mistakenly placed. They rate an open season at the same time as deer. They should have tags like deer. One bear should usually be the season limit for each hunter. Truly enough, bearskins are at their best and meat at its worst in the spring right after hibernation, but the risk of taking sows with cubs later on is too great.

Bear trapping should be prohibited, but running with hounds is all right if the dogs do not get side-tracked on deer. A few states do or recently did permit deer hunting with hounds, the excuse being that it is the only way to get any. However, the hounding of any species of game animal deserves careful attention.

By fall, cubs are independent. Few would shoot a cub—they are too cute—but I do not know that they rate special protection. It is a local matter.

Occasionally bears do damage. They kill pigs or sheep. A bad bear is bad enough, and owners of domestic animals should have a right to protect their property; financial reimbursement is not enough. Dog taxes were presumably devised to reimburse for sheep killing, but for all that, dogs pretty well ran the sheep business out of New England and New York. My grandfather raised some sheep almost a century ago, and dog protection was too much trouble.

So, for bears and any protected carnivores, something must be done to protect stock from them, or pay well for the damage.

No other American bears except the Alaskan browns may rate an open season. Grizzlies should be rigidly protected unless they are killing stock (or people). Possibly Alaskan grizzlies rate an open season along with the brownies. I am physically afraid of grizzlies. When in one of the grizzly-ornamented National Parks, and away from the highways, as I usually am, I am rather likely to be lugging a handgun not lighter than a .45 automatic. I know how to keep away from grizzlies, I hope, but they have attacked and killed people who were leaving them alone. If one attacked me, I would try to survive. If I got arrested, that would be that. One can defend himself in court but he cannot do much about it if he is dead.

For the present, I am violently opposed to any open season on polar bears. We should give them room and leave them alone.

Cougar management is almost identical to black bear management, except that cougars are now in worse shape. There should be no trapping, but running with dogs in the winter is permissible. Treed cubs or pregnant females should be left in the tree. Cougar hunting with dogs is almost the only method, because the cats are too sleuthy to be seen very often when hunting other game.

Canadian *lynxes* and *bobcats* seem to be holding their own. They rate a season along with other fur-bearers.

Outside of Alaska, our *wolves* are gone excepting a few on Isle Royale, and further excepting a few red wolves in the South. Though wolves are big, strong, intelligent creatures that can be destructive, they should not have been cleaned out of any of the big parks, federal or state, and some should be judiciously brought back. Our ancestors lived with wolves for thousands of years, and I am unwilling to admit that they were any smarter than we are.

Coyotes rate control, but it has been overdone. I have heard that there are some wild ones living in every state except Hawaii, but including

Rhode Island and Delaware. Within the past ten years a friend in New York had an appointment at Columbia University about 8:15 a.m. It was December, and just daylight. He was a bit early, and he spotted a coyote trotting across the Morningside Heights campus. He watched it briefly, and it sat under a spruce tree as the early-class students erupted. Some passed within thirty feet, but if they saw the animal, of course they thought it was a wandering dog.

Crossbred "coydogs" and all uncontrolled dogs can do very serious damage, and should be exterminated if there is any way to do it. Poisoning is out, except for rats or other destructive rodents. Trapping is logical, but coyotes do not like to be trapped and are otherwise pretty smart. Of course, anyone who has never heard a coyote "sing" has missed great music. It is third to the wolf's howl and the loon's wail, but still very fine. There is still room for coyotes in the Great West. This is especially true if there is room for even one on the Columbia campus!

Coyotes are natural rodent hunters, and in Montana I saw the most asinine coyote control. Federal predator hunters trapped coyotes in prairie-dog towns. The coyotes came there only to catch "dogs." When the coyotes were cleared out, the hunters had to go after the prairie dogs and other rodents. At the time, I was working for the U.S. Fish and Wildlife Service. Our Refuge Division was dedicated to the saving of animals; our Predator and Rodent Control Division was dedicated to killing them!

I carry no torch for most rodents. The common rat is the world's most destructive mammal, and we should be careful indeed about killing animals that largely live on those destructive rodents. Coyotes may be the Number 1 rodent killers. There is the occasional "bad" coyote, but proportionally more "bad" humans, and it is poor judgment to condemn a whole animal species because a few are delinquent. At one time the civil-service predator controllers were given "credit" for the numbers of the animals they took. Easy-to-get pups rated as high in the front office as did the most arrogant sheep-killers. A hunter might be far more valuable if he spent a month to get one "bad" animal.

Ignoring the rodent situation for now, one of the most important big-time management improvements would be to eliminate federal predator control totally. One or two of my Idaho State University graduates are in this division, and are too good to be thus employed. If they were turned loose on domestic rats, I'd be all for it. A century ago, professional "wolvers" had some values. They are a menace at the present time.

The rest of the carnivorous furbearers vary from rating total protection to being a nuisance.

The *wolverine*, possibly the largest American weasel, has been almost exterminated. In twenty-five years, I have heard of two in Idaho, and one of them was killed. They are now protected, if there are any to protect. Still, if there is any animal totally "bad," perhaps *Gulo luscus* is it. I have known a couple of professional Ontario fur trappers who had to compete with wolverines on trap lines. If one got on the line, he had to kill it or get out. For all that, these magnificently despicable creatures rate something better than extermination. They can be saved in Alaska and parts of Canada. The wolverine's scientific name, incidentally, translates "one-eyed glutton." The specimen responsible for the name had only one eye (a fighter!), and the classical name for "glutton" was the result of a translated Indian name that meant the same thing. Further, wolverine fur sheds frost better than anything else known.

Sea otters, also gigantic weasels, were almost exterminated by fur hunters, among whom the Japanese are said to have been the most savage. Some have come back off Alaska, and also off the Monterey section of California. I have heard that fishermen are clamoring for their blood. It is just possible that federal management may permit some sea-otter harvest, parallel to the limited seal "fisheries." Seals will hold their own if the Japanese can be controlled. And the otters can be built up to perhaps match them.

Land otters are also in rather precarious shape. They are very smart animals and one of the hardest to trap. That has perhaps saved them from extinction in some places. There are comparatively few places in the U.S. or Canada where open seasons on otters are justified.

Otters are fascinating as well as beautiful. They are also, apparently, not hard to domesticate. When I was stationed in Winona, Minnesota, a gentleman named Emil Liers, in the neighboring village of Homer, raised and sold otters. They were as gentle as setter puppies. Mr. Liers had a couple of otters that would dive off the bow of his skiff, catch fish, and bring them to him. They also retrieved ducks, like a spaniel.

Though they are fish eaters, otters feed on any sort of water creatures they can catch, and that takes in considerable territory. They especially like crawfish. Slow breeders, and never abundant anywhere, it is doubtful if they ever measurably diminished game or food fish.

Otter fur is the most durable of any that exists, according to the old *Peterson's Index*. That refers to the unplucked fur. When plucked, it is very similar to plucked beaver, but shorter—about plucked Alaskan seal length. One needs to know a little about fur to appreciate *un*plucked otter. It is beautiful in either condition. Further, if a high-school girl is able to scrounge some otter fur, her grandchildren may be wearing it with pride. Like the lace on grandma's wedding gown, it is not going to lose style.

For all of this, otter fur may be forced out of style in order to save them. My wife has a very fine otter cape with a muff and Russian-style cap to match. Though the fur has breath-taking beauty, I prefer my otter skins to encase the live animals, and I especially enjoy watching them rear half out of water (and half an otter looms fairly high) as they study an admiring human. When I was stationed as a seasonal ranger on Yellowstone's isolated Shoshone Lake, one summer an old otter and two half-grown pups played around rather frequently. They occasionally swam close to camp. Sometimes they cut across our canoe route. They should exist in the parks, but may not otherwise without meticulous care.

The other famous big fur weasels are the fishers and martens (sables). Both have been experimented with in captivity. They *can* be raised, but the costs are prohibitive. Both have very peculiar breeding complications. A fisher's gestation period is close to a year, and the fertilized ovum is dormant for months before it grows perceptibly. The martens are similar but the gestation period is shorter.

Fishers (apparently the name came from some sort of a crude Indian translation) do not necessarily do much or any fishing. Like otters, they eat anything catchable. Of course they swim well, but unlike mink and (especially) the otters, they are not water animals. They have been exterminated in most of the U.S., short of Alaska. When I was on the Chequamegon National Forest, 1933 to 1935, I knew of one fisher that had been caught in Wisconsin since the turn of the century, though there were still some in Minnesota at that time. Gone in Idaho, there have been some importations from Canada. Fishers (believe it or not) kill porcupines and manage to survive the process. Perhaps some are eventually done in by quill infection, but it takes considerable doing. In the more isolated timber areas of the West, enemy-less quill pigs do much damage. Their quills also kill valuable animals. In 1916 I saw a fox that died from quill infection, and I found a bighorn ewe in Nevada dead from a similar cause. Porcupines were rare in that part of Nevada too.

I have not heard how the Idaho fisher plant is succeeding, if at all, but I hope it is successful. Trapping them was not prohibited until all were gone, but limited harvest could be possible; good fur animals should rarely be permitted to die of old age. Few bigger predators would tackle a fisher. One of the very big weasels (up to 20 pounds), he is a scrapper.

Fisher fur is of fox or skunk length, and has its own brand of beauty. After keeping an eye on them for perhaps a decade, I picked up four good fisher skins that my wife now sports in the form of a "shrug." Prices went down because the animals went off the market. About 1920 in "Down East" Canada, I saw good raw skins sold for $120 each. Of course, mere man cannot understand styles of any sort, and fur styles least of all. This has advantages, as it gives the animals a chance to catch up. It also gives anyone who likes fur a chance to pick up bargains when the demand is down.

Good fur is always good fur, as far as the public goes. This because that public has not taken the trouble to learn much about it. The couturiers set the styles, and the fur-retailers follow them. Good furriers give customers an honest deal, though all good fur and even some that is not so good runs into money. There have been overly sharp furriers who will overcharge or sell fake stuff when they can. It pays to patronize the best dealers, or get information from someone with a little background.

A smaller and more beautiful cousin of the fisher is the *marten*, or sable if one would make like an aristocrat. The Russian (more properly Siberian) sables of top quality produce the world's most valuable furs. I have read that some of the most elegant ladies crave Russian sables when they have become tired of mink!

I have noted that martens are very easy to catch. They are primarily tree animals, and red (pine) squirrels are their favorite food. A marten may take a squirrel in a stern chase, and I assure you that a squirrel traveling for his life can really travel.

Also slow breeders, martens must be trapped with the greatest precision, or they are gone. However, they seem to cheerfully go into any kind of a trap. In Quebec, in the fall of 1916, I saw one. He was a spring kit that had been caught in a rabbit snare. He got one snare around his neck and broke it, wearing it like a collar. He got his front legs through the next one, and the guide, who was taking young rabbits for the pot, found him alive and unhurt. Of course he was released in the hope of being caught in November, as he probably was.

While on the Chequamegon in Wisconsin, I got one record of a marten. A smart little girl spotted it, and the identification was positive. (In fact, bright children from about nine to twelve or thirteen make the most reliable nonscientific observers that I know about. When older, they may not lose any observational ability, but frequently their interests change.)

The big parks form the best marten preserves. Around Yellowstone, it is not unusual for one to drift through a camp. Most tourists do not have the most remote idea what they are. I saw one, about 1952, on the Targhee National Forest just southeast of Yellowstone Park, that was unbelievably large—fox size! My very knowledgeable horse spotted him first. Then I saw him drop from an aspen onto a large rock. He eyed me for some seconds while I marveled at his dimensions. Then we both went on to take care of our respective affairs. If this animal did not get into the park, he probably was skinned the next winter.

From that general area a few years back, I picked out the four best skins among a catch of some fifty martens. The trapper's proximity to the park was his only reason for getting that many, but they are not uncommon in the more remote woods of Canada.

I will largely ignore *skunks*, except to repeat that, on the Upper Mississippi Refuge, skunks get snapping turtle eggs and the turtles got ducks. Skunks produce good fur that goes up and down in value. When in high school and somewhat earlier, I always caught a few from November to when they "holed up" into semi-hibernation. A good black one was worth a dollar. If I got a dozen and they averaged 75¢ each, I was doing right well. Skunk oil sold for 50¢ a pint! It was supposed to be good for arthritis, or "rheumatism" as it was largely miscalled. It was actually used internally for a "cold"!

Skunks are on Idaho's varmint list, but seem to survive in both the big black and little striped (civet cat) species. They have been farmed some, and of course make affectionate pets. A veterinarian can take out a skunk's scent glands in minutes. I have even seen one pet skunk that was not de-secented, which never gave any trouble. Most dogs give these pets a wide berth. It is instinctive distrust. Of course a de-scented skunk is helpless against any enemy.

Skunk scent is an important perfume fixative. Now that deer musk and ambergris are so scarce, its value may be greater. However, as a normal part of the rural landscape, they are odorless if you leave them alone, as you usually do. I do not mind their scent unless it is so thick that I can taste it.

Wild mink still exist as important fur animals, and get along with a sensible open season. They are somewhat adaptable. A farmhand working for one of my uncles caught one in a rat trap set under the corn crib. It was winter, and of course the mink was skinned. Commendably enough, he had left a nearby stream and was hunting rats. But mink will kill chickens, as will skunks.

Some years ago, a man in New York City was apprehended while catching mink in Van Cortlandt Park! He was running his traps at night and making a winter living at it. He had an out-of-city summer job. This got into the papers, because once the authorities caught him, they didn't know what to do about it. Shooting was illegal, and so was fishing, but he was trapping! Of course a new municipal ordinance was swiftly passed.

Mink are far from dumb, but not especially hard to catch. If I found one's line of travel, I usually got him on his next trip. Occasionally one would blunder into a muskrat trap, when he, like myself, was after the rats. When I was young, a mink was minor wealth. I never sold one for less than $1.50 and often got twice that, admitting that I did not often get a mink!

Mink, of course, are now largely "farm" animals, for mink is one fur species that has stayed popular. Though there are many mutation colors, many prefer the dark wild ones, so they are not going to be exterminated.

True *weasels* (ermine or stoat) are still in the market and somewhat popular, but scarcely worth catching and skinning in the U.S.A. (When Queen Elizabeth II was crowned, I believe she wore a standard ermine robe, though many of the accompanying grandees had to settle for white rabbit fur.) "Summer ermine" is good fur, but I doubt if it is caught in the summer. (Weasels did not always turn white in southern New York.) Incidentally, the big New York weasel is one of the best and biggest, and ranges far from New York. The least weasel would scarcely be there if he was any smaller! I believe his fur is all right, but he is mole size.

While of course the weasel family produces the finest furs, the rodents manage the most square yards (or square miles) of it. *Muskrats* are the most numerous, and produce fine fur. By my standards, they furnish the best reasonably priced fur, if any can be called reasonably priced. Sometimes dubbed "stenographer's mink," it is presently popular when "let out" and blended to resemble mink. Still, muskrat is good enough fur to just rate as muskrat.

"Rats" vary somewhat in size and differ geographically. The last figures I saw listed Louisiana as the best muskrat state, producing far more dollars' worth of pelts than any other state. Alaska, because of its latitude, produces the best fur, but not the most of it. Further, southern muskrat skins are light and drapy.

The biggest muskrats I have personally seen came from New York's Montezuma Marshes. They were thick-skinned and very durable. I also saw some big ones out of Tule Lake, California, where I personally handled 65,000 skins. Primarily a waterfowl refuge, this area produces a lot of fur.

Muskrats are adaptable, and will do well where their habitat is not drained out. Mink are their worst predatory enemies, as a mink can go right into a rat lodge or burrow. A muskrat is a true rat and a fighter, but he has no chance against a mink.

Muskrats are somewhat cyclic, and open seasons should vary somewhat. Again if you will recall our suggestions as to "rat" influence on waterfowl marshes, their incidental usefulness should determine the season. Spring skins are the best. The numbers will be less, however, as there is some winterkill and some mink predation. Further, skins are top value and the animals easiest to catch during the spring breeding season. At that time the rats are at their scrappiest, and may tear up an animal in a trap unless the set is such that he drowns. If other things are remotely equal, I do not like any sort of wildlife harvest during a breeding season. Contrarily, muskrats in a suitable environment can scarcely be exterminated. Barring the cycle, there always seems to be plenty of breeders. They build up fast.

The other really important American fur rodent is of course the *beaver*. He is pretty much an overgrown muskrat except for his differently shaped tail. The beaver's tail is of less use in forward swimming but very valuable in diving and for signaling.

Beaver fur fluctuates in value as does most other fur, but it is fine fur and scarcely ever really out of style. Usually it is plucked, and from a distance resembles the shorter plucked otter. (Plucked raccoon fur also resembles plucked beaver, though a touch reveals the difference.)

At the turn of the century, beaver in my native New York were close to extermination. Under some protection, they were brought back to minor commercial importance. While I was teaching at Syracuse, some $20,000 worth of raw skins were produced each year. Similar improvements were common all over the U.S. and Canada.

Unlike muskrats, beaver are easy to exterminate. Their work is conspicuous, and they are easy enough to trap (though hard to hold unless they are swiftly drowned, which is also not difficult).

Further, some harvest or control is essential, as they will eat themselves out of a home. My considerable experience with them shows that they demand the willow family, Salicaceae, for food. The poplars, and especially aspens, are favored. They are happy enough, however, with any *Populus* or any *Salix*. There are other things that they eat with some interest, including red asier dogwood. When their regular food gets scarce, however, they move. Sometimes downstream, sometimes crosscountry. Possibly they know where they are going, perhaps not. In any case, they may not arrive. A beaver is a lummox on land, easily caught and picked up by the tail. Sometimes they fight, and I assure you that a beaver can bite, but they are easy to tame. A kitten beaver is a cuddly creature who is something of a trial when he crawls out of the creek and onto your lap!

When in Syracuse, 1924 to 1928, I had occasional business in Westchester County near Briarcliffe Lodge. Some of the wealthy estates were on streams and maintained half-domestic beavers, though I did not see them picked up or petted, for they are very dampish pets at best. The shrubbery had to be carefully fenced and the trees protected by heavy wire screens. In the surrounding wooded hills, however, there were plenty of aspens. Once or twice a week, a long-suffering chauffeur or gardener would be sent to the woods for a station-wagon load of aspens for beaver bait. Even the boss or his son might help! The chopping was crude but they managed to get results. The beavers would all but climb on the wagon if they were hungry, as they usually were. I did not ask if they got permits to kill some if they were too numerous, and I never saw or heard of similar beaver-baiting elsewhere. It was very amusing, and some of those people maintained whitetail deer, on a small scale, on the same estates. Money has its advantages, and this sort of small-time game farming has my approval. Some California suburbs treasure coyotes for their music, admitting they eat the occasional pet cat! At times suburb animals may help to repopulate their surroundings. Perhaps where there is nothing except urbia or suburbia, game management must be there or totally lacking.

Foxes are usually protected as fur producers or sport animals. Adaptable as well as unbelievably intelligent, they will survive with little attention except for a routine open season. (Perhaps four months after mid-October is a season to consider.) Occasionally they can be destructive, and my Chapter 10 under the harvest section mentions long-gone fox bounties in New York. However, foxes are rarely "bad" as to either domestic stuff or game birds, though castigated as both quail and pheasant killers. Thus exterminating foxes over whole counties—and they can be exterminated—does not increase the game birds. Game birds have lived with foxes longer than they have with humans, and much more happily.

Raccoons and opossums likewise vary from valuable sport animals to varmints. 'Coons are in the latter category in Idaho, but are sharp enough to hold their own if the environment is suitable. (In fact, some survive in very unsuitable terrain.) As fur, meat, and sport animals, they rate a fall and early-winter hunting and trapping season. A raccoon, though a smart animal, is as easy to trap as a fox is not. Their range has spread and they get on just outside of suburbia or even in it.

While we are dealing with valuable fur animals, a word on imported *nutrias* is essential. Though their fur approaches beaver in quality, they were a mistake. I have not looked up recent figures, but it looks as if they are here to stay in the swampy South, and maybe they can successfully drift into colder marshes. My only suggestion is that we should eradicate them if we can.

Cottontail rabbits are the most numerous American game animals, and are likely to stay that way. They adapt. A nest of cottontails was successfully reared on the University of Michigan campus when I was doing some graduate work there. They were in a very small patch of shrubbery. Many dogs were blundering around, and there were some cats, but the bunnies made it. Rabbits have some cyclic variations, but less than their true-hare cousins, the snowshoes and jacks. (An Englishman might say that our cottontails *are* hares, and that only the genus *Cuniculus* should be called rabbits, but that is more systematic folderol!) We will continue to have some rabbit hunting with no management except an October to late winter season. Sometimes it is safe to hunt them through February.

Game *tree squirrels* are parallel to rabbits in management, though obviously you need food trees, and home trees. All the nut and acorn trees, blue beeches ("hornbeams") and most fruit trees help support squirrels. Crude timber management, where there are some dead and hollow trees, is a further advantage.

Gray and fox squirrels are tame in parks. Our parklike campus harbors many fox squirrels and some are in my back yard. But they can get wily indeed when hunted. And they are even better eating than cottontails. All they need is food, timber, and a fall open season.

There is no open season on tree squirrels in much of the West. Idaho has no really wild tree squirrels except the little reds (chicarees). I am rather sure these park fox squirrels cannot take to the real woods. Tree squirrels plant coniferous trees and feed martens, reasons enough to protect them. So squirrels are primarily Eastern, Midwestern, and Southern game animals. I like to hunt them in the proper environment, but I doubt if the average Westerner, or reformed Easterner like myself, would bother with them even if they were legal in the West and numerous enough to be worth hunting.

—22—

Enforcement Problems

UNDER EVEN REASONABLY civilized conditions, laws and law enforcement are essential. Sadly, game laws, like traffic laws, are highly technical and easy to break. Too many do not worry about ignoring regulations if they get away with it. Some people are conscientious; others are like the medieval monks whom Boccaccio cited as following the doctrine, "A sin concealed is half forgiven."

Though I have never worked exclusively or even largely on law enforcement, I have given it considerable attention. For about a dozen years as a federal biologist, I was also a federal law-enforcement officer. At the same time I had authority in six different states, and right now I am an *ex-officio* Conservation Officer in Idaho as well as a Bannock County Deputy Sheriff. Many law violations are petty and dull, but big cases can be lively enough. Many young men trained professionally in game management have to spend some time as a game warden, and the experiences do them no damage.

Unfortunately, perhaps, the first gesture toward game management is usually to pass laws restricting the taking of certain game species.

I know men in Idaho who recall, if not the first game laws, at least the first gestures toward their enforcement. In my native New York, I was a big boy before I ever heard of anyone being arrested for a game-law violation. (That chap was not convicted, though I knew he was guilty as charged.) So, in this country, game-law enforcement is relatively new.

Probably the passing of laws never saved any game, fish, or fowl from extermination. Still, laws are important. They even scare some people into not hunting at all! When I was a biologist on the Upper Mississippi Refuge, the duck bag limit was generous enough, but there were species restrictions. The totals of canvasbacks, redheads, buffleheads, and ruddies were restricted to perhaps four in aggregate and not over one of each, and there was no open season on wood ducks. On some public shooting grounds, wood ducks were very numerous. Also easy to shoot. And these hunters never knew their ducks.

Most ducks are not hard to identify. If a hunter is within reasonable scattergun range, he should be able to spot the species, often the sex, and sometimes the approximate age of a duck. Even their voices give them away. A female redhead is the hardest duck to spot on the wing as I see it. Adult drake redheads shout their identity, but their wives might have inspired Gertrude Stein to write eccentric duck verse. It could have started: "A duck is a duck is a duck is a duck." If you see a duck and are sure it is nothing else, call it a female redhead and charge it against the redhead limit if you collect it. (Probably you will, as redheads are not very bright.)

Most states dispense beautiful colored brochures identifying ducks, for not over four bits. Hunters should have this descriptive literature in some form. Then, when hunting, they should also call the species before they shoot. Game-management majors should learn their species either in the laboratory or the swamp. I once saw a federal game warden call a merganser a canvasback, and it could have caused him embarrassment if his audience had been a canny hunter instead of an indulgent biologist. Nor did I correct him directly, though I took pains to see that his immediate superior worked to improve his knowledge. That suggests the importance of judgment. Not that I was necessarily right, but it is my own belief that humiliation usually should be avoided. Further, following the same train of thought, it is possible that it is better to educate a slightly erring hunter than it is to arrest him. There are instances when a law-enforcement officer fails to bear down on a minor technicality and makes a friend. If he makes an arrest and gets a conviction, he may have created a departmental enemy for a half-century. Game departments need friends.

Enemies are especially irksome because game-law violations are hard to detect. Further, judges frequently do not like their dockets cluttered with what they consider minor nuisance cases. Naturally, judges may need educating, and some are slowly gaining.

One of the best federal officers I ever knew claimed that it took exceptional personnel and organization to apprehend 5 percent of the game-law violators. He was primarily concerned with waterfowl at Tule Lake, California. In general, countrywide, my educated guess suggests that not over 2 percent of small-game violations are picked up. Big-game violators, and especially market hunters selling deer and elk carcasses, run bigger risks. The contraband is bulky, and dealers (we really want to arrest those dealers!) may "squeal" on their hunters to get their own penalties reduced.

If poaching hunters are smarter than "the law," they may never get caught. About 1951 I saw something of the most notorious game-law violator I ever even heard about, and that takes in considerable territory. He was old and we will call him Uncle Dick. He is dead, and I will not mention his name or exact location, but it is essential to note that he lived in Idaho, not far from the Wyoming boundary. I could have arrested him myself for illegal game possession in one instance. His general guilt was great, but this particular offense was trivial, and peculiarly enough, he never actually did any material damage. (In fact I could write a chapter entitled "Game Management by Poaching," but such a piece belongs more logically in one of the sporting slicks.)

Uncle Dick was telling me something about his elk poaching. He raised a big family and they ate elk meat regularly for thirty (maybe forty) years, twelve months a year. I asked him if he had killed five hundred elk during his life. He promptly answered: "More than that." When I asked if he had killed a thousand elk he hesitated a bit, did some finger counting, and said "I might 'uv."

His position was strategic. All his neighbors knew about his violations. He never sold meat, but if some friend needed some, he cheerfully donated a quarter. If he ran out, he shot more. The local conservation officer knew about it too, but he was an Idaho officer and Dick did his poaching in Wyoming. Besides, there were too many elk in that part of Wyoming. I have mentioned that a few years ago the Yellowstone authorities quite properly butchered five thousand elk to prevent serious winter killing. These were really part of the same gigantic elk horde that wanders around Yellowstone and Grand Teton National Parks. If there had been, through the years, some twenty-five Uncle Dicks in operation, that famous "elk slaughter" might not have been essential.

In short, an Idaho resident was poaching outside of Idaho, and the Idaho officers did not bother about it. Not that they would admit it. There is small reason to admit anything that might get you criticized! But I know they could have had him on illegal possession, because I could have had him myself. These regular officers had other fish to fry, and so did I. Pinching the old boy would not have changed him any. He would have continued his violating as soon as he got out of jail. The Wyoming authorities hunted him years on end, but he was smarter than they were and always stayed a jump ahead. As soon as he slid back over the state line, they lacked jurisdiction. Or just possibly, being intelligent men, they were equally aware that there were too many elk, so they also fried other fish. If Uncle Dick violated on federal land (as he did) I am sure that federal officers, who could ignore boundaries, might have apprehended the old rascal if they had really tried. If I had been one of those federal officers, and had been specifically ordered to bring Uncle Dick in, that would have been that. Otherwise, I would have been somewhere else when he went on a foray across the border. Of course I would also have taken pains not to be caught being somewhere else!

This old poacher also took the occasional deer, and it was on deer I could have taken him on a possession charge. Possibly he took moose, since he was utterly incorrigible as far as game goes. Moose are relatively scarce and easily identifiable, and I would arrest my favorite grandmother if she took one illegally, under the citizen's-arrest code if I had no other authority.

Enforcement officers in the field are theoretically not supposed to rely on their own judgment. At least that is how I have been instructed. Judgment is for a judge, or a jury. Practically, it does not work that way. I could write page after page citing instances where field judgment promoted law and saved friends. Laws are passed by elected officials who are broadly competent and mean well, but they rarely know about field enforcement problems. Thus I insist that both state and federal game departments can be made or broken by law enforcement in the field. Judgment must not be confined to the courtroom.

Interestingly enough, during my years as a federal biologist I never heard of any crookery in federal game-law enforcement, though it was possible, in connection with waterfowl bootlegging. The federal men I knew and heard about were honest. I have mentioned one who should have known his ducks and did not, but he would not have been bribable. One smart young federal man arrested a U.S. Supreme Court Justice! This was years ago, when "duck stamps" were relatively new. The old legal eagle did not have one and did not know that he needed it. Since he had always borne down on the principle that ignorance of the law was no excuse for breaking it, he went into federal court and paid his minimum fine like a little man.

This case caused considerable comment as well as amusement in the U.S. Fish and Wildlife Service where I was employed. I sat in on a discussion that included a couple of very competent enforcement men, each with thirty years' experience. They thought that the young man should have turned the justice loose, insisting that he immediately go to a post office and buy a stamp, sending him (the game warden) an affidavit that the stamp had been bought, and the place and date of the purchase. He should of course have reported this action to his immediate superior, explaining that if more drastic action was needed, the superiors should carry it on, since this justice was well identified.

I agreed with these old-timers. If it had been my problem, I do not know what I would have done. Law men, in the field, unlike judges and jurors, lack the time to ponder, or perhaps search the libraries. Sometimes there is violence. The officer does not have even a second to decide what may be self-defense and what may be brutality. He lugs a gun as well as a badge. Lone federal game men have been killed by waterfowl bootleggers, though in pairs they have all survived, so far as I recall. I knew one loner who had been shot twice, in two different fights. He shot his way out with his left hand when his right was crippled. He was shot in the stomach the other time and narrowly escaped death. After that, he was very cautious! He slept with one light handgun, usually carried a heavy handgun, and kept both a shotgun and a high-power rifle in his car. When I knew him he had been transferred from this extremely dangerous anti-bootlegging assignment, but his caution did not relax. His ambidexterity and deadly shooting saved him twice, though he admitted some luck. One never knows when luck will run out.

I avoided fights in my law-enforcement days, but a couple of times it was a near thing. It is axiomatic that violence should be avoided, but it is equally axiomatic that a violator must not be permitted to escape. The law must meet violence with more powerful violence. I feel that this is true in all fields. As I write there have been recent campus disorders, though not in our well-administered establishment. And I am writing during what could be one of those "long, hot summers" in the metropolitan ghettoes. Possibly laws in general and game laws in particular are necessary evils. If so, they are still necessary. I repeat that game laws may never have saved anything from extermination, but no one will doubt their usefulness. If law enforcement breaks down, everything breaks, everywhere. Sure there are errors, since law men, like others, are humans. We have to eliminate what errors we can and be educated to support the laws, or change them.

Since game management is influenced by a multitude of human viewpoints, its legal aspects may rate certain exploration because of existing lawless tendencies. As I write, there has been a spate of rioting and complaining over two or three years, and law enforcers, both civil and military, have been enjoying little popularity among a small but noisy minority. Game-law enforcement has not increased in difficulty as far as I have noticed, because this vociferous minority have been concerned with bigger issues, but law enforcement is law enforcement, so any trend is possible.

At present, various "anti-establishment" critics have been noting that we are in a "violent" period. (Game management is part of the "establishment," and the most important part to a specialist in it.) The violence curve is historically variable. Still, its general direction has been down. During the well-documented past, men were usually personally armed, and it was not unusual for women to carry small but deadly dirks. "Gentlemen" carried swords. Lesser humanity managed with quarter-staffs, or some sort of cudgels. Pistols or sword-sticks or both became popular during later periods.

My gun collection has promoted some study of weapons in general, and I formerly knew people who would have considered our present existence very mild and safe. One of my grandfathers was a Methodist clergyman, but he frequently carried a cap-and-ball revolver. I was only about eight when he died, and did not manage to get this historic weapon, but I knew about it. One of my older uncles, who was accustomed to lug considerable currency, also lugged a .38 as habitually as his key-winder watch and jack knife, and the knife was pretty close to weapon-size, too. My father rarely carried a weapon, but his 12-gauge double stood in a corner by the kitchen door, with a couple of coarse-shot shells on a ledge beside it. We also had an excellent watchdog. I could go on indefinitely about the attention to personal arms into the present century to say nothing of earlier conditions. I have a copy of Sears, Roebuck's 1902 catalog. They advertise forty-eight different handguns. One is a relic and several are target weapons. All could kill. And on page 331 they list a ladies dagger with a pearl handle and the finest steel, double-edged blade! Sears did not advertise stuff that did not sell, but they quit daggers not many years later.

At present, there is some indication that the lawlessness curve is going up, parallel to the violence curve. Personal weapons-carrying will therefore go up with them. A hunter who owns a shotgun is supplied with the best home defense that exists. State and local laws determine its legal use. Usually, a householder, be he owner or renter, can use any necessary force to defend his home if a depredator is *on* his property. A thief or rioter may be legally "home free" if he gets to a public street. You may then run him down and knock him out, but not shoot him. Though I believe it is changing, the present practice is often to turn the criminal loose and convict the honest citizen.

These trends affect the enforcement portions of wildlife management. Softness toward violators in general will add to the existing difficulties. The swiftly developing interests in the natural environment will subtract from these difficulties. The results are guesswork, but I am inclined to be optimistic. This may be wishful thinking. I realize that I am old-fashioned as well as old, a "square" in the present jargon of youth. I still hope to see the punishment fit the crime, and if there is an argument, I support the police "pigs" rather than the rioters they are trying to contain. The "establishment" is often wrong, but we are a part of it, and must string along with it until it can be changed according to law. Here again I am optimistic. Law maintenance in general and enforcing natural resources laws in particular will be difficult enough, but we will muddle through.

I would terminate this somewhat vague chapter by emphasizing that education is the only substitute for law. If one is trained to accept a government of laws, he is unlikely to run afoul of those laws. Little people must not be trained away from ambition. Irrespective of race, color, or creed, however, our American "proletariat" have the best opportunities for success of any citizens anywhere. This is admitting the big British Commonwealth nations are equal or close to it. But little people, unfortunately, are just that. Conversely, U.S. little people can still legally possess guns, and can legally use them. Hunting opportunities have been getting more limited, because of too many people and too much money, but hunting is still legal. It is not free, and never again will be free in the foreseeable future, but it is cheaper than in most foreign countries. So, there will be opportunities to hunt legally if one is sufficiently interested and will pay the price. That price may not all be in money, but it must be paid, one way or another.

Perhaps certain critics will not agree with my views on freedom and equal opportunity. I am basically concerned with game management, but it applies to pretty much of everything and to everyone, in the social, economic, and educational fields. I may be asked what I, a retired biology professor, know about poverty, lack of opportunity, and educational privation. The simple answer is, "plenty."

I was farm-raised and had to walk two miles (measured and not guessed!) to a one-room district school. I had to travel eleven miles under my own power, and pay tuition, to get to high school. I was the third student and first boy from that district to graduate from high school. I was the *first* student from the district to get a college degree. And I earned or borrowed every dime that went into my higher education. My father was poor, though average or higher in the community. He was a farmer, and no farmer at that time saw any reason for raising a son except to have him work on the farm. Education, above the "3 Rs," was for people who could afford it. We could not!

My pursuit of education was stubborn and ruthless. My mentality must have been average or better and my physical stamina was definitely above average, or I could not have made it. So anyone can do the little that I did, if he works as I did. That includes the ability to get and use a good double shotgun! Of course this further assumes a certain minimum of brain and muscle. Most real poverty, sadly indeed, is largely choice. Except from choice, it results from poor judgment, again assuming average mental and physical equipment. At an advanced age, my ruthlessness continues to the extent that I have scant sympathy for the "submerged." There *are* sad exceptions, but most of these submerged folks could swim out if they had the essential determination.

Index

Index